The Shadow of Death

The Shadow of Death

LITERATURE, ROMANTICISM,
AND THE SUBJECT OF PUNISHMENT

Mark Canuel

PRINCETON UNIVERSITY PRESS

PRINCETON AND OXFORD

Copyright © 2007 by Princeton University Press
Published by Princeton University Press, 41 William Street,
Princeton, New Jersey 08540
In the United Kingdom: Princeton University Press, 3 Market Place,
Woodstock, Oxfordshire OX20 1SY

All Rights Reserved

ISBN-13: 978-0-691-12961-7
ISBN-10: 0-691-12961-4

Library of Congress Control Number: 2007920513

British Library Cataloging-in-Publication Data is available

This book has been composed in Sabon

Printed on acid-free paper. ∞

press.princeton.edu

Printed in the United States of America

1 3 5 7 9 10 8 6 4 2

For my brother, David

Contents

Illustrations ix

Acknowledgments xi

Abbreviations xiii

Introduction
Cain's Legacy, Nietzsche's Complaint 1

Chapter 1
"The Horrors of My Dreams" 11

Chapter 2
Uncertain Providence and Certain Punishment: Hannah More 34

Chapter 3
"Shuddering o'er the Grave": Wordsworth, Poetry,
and the Punishment of Death 55

Chapter 4
Jane Austen, the Romantic Novel, and the
Importance of Being Wrong 81

Chapter 5
Coleridge, Shelley, and the Poetics of Conscience 115

Chapter 6
The Two Abolitions 142

Coda
The Culture of the Death Penalty 168

Notes 177

Selected Bibliography 193

Index 203

Illustrations

Figure 1. William Blake, "The Execution of Breaking on the Rack"   149
Figure 2. William Blake, "The Flagellation of a Female Samboe Slave"   150
Figure 3. William Blake, "A Negro Hung Alive by the Ribs to a Gallows"   155

Illustrations by permission of the Milner Library, Special Collections, Illinois State University

Acknowledgments

I began trying out arguments related to this book while I was a graduate student and supposedly devoting all of my time to my dissertation. Although few traces of that work now exist, I appreciated the opportunity to share those early starts at meetings of the North American Society for the Study of Romanticism. Helpful suggestions by panel participants—including Alex Dick, Marjean Purinton, and Sharon Setzer—put me on the right track. More recently, the book started to come together with the generous support of a Michael J. Connell Foundation Fellowship at the Huntington Library in San Marino, California. At the Huntington, Scott Black, John Brewer, John Eglin, Cathy Jurca, Zacary Leader, and Tom McLean concocted the perfect mix of intellectual stimulation and welcome diversion. Collections at the University of Chicago's Regenstein Library, the British Library, and the Daley Library at the University of Illinois at Chicago were also invaluable. As always, the University of Illinois at Chicago provided essential financial support during my travels.

I am particularly indebted to Steve Engelmann and Lisa Freeman; they read through the whole manuscript, and I feel honored by the close attention they paid to it, providing appropriate amounts of cheerleading, skepticism, and helpful corrections. The two superb and insightful readers for Princeton University Press urged me to revise, defend, or modify a range of points that I make here; Kevin Gilmartin, Sharon Holland, and Mary Beth Rose read individual chapters and helped me think through points in them. Sharon Holland's work on different facets of this project provided both support and challenge to various parts of this book; Dwight McBride's conversations with me continually provided inspiration. I am grateful for Hanne Winarsky's unswerving confidence as this book's editor, and for Sherry Wert's ideal combination of lenience and rigor as copyeditor. And here I heap together a list of names of those who generously offered assistance ranging from encouraging words to helpful references: Jennifer Brody, Toby Causby, Dwight Conquergood, James Crane, Lenny Davis, John D'Emilio, Andy Franta, Greg Jackson, Kirstie McClure, Lisa Merrill, Walter Michaels, Kristy Odelius, Matt Repking, and Karen Weisman. I thank my mother and father for their love and support; I dedicate this book to my brother David.

Acknowledgments

Part of Chapter 4 appeared as "Jane Austen and the Importance of Being Wrong," in *Studies in Romanticism* 44 (2005): 123–50; *Studies in Romanticism* and the Trustees of Boston University generously granted permission to reprint this material.

Abbreviations

BSP   Montagu, Basil. *A Brief Statement of the Proceedings . . . Upon the Several Bills Introduced with A View to the Amendment of the Criminal Law.* London: Longman, 1811.

EBW   Burke, Edmund. *Works of the Right Honorable Edmund Burke.* 12 vols. Boston: Little, Brown, 1894.

HCL   Stephen, Sir James Fitzjames. *A History of the Criminal Law of England.* 3 vols. London: Macmillan, 1883.

HW   Hazlitt, William. *Collected Works of William Hazlitt.* 21 vols. Edited by A. R. Waller and David Glover. London: J. M. Dent, 1902–4.

MSR   Romilly, Sir Samuel. *Memoirs of the Life of Sir Samuel Romilly.* 3 vols. London: John Murry, 1840.

OCL   Romilly, Sir Samuel. *Observations on the Criminal Law of England, as it Relates to Capital Punishments, and on the Mode in Which it is Administered.* 2nd ed. London: T. Cadell, 1811

OLP   Romilly, Sir Samuel. *Observation on a Late Publication, Entitled, Thoughts on Executive Justice.* London: T. Cadell, 1786.

PML   Bentham, Jeremy. *An Introduction to the Principles of Morals and Legislation.* New York: Hafner, 1948.

PMP   Paley, William. *Principles of Moral Philosophy.* New York: Garland, 1978. (Original ed. 1785.)

RP   Bentham, Jeremy. *The Rationale of Punishment.* London: Robert Heward, 1830.

SSR   Romilly, Sir Samuel. *The Speeches of Sir Samuel Romilly in the House of Commons.* 2 vols. London: James Ridgway, 1820.

TEJ   Madan, Martin. *Thoughts on Executive Justice.* London: J. Dodsley, 1785.

TL   Bentham, Jeremy. *Traités de legislation.* Edited by Etienne Dumont. 3 vols. Paris: Bossange, Masson, et Besson, 1802. (Translations mine.)

The Shadow of Death

INTRODUCTION

Cain's Legacy, Nietzsche's Complaint

> There is no formation of the subject without a passionate
> attachment to subjection.
> Judith Butler, *The Psychic Life of Power*

In 1821, Lord Byron wrote a drama in which the central character kills his brother and is sentenced by a judge to a life of hardship. While spurned and cursed even by the members of his own family, the judge grants the young man a lenient but nonetheless conspicuous punishment. When the murderer asks for death in order to "redeem" his dead brother, he is told that his death cannot "heal murder." Instead, he must bear the sign of his crime everywhere. He must "fulfil [his] days" and—it is hoped—reform his behavior.[1] Perhaps it is already obvious to readers of Romantic literature, but the drama to which I refer is *Cain: A Mystery*: in my transposition of terms, the young man is Cain, murderer of his brother Abel; the judge is the Angel, speaking the law of God. The reading of the drama according to a series of secular analogies, though—interpreting God as legislator, the curse as an alternative to the punishment of death—is not actually my own. By the time Byron wrote this work, the practice of making the Cain and Abel story from Genesis 4 into a legal allegory about the wisdom of opposing the death penalty utterly permeates thought on judicial punishment in Britain. It is thus hard to believe that Byron conceived of his drama without knowing the implications that legal theorists habitually traced out of the story of the world's first murderer.

No passage from the Bible—or from any other text, in fact—seems as popular among late eighteenth- and early nineteenth-century penal reformers as this one. The punishment for Cain's terrible offense is not mere retaliation; it is a substantially reduced, yet still severe, sentence. For this reason, British reforming jurists saw it as an ideal for their own version of criminal legislation. In the fourth volume ("Of Public Wrongs") of his *Commentaries on the Laws of England* (1769), Blackstone uses the story to argue that Cain's fear of being murdered by others demonstrates the importance of a "sovereign power" over legal punishments—an authority that can protect criminals from vengeance.[2] (It is interesting that we can find comparatively less attention to God's words from verse 15, "Therefore whosoever slayeth Cain, vengeance shall be taken on him sevenfold," which might weaken the authority of liberal views on the issue.[3]) Other writers are more specific about the lenience demonstrated by the beneficent sovereign power described by Blackstone. Perhaps the best textual evidence we have of *Cain*'s relation to the debate about capital punishment is that Byron's friend and physician John William Polidori (best known for his Gothic fantasy *The Vampyre* [1819]) employs Cain allegorically in his essay "On the Punishment of Death"; Byron read and edited the essay, and it was published in 1816.[4] God's punishment of Cain, Polidori writes, proves "lenity" to be "the best corrector of vice"; the death penalty only reinforces "a spirit worse than the crime itself."[5] Cain's punishment continues to inspire reformers throughout the early decades of the nineteenth century. In a publication from the Society for the Diffusion of Information on the Subject of Capital Punishments (founded in 1829), J. Sydney Taylor speaks of God's forbearance in punishing Cain; Lord Nugent opposes the death penalty for murder because the "almighty himself" has spoken against it in favor of a "penal and outcast condition."[6] (God, in other words, favors transportation.) The list of variations on this theme could go on for many pages.

Byron's own version of the Cain and Abel story is a work with multiple layers of political and religious commentary, but, with the evidence I just cited in hand, we need to consider its importance not only as a text that blasphemously flouts the religious conventions of the author's day (as many interpretations suggest), but also as a decisive statement about the combined purposes of legal punishment.[7] While Byron's Cain may in some ways seem to be the archetypal Satanic outcast—and thus an image of the author himself—he is also the perfect example of an appropriately punished criminal.[8] And while Byron's God is one who demands a proper rite of sacrifice, he is also finally the upholder of wise and just law.[9] The drama thus offers a condensed but compelling instance of this book's subject: the Romantic opposition in Great Britain to the widespread use of the death penalty and consequent revision of the aims of legal punishment. The following chapters investigate the preeminence of Romantic writers in defining one of the earliest comprehensive assaults on the death penalty. My central claim is that this movement, while certainly one of the great humanitarian causes of the age, is in fact inseparable from a far more wide-ranging revision of punishment's meaning. Punishment's "meaning," however, can be summed up not as a philosophy or doctrine but rather as a troubling conjunction of contending rationales, recommending a sense of lenience and economy on the one hand, and a sense of severity and rigor on the other. In a flash, all of this becomes visible in *Cain*, as Byron slyly imports the terms of the death-penalty debate within the Biblical scenario and brings the tensions embedded in reform to life. Cain's wish to "redeem" his brother's life with his own rehearses a classic argument of death-penalty advocates, to this very day. Meanwhile, the reformed punishment imposed by Byron's God—just like that of the ideally reformed British legislator—is more merciful, yet utterly indelible and inflexible. It is a protection and a curse, a guarantee of life and prolonged suffering. (And it is precisely this depiction of God's severity that leads William Blake to answer Byron with *The Ghost of Abel* [1822]; Blake's Jehovah offers a "Covenant of the Forgiveness of Sins" rather than retribution.[10])

In the more expanded discussions that follow, I concentrate on the way that Romantic advocates for reform articulate punishment as a relationship or negotiation between rationales rather than as a perfectly seamless whole. It is this set of moral-political directives, rather than any coherent system or philosophy, that constitutes British Romanticism's contribution—from Romilly's heroic speeches against the death penalty in the last decades of the eighteenth century to Peel's "consolidation" of criminal law in the nineteenth—to the history of criminal law. It is also this set of moral-political directives that constitutes Romanticism's enduring legacy, visible in modern notions of punishment that continue with us in our own age. As Chapter 1, "The Horrors of My Dreams," argues, legal reformers such as Samuel Romilly and Jeremy Bentham insist on the essentially utilitarian notion that punishment can be judged according to its effects: it should economize on pain as much as possible, measuring out only as much penalty as individual reform and public good requires. At the same time, these very writers view such a utilitarian commitment as inseparable from an essentially retributive notion that punishment demands a certain and legible patterning of legal sanctions proportioned to the offender's guilt. One perspective threatens to banish punishment altogether: Bentham, for instance, suggests that the fine of a shilling might in some cases be sufficient to deter someone from murder. The other perspective, upholding the terrifying rigor of inflexible penalties, threatens to undermine the interests of the same political subject it claims to protect. Romantic writers thus establish punishment as a problem or a process: it is a ceaseless negotiation between inseparable but often conflicting perspectives, supported by inseparable but often conflicting justifications.

This book's subject borders on an important line of discussion that has predominated in studies of eighteenth- and nineteenth-century novels and poetry. It might even go without saying that these chapters would not have been written without the work of Michel Foucault, in *Discipline and Punish*, to precede and inspire them. But rather than simply building on his influential claims, my account aims to depart from them in a significant way. In Foucault's celebrated history, penal reforms appear only as an interlude between the two more famous descriptions of the "body of the condemned" and the "disciplinary subject." The eighteenth-century emphasis on the revision of the penal law, in Foucault's view, only amounts to an ephemeral preoccupation with an abstract "carnival of signs." The work of eighteenth-century jurists eventuates primarily in a revision of "juridical" apparatuses rather than "political" or institutional structures. Only these institutional structures—so resonantly described in Foucault's account of panopticism—achieve the privilege of operating at the more intimate level of individual subjects who incorporate the rules of the institutions governing over them.[11]

It is worth emphasizing, I think, not only that few readers remember Foucault's account of eighteenth-century jurists at all, but also that he makes this section so forgettable by casting the work of juridical forms in terms that appear more evanescent and temporary than the work of institutional disciplines. Rather than fleeting "signs," institutions leave "traces" on the subjects organized under their collective regime. Foucault's appeals to the "trace," to the "detail," in his account of institutions eventually operate at a virtually prediscursive level, as if it were merely self-evident that institutional forms would leave marks that were more or less indelible on their subjects.[12] In Foucault's work and the work inspired by it, the modern subject inevitably looks like a version of the architecture she inhabits, while the same architecture comes to look like an idealized version of her own consciousness. Foucault's rigorously materialized or empiricized formalism thus makes persons and the environments they occupy into perfect versions of each other, so that the actual work that forms do—architectural, linguistic, and so on—can be ignored.

Political theorists have frequently applied Foucault's work to account for modern institutional developments in a range of different contexts, all of which are aimed at "achieving total control over the behavior of subjects."[13] In the study of Romanticism, moreover, this dimension of Foucault's argument has influenced some of the most sophisticated and important examples of historical reading. From Clifford Siskin's *The Historicity of Romantic Discourse* and Alan Liu's *Wordsworth: The Sense of History* to Deirdre Shauna Lynch's *The Economy of Character* and Thomas Pfau's *Wordsworth's Profession*, discourses and institutions come to be replicated within individuals in order to shape or discipline a normalized interiority.[14] The result is an institutionally modeled British citizen, economic negotiator, proper lady, cultivated humanist, professional writer, or some other analogous formation of the subject. The particular intervention I make in this book—which is in agreement with many aspects of Gillian Rose's critique of the Foucauldian separation of law and power in her *Dialectic of Nihilism*[15]—works against the curious result of this line of argument in Foucault and his interpreters, which is

4

that important juridical reforms seem not only like events without meaningful effects but also like the basis for a massive theoretical obfuscation of the political, the institutional, or the disciplinary.[16] (Foucault adds confusion by claiming that institutional discipline "replace[d]" generalized punishment, even though the jurists and institutional reformers, like Romilly and Bentham, constitute one single group of reformers at one moment.[17]) I see the reform of punishment in different terms: it is a discourse that shapes, and is shaped by, a range of political and literary texts; it is a discourse with decisive importance in its time, and with startling—indeed, disturbing—longevity.

Perhaps it may initially seem interesting enough to note that punishment as a juridical concern has not disappeared in our own day; its sanctions, its fairness, and its applicability to similar crimes inflicted by persons of vastly different capacities or backgrounds continue to provoke debate. This is especially the case with the death penalty, the place of which must be considered not merely as a theatrical exhibition (as in Foucault's account), but as a penalty within a scale of other sanctions, given the stamp of approval by an apparent consensus among moral-political agents in a democratic regime. (At present, even regimes that do not legally allow the death penalty nonetheless exhibit a substantial popular support for capital punishment.[18]) My interest in punishment's sustained presence contrasts, then, not only with the work of Foucault, but also with the range of postmodern writing on sovereignty by Giorgio Agamben, Judith Butler, Michael Hardt, and Antonio Negri, among others.[19] Although I find some ground for agreement with this work (and reflect that agreement in quotations or citations from it), the fundamentally deconstructive interest of postmodern theorists in the constitutive inclusions and exclusions of "biopolitics" contrasts with my focus on problems of justice. My concern is not with the ontological foundations of the state, but with its technological means of social order.

The main line of discussion that I pursue in the following chapters does not simply note punishment's persistence, although that may be an ample demonstration of its importance. Instead, my argument focuses on the conspicuous position of the discourse of reformed punishment within a historically specific set of textual productions. In particular, I see a range of political and literary texts as important participants in a collective attempt to render the interlocking (yet contending) justifications of modern penality into politically persuasive or aesthetically compelling forms. In one sense, taking account of the specific character of the reformers' arguments brings us back still further, past Foucault, to the picture that Friedrich Nietzsche draws of punishment when he complains in *On the Genealogy of Morals* (1887) of "how uncertain, how supplemental, how accidental 'the meaning' of punishment is, and how one and the same

Introduction

procedure can be employed, interpreted, adapted to ends that differ fundamentally."[20] Nietzsche seems more interesting to me at this moment than Foucault is, since he sees the kind of punishment that Foucault leaves aside as an artificial construction, yet a powerful and lasting one.[21] But in another sense, the work that I do in this book brings us to a more refined way of *reading through* Nietzsche's complaint, into the inner logic of texts that are permeated by the differing meanings, supplemental to and inextricable from each other, that stand at the focal point of the *Genealogy*'s critique. If, following Nietzsche, modern regimes of punishment can be defined in terms of their unsettling or jarring mixture of rationales, my claim is that those rationales must be opened to further inquiry in order to grasp their historical importance and analyze the consequences of their continued viability.[22]

Penal reform, it turns out, was central to the careers of Romantic writers: Byron, William Hazlitt, Charles Lamb, Percy Shelley, and William Wordsworth were among those who wrote works explicitly devoted to the subject. Besides allowing us to discuss an aspect of Romantic texts that is underrepresented in scholarship on the literature of the period, attention to the abiding interest of late eighteenth- and early nineteenth-century writers in penal law helps us to understand one aspect of the political functions of that faculty of mind that we so frequently associate with Romanticism: the imagination. If works of the period understand punishment not as a theory but as a negotiation or relation between different rationales, "imagination"—its work and its products—comes to be what names and conditions the relation between them. As the example of Hazlitt's 1812 essay "On the Punishment of Death" shows in the first chapter, imagination can reside within contending justifications for punishment, both utilitarian and retributive; it establishes a sought-after engagement between political subjects and the finely calibrated set of sanctions that help to guide or shape conduct. This is why it is fair to say, I think, that the subject of this book, unlike Foucault's and those works influenced by him, allows us not merely to see persons and socially organizing forms as mimetic versions of each other, but to see the work that forms do on, and with, persons.

Although I have much to say about the specific role of literary works in framing rationales of punishment, the chapters on those works show how poems and novels have a place in discussions of penality that differs in substantial ways from that of political argument. While the political texts that I study attempt to bring different penal rationales into a balance or equilibrium, literary works do not necessarily transfer that apparent balance into fictional forms. It would be most accurate to say that they offer vigorously defined perspectives within that balance, from the utilitarian sympathies of Austen's heroines to the retributive rigor of Shelley's

Adonais or *The Triumph of Life*. Those perspectives, in turn, become the loci of imaginative power: in *Mansfield Park*, Fanny's quest for sources of "painful solicitude" is inseparable from her status as an engaged reader, perfectly demonstrating the aim of punishment as reform. Shelley's account of the penal sanctions requisite for a "sane polity," by the same token, is inseparable from his defense of those sanctions as an "art" of retribution, endowed with brilliant variations in "shade" and "color." Thus, even as political accounts of penal reform seek to engage the imagination in their defense, the writers of poems and prose fiction work in a complementary fashion. They become attached to the issue of punishment, it may be said, in order to demonstrate a particular dimension of the imagination's power, thereby revealing the priority of fictive constructions within political theory's own domain. The basic function of penalty requires the imaginative work at the heart of fictional constructions.[23]

Before turning to such instances in Romantic literary production, however, Chapter 2 moves us toward an understanding of the pervasive commitment to penal reform by offering a striking counterexample. In Hannah More's writings, the reform arguments and their implications are frequently viewed with both attraction and repulsion. Enthralled by the possibility of teaching children to plan futures informed by coherent penal regimes, she puts tales in her *Cheap Repository Tracts* (1800) that depict young people appropriately chastened by legal sanctions for their "foolish" and "sinful" conduct. To follow the lessons of the *Tracts* is to be guided away from the punishments of "Tyburn" or "Botany Bay" and toward the blessings of success and security. More's evangelical sympathies simultaneously pull against these lessons, however. In some of her tracts, her messages are simply confused; utilitarian commitments emerge at cross-purposes with the conviction that individuals cannot know the wisdom of Providence. Even so, her novel *Coelebs in Search of a Wife* (1808) achieves a decisive resolution to all such confusion. Although the text is riddled with punishable crime, faith in God ultimately guarantees "compassion" rather than fault, and a cleansed "spirit" rather than guilt. As the agents in her work gradually harden into the confines of Christian allegory, More purges all of the attractions of the realist novel that she at first seems to be writing: the erasure of crime and penalty, making each agent into a replicable model of heavenly virtue, also results in the erasure of character.

In Chapter 3, I explore a range of complex poetic statements on the death penalty that punctuate Wordsworth's career. In his Salisbury Plain poems, Wordsworth speaks out against the cruelty and injustice of official killing—through war, slavery, and capital punishment; his much later *Sonnets upon the Punishment of Death* (1841) adopts an opposing view. It rejects all "show humane" and instead asks legislators to honor God's "perfect Intelligence" by imitating His power to destroy human life. Both of these extreme positions are subtly modified, however. Despite the reformist agenda of the earlier poems, Wordsworth imagines scenes of legalized violence that will punish the guilty "Oppressor"; by the same token, the later sonnets support the death penalty, but only insofar as it furthers "social good." Even this limited support presents a substantial risk for the poet, moreover. Wordsworth implies that executions threaten poetry's quality as an imaginative entity; the Gothic effects related to the death penalty are suited only for the "grovelling mind." The sonnet series thus comes to a close by shaking its overtly stated purpose, hoping for a day when the death penalty will actually be abandoned "for lack of use." Both vantage points, I argue, are informed by the contending forces within Romantic penal reform: forces that oppose the pervasive and indiscriminate use of the death penalty, yet ambivalently allow its retention within a coherent set of sanctions proportioned to the severity of crimes.

Wordsworth's apparently opposing positions on the death penalty are in fact modifications of each other: a commitment to the value of retributive sanctions, and a commitment to the effect of those sanctions on the repentant criminal and on political subjects more generally. His poetry thus provides an appropriate way to begin discussing works that imaginatively reinforce these supplementary and inextricable positions. As I show in Chapter 4, Jane Austen's *Mansfield Park* (1814) presents penalty in rigorously utilitarian terms: error and punishment not only reform character but also create it. Although Fanny spends much of her time in the novel in a state of mortification from actual or potential offenses, the chastisement and suffering she endures nevertheless guarantee her visibility and social value; she thus anxiously seeks the very errors and consequent punishments that she supposedly wishes to avoid. Throughout the novel's series of adventures, Fanny repeatedly insists upon suffering penalties even for actions that are not her fault. Meanwhile, other characters, like Julia or Mary Crawford, disguise their faults or "sins" and any blame for them; their avoidance of fault deprives them of personal "disposition" and threatens to drain them of any distinguishing features. One of Fanny's final gestures in the novel is particularly revealing: she brings her sister Susan with her to Mansfield not to obtain relief from troubles at home, but to participate in a pleasing "anxiety" and "dread" of penalty. Austen's insistence on framing penalties as uncompromised benefits to the human subject, I argue, makes *Mansfield Park* an extension of the Gothic novel's more explicit critique of capital punishment. As in Mary Shelley's *Frankenstein* (1818), the Gothic novel makes the death penalty resemble a machine or monster indifferent to human concerns. Austen's fiction also coincides with the critique of the death penalty in the historical novels of Sir Walter Scott. In *The Fortunes of Nigel* (1822), the death penalty continuously hovers at the borderline between the antique and the modern; the very condition of narrating historical fiction with a "great variety of shading and delineation" requires a distance from the "ancient manners" typified by the arbitrary, unvaried use of capital punishment.

Chapter 5, "Coleridge, Shelley, and the Poetics of Conscience," explores literary representations of conscience, a term that occupies a central position in the reform of penal law. Conscience is traditionally understood in opposition to merely external applications of the law, yet legal theorists such as Martin Madan see it as subversive precisely because it aims to substitute itself for law. Literary texts of the Romantic period make conscience into a particularly supple term that spans these alternatives: it is occasionally a frame of mind resistant to the influences of external sanctions and—most interesting of all—occasionally a terrifying reinforcement of retributive justice itself. In Coleridge's *Osorio* (1797), conscience is "the punishment that cleanses hearts," a punishment that paradoxically emerges inside the political subject initially, but that finally reasserts itself as an indelible external force. Shelley provides an appropriate point of comparison and contrast because he invokes the discourse of conscience, yet eradicates it from any determination by the political subject's judgment. In Shelley's writing, that is, conscience scandalously becomes exercised within and by poetry; poetry accumulates a moral-political force, heaping "shame" and "scorn" on those who cannot comply with its ideals. Opposing the death penalty as a threat to his art's integrity, Shelley's late poems, like *Adonais* (1821) and *The Triumph of Life* (1822), nevertheless make that integrity inseparable from a retributive imposition of shame on virtually any being that comes into contact with his poetry. Constantly associating the rhetorical force of his works with the burning or branding of offenders, Shelley conjures up a disturbing yet potent way of portraying the submission of readers, politicians, critics, and fellow poets.

My final chapter broadens the parameters of the discussion to reveal a previously unrecognized connection between the abolition of the death penalty and the abolition of slavery. Prominent white liberals of the period—Romilly, Thomas Clarkson, William Wilberforce, and others—were advocates of both causes, but the connection goes much deeper than that, since tracts on one abolition continually refer to the other. Death-penalty abolitionists borrow the sympathy offered to black slaves and ask their audiences to apply it to convicted criminals who should be saved from the gallows. Still more important, slavery abolitionists—in a seemingly contradictory direction—imagine the freedom of the slave to be contingent upon a presumed criminality; their suffering under slavery, then, is deemed to be of "unmerited severity" rather than fundamentally unjust. The connection between these two abolitions, I argue, helps to explain

Introduction

why authors like Sarah Scott and William Cowper connect the abolition of slavery to a more broadly reformed legal order. Even black abolitionists like Olaudah Equiano make the innocent slave into the exemplary "arraigned and condemned" subject of an ordered system of penalties. Whether in political texts, the graphic arts, or literary works, black slaves are considered potentially free political subjects only by virtue of their punishability: thus "peace for Afric," as Cowper writes, will be obtained only if "fenc'd with British laws."

I end this book with a brief coda on debates about, and representations of, capital punishment in America today. Whereas Romantic writing tends to expose contending rationales of punishment, American debate has tended to sever one from the other; an empty formalism defends the death penalty as an instance of retributive justice, whereas opponents of the death penalty criticize it as if all punishment could find its reference point in human utility. I take contemporary American film as a particularly revealing dramatization of this poverty in political discourse. While at once implicitly recognizing the unfairness with which the death penalty is administered, Hollywood films such as *Dead Man Walking* and *The Life of David Gale* typically fall short of explicit critique of capital punishment. In other instances, films like *The Green Mile* even celebrate and sacramentalize the death penalty with more fervor than Wordsworth ever could have done. This is not the fault of the films themselves. The films are instead symptoms of a pervasive inability of political discourse to confront the legacy that structures its own terminology and limits its opportunities for change.

1
"The Horrors of My Dreams"

> They're dreadfully fond of beheading people here: the great wonder is, that there's any one left alive!
> Alice, in Lewis Carroll, *Alice's Adventures in Wonderland*

Early in his *Memoirs* (1840), Sir Samuel Romilly gives an account of some terrifying images first experienced in childhood, yet powerful enough to trouble his mind in adulthood:

> The Prints, which I found in the lives of the martyrs and the Newgate Calendar, have cost me many sleepless nights. My dreams too were disturbed by the hideous images which haunted my imagination by day. I thought myself present at executions, murders, and scenes of blood; and I have often lain in bed agitated by my terrors, equally afraid of remaining awake in the dark, and of falling asleep to encounter the horrors of my dreams." (*MSR* 1:11–12)

Romilly—arguably the most celebrated reformer of criminal law at the turn of the eighteenth century—registers a fear of capital punishment as a thing of the past, even while confirming the enduring power of its "hideous images" in the present. It may be interesting enough that the author, even after his own efforts have significantly reduced the use of the death penalty in the British penal system, nevertheless calls it to mind so vividly and urgently. But we also notice that this particular instance is in fact one of many; the most striking attribute of the *Memoirs*, is Romilly's insistent connection between his "natural inclination . . . for peace and tranquility" and his equally powerful inclination to cultivate fears of misfortune and ruin (*MSR* 1:13). He reminisces about his youthful tendency to take pleasure in "indulging" his terrors; "[I] reproached myself," he writes, "if ever I felt a moment of security" (*MSR* 1:12). In his public life, furthermore, he is "haunted" by his fears of failure as a politician and speaker (*MSR* 2:146). In these pages, a sense of serenity is never far from an enduring threat.

Romilly's *Memoirs* provide a fitting introduction to this chapter, because they so brilliantly display a typically English sense of the "horror" of the death penalty: a horror that is not merely eliminated through the march of reform, but is in fact appreciated, sustained, and narratively reinforced. The potent and complex maneuver of that text, in other words, does far more than simply delineate a psychological phenomenon. It gives voice to a decidedly modern moral-political disposition, one in which the enlightened recoil from the savagery of ritualized punishment accompanies a new, muted, but persistent fear, a fear inspired by the threat of pain or death that underwrites the author's very sense of "peace and tranquility." Romilly's reminiscences, as the following pages will show, bear the marks of a much more pervasive and influential discourse on the abolition of the widespread use of the death penalty and the reform of punishment that Romilly so fervently championed. In the broadest of terms, this chapter traces the Romantic opposition to the death penalty as a species of humanitarian reform that simultaneously—and more importantly—aimed to redefine the relationship between political subjects and legal structures, and thus to redefine the very meaning of punishment more generally. That meaning, I will suggest, could not be reduced to a simple formula; it involved potentially conflicting but inseparable goals—goals that have came to define the system of punishment with which we live today.

The use of the death penalty in the late eighteenth century initiated a productive crisis in the construction and conduct of criminal law. By some estimates, Britain had more capital crimes—by the eighteenth century, punishment with hanging accompanied by any number of post-mortem penalties like gibbeting or dissection—than any other nation. And the penalty of death seemed to its critics to demonstrate the survival of barbarous practices in modern government that stood in "violation of the laws of nature, and the precepts of our religion" (OCL 27). At the same time, however, it was shown to be utterly inefficient. Romilly cited statistical figures in an 1810 parliamentary speech to show that in the seven years prior, 1,872 criminals were convicted of capital offenses, and only one executed (OCL 7–8); similar sets of figures punctuated the writings of reformers like Edward Gibbon Wakefield in the early decades of the nineteenth century. Despite the vast accumulation of capital offenses (also known as the "Bloody Code"), many criminals went largely unpunished: "It is the uncertainty of punishment, of which too great severity is one main cause," Wakefield wrote, "that makes the law proclaim, as it were, impunity of crime."[1] The accumulation of capital statutes, which punished thefts of everything from horses to lace, was widely read as the effect of "Mammon," Britain's proliferating commercial interests.[2] But Wakefield's claim confirms what Henry Fielding had observed many years earlier: capital statutes endangered the very property rights that they were designed to protect.[3]

It is impossible, then, to describe the Romantic opposition to the death penalty as if it were generated solely from a sense of outrage over the cruelty of the gallows; rather, as I have already begun to suggest, it was inseparable from a new way of thinking about the nature of punishment itself. Capital punishment had been aimed at imposing a certain kind of awe upon its terrified spectators—an awe that frequently devolved into chaotic or carnivalesque opposition. But reformers of the age, like Romilly, Basil Montagu, and Jeremy Bentham, sought to forge an unprecedented level of engagement between structures of legal authority and the lives of individual political subjects. No longer designed to make those subjects bow in submission to a terrifying display of authority, the law would both acknowledge and capture the energy of seemingly intractable sympathies. At the same time, those very sympathies—those very individual and intimate subjectivities held under the law's jurisdiction—could be seen in a newly dependent relationship to the penal law itself, to such an extent that individual right would in fact be constituted through it rather than against it. In Francis Jeffrey's words, the reformers sought to produce a "necessary reciprocation of crimes and rights," so that "we can only be said to have a *right* to do . . . things, because the law has made it a crime for any one to disturb us in doing them."[4]

What I regard in this book as characteristic of the thought of the Romantic period, then, is not a new theory of penalties—not a theory of which punishments work best to solve which crimes, and not even a theory about how to devise such a system. Romantic penal reform was thus distinguishable from earlier attempts to eliminate crime through spectacles of violence or, as in Fielding's account, through a "restraint" on luxuries and vice.[5] Instead, it was a way of opening up and traversing a new *space* between legislators and subjects. No one was more successful than Romilly himself at voicing the need for criminal law to reflect the manners and feelings of the British people, whose lenience seemed to be abundantly proved by statistics citing the declining use of the death penalty. But the lenient curbing of the death penalty needs to be viewed in the context of an attempt to invest the law with a new level of authority. Punishments had meaning only insofar as they were effective among the political subjects over which they held their authority; at the same time, criminal law came to be attributed with a new degree of power to give shape to the manners and beliefs from which it apparently arose. This space, between minds of political subjects and freshly minted laws, would be occupied by and through the work of the imagination—the imaginative work of both subjects and legislators. Thus to think of revised operations of the penal code was to think of revised operations for this faculty of mind standing at the center of Romantic writing.

Chapter 1

Romilly and Reform from Within

Capital punishment could be seen as a symbol of British brutality even though it was infrequently used; it destroyed the body and degraded the mind, even while it was widely recognized as inefficient or even useless. It is nevertheless the case that the rising opposition to the death penalty faced two prominent and successful lines of argument in its defense. One of them defended the written law against its practice; the other defended current practice against the written law. Neither is without interesting complications, and neither could be easily repudiated by the reformers. Martin Madan, whose *Thoughts on Executive Justice* (1785) Romilly repeatedly opposes—and in fact blames for single-handedly bringing about an increase in the number of executions—attributes the weakness of the current system on the death penalty's irregular application (*MSR* 1:89). For Madan, there is nothing wrong with Britain's present system of criminal laws; it is simply that they are not systematically imposed. Likening British laws to the laws of Vienna in *Measure for Measure* (1604), he asserts that the high crime rate could be attributed to the fact that the "dispensers . . . rarely put them in execution" (*TEJ* 15, 18). Madan, of course, has little interest in the Duke's merciful pardons in Act 5, the culmination of the play's pervasive ambivalence about strict adherence to the law. Instead, he simply insists that the current "scandal" of criminal law is that the judge repeatedly suspends capital cases and thus "sets himself above the law, and presumes to exercise an authority with which the constitution has not entrusted even the crown itself" (*TEJ* 46). The solution is to assure that sanguinary laws are "duly, constantly, and impartially enforced and executed" (*TEJ* 3).

It cannot escape our notice that Madan fears the judge acting as if he were superior to the law: even while swearing to uphold the conventional legal order, the judge's "conscience" is a distinctive form of interference that could break the law in accordance with another law supported by internal conviction (*TEJ* 103). But Madan allows no place for conscience, a work of the mind that I shall have more to say about in my discussion of Coleridge and Shelley in Chapter 5. Rather than insert himself "between the judgment and the execution," the judge should instead "resign his place and not trifle with the law" by disrupting its regular, unswerving application (*TEJ* 103–4). When Ann Radcliffe in *The Italian* (1797) has her villainous monk Schedoni defend the death penalty's "Justice" against the "weakness" of those who allow "laws" to be "neglected," she is almost certainly thinking of, and satirizing, Madan and his followers.[6] But William Cowper is perhaps more sympathetic toward Madan in *The Task*

(1785); he observes that "thieves at home must hang" (and repeatedly seeks a "noose" for all thieves' necks), but he also criticizes the lax treatment of the rich: "He, that puts / Into his over gorg'd and bloated purse / The wealth of Indian provinces, escapes."[7] The more nooses the better: in the place of judge-made law, Madan envisions the operation of laws as "forms" that beautifully "maintain [the] consequence and dignity" of the judge's position precisely by restricting the weakening effects of independent judgment (*TEJ* 84–85). His suggestion, in other words—taken up by the likes of Chief Justice Ellenbrough and Lord Chancellor Eldon—is that the very ability to question the law might be the source of the nation's ills; a solution to those ills can be found in the pure abstraction of a law immune to all critique.

But there was yet another influential argument with which reformers needed to contend, found in William Paley's *Principles of Moral and Political Philosophy* (1785). If Madan claims that the problem is not with the laws but with the application of them, Paley insists instead that the problem is not with the application but with the laws themselves, to such an extent that the actions of judges might entirely occlude them. In a sense, Paley is not far from the aims of reformers when he opens his chapter "Of Crimes and Punishments" with the claim that the aim of punishment is "not the satisfaction of justice, but the prevention of crimes" (*PMP* 526). Yet, because of a "defect" in the laws "in not being provided with any other punishment than that of death" (*PMP* 543), it is entirely in the "magistrate" that Paley wants to invest "the mitigation of punishment" and "the exercise of lenity" (*PMP* 532). He thus describes the law itself as a bearer of "tenderness" or "wisdom and humanity," at the same time that those qualities are not so much properties of the law as they are qualities of the individuals who administer it (*PMP* 533).

Paley's argument is a powerful and convincing one, Dr. Johnson's frequent intercessions on behalf of friends in trouble—including his failed attempt to save the penal reformer Dr. William Dodd from execution for forgery—reflects basic agreement with it.[8] "Whatever be the crime," Johnson wrote in a letter pertaining to the Dodd case, "it is not easy to have any knowledge of the delinquent, without a wish that his life may be spared."[9] This view also finds common ground with Edmund Burke's. While still regarding the accumulated statutes of criminal law with all the reverence he pays to English custom and tradition in the *Reflections on the Revolution in France* (1790), Burke suggests that custodians of the law need to make minute adjustments to it rather than strictly enforce it. In "Some Thoughts on the Approaching Executions," for example—a series of letters and observations on the proper punishment for the 1780 Gordon rioters—Burke asserts that the magistrate must not simply adhere to the law by executing criminals who are tried and convicted. He must do so with heightened attention to what will achieve the desired effect within a given audience. The main difference between Burke and Paley on this issue is not a large one. Paley openly acknowledges a "defect" in the law; Burke knows that there is such a defect but wants it to be hidden by a sly bit of subterfuge, not unlike the "politic well-wrought veil" in the *Reflections* that glosses over disruptions in England's rocky "order of succession."[10] Rather than follow legal provisions—provisions that would produce mass executions—he asks the government to select several of the "fittest examples," but no more than six to be hanged in six different places. The more lucky criminals, "the rest of the malefactors," would have their sentences commuted to prison terms and service in the navy.[11] Burke can thus correct a defect while also maintaining respect for the system of legal conventions that Madan defends.

This kind of argument, according substantial power to the judge in order to correct the law's violence mercifully, still has its advocates today.[12] It is also not entirely inconsistent with other commitments that Paley voices in the *Principles* on behalf of religious freedom (*PMP* 554–86). The leniency of the judge would seem to be reflected in the leniency of government toward various kinds of dissenter, and we cannot be surprised to hear later writers on tolerant government (like Jeremy Bentham) quoting Paley as one of the primary authorities on the issue.

But reformers of the penal law needed to oppose themselves to both points of view—the perspectives of both extreme rigor and extreme mercy—and the response of the range of writers I discuss here is something that I want to define as quintessentially Romantic. Romilly's critique of criminal law was central to this claim, and one of the purposes of this chapter is to identify him as one of the great heroes of criminal law reform at the turn of the eighteenth century—quoted admiringly for ages after his career came to an abrupt end with his suicide—and to show exactly why this was the case. One line of attack that Romilly takes is to oppose Madan's position because it simply ratifies an obsolete system of accumulated penal laws. The accretion of hundreds of years of statutes added up to a seemingly chaotic agglomeration of confused legal categories, making a crime at one time of day or in one place not a crime at another time of day in another place—or making two vastly different offenses like theft and murder amount to the same thing and receive a similar penalty.[13] The problem with Madan's position, according to Romilly, is that the practice of law is made by such means into a "science of memory," an attempt to recall a preserved relic from the past that violates the "feelings and understandings of men" (*OLP* 38). Romilly's campaigning against the widespread use of the death penalty thus aims to make the laws "less inhuman than they are" (*OLP* 105), but this is not with a merely abstract sense of what is "human"; Romilly continually calls upon his countrymen to reform the nation's laws by looking within themselves. Traditional modes of punishment have only tended to "revolt the feelings of mankind, and to furnish foreigners with a reproach against our national character" (*SSR* 1:431). The current penal law threatens not only to serve as a reproach against that character but also to exert a corrupting influence on it, leading to an irreversible "deterioration of moral feeling" (*SSR* 2:326). The trend, however, can still be reversed: Britons can accomplish this by bearing witness to their own revulsion and outrage, reflected in their own practice of applying "lenity" to the death penalty (*OCL* 7–8). This lenity, in turn, should encourage them to shape laws that are more consistent with the true, uncorrupted "character of [the] nation" (*OLP* 38).

Romilly was surely not the first to have framed a reform of criminal law on these, or at least similar, terms. Henry Dagge, in his *Considerations on Criminal Law* (1772), suggests that Christianity could serve as a model for law reform, since "the Principles of Christianity breathe nothing but the most extensive benevolence, the most disinterested charity, and the most diffusive moderation."[14] Manesseh Dawes's *An Essay on Crimes and Punishments* (1782) in a somewhat more secular fashion urges its readers to consult morality and religion as a guide to their reform of punishment, and still more generally as a guide in forming their "duty as citizens, parents, friends, children, masters, and servants."[15] But Romilly, like Cesare Beccaria, Bentham, and others who so profoundly influenced him, disarticulated the issue of punishment from religion even more thoroughly, and this was what made him a hero, as controversial as he was inspirational, for later reformers. This aspect of his work did not go down easily with everyone: Hannah More found it difficult to wrestle with a notion of punishment that usurped the role of Providence, as I will discuss in the next chapter; and Romilly constantly found himself under siege by those who accused him of selling out to continental, particularly French, "theory" (*SSR* 1:342). Similar things were said about Bentham, of course, and about the Edgeworths, with whom Romilly was a regular correspondent. But Romilly's plea to the public, and more specifically to the present state of national feeling, appealed to liberals like Sir James Mackintosh, who campaigned to "make the laws popular—to reconcile them with public opinion," and who declared himself to be one of Romilly's most ardent followers. His memory, Mackintosh insisted, would "remain consecrated in the history of humanity."[16] Byron's friend Polidori likewise hailed Romilly as a leader in "the cause of humanity" and "a man whom every patriot must revere."[17]

Chapter 1

Punishment and the Point of Form

The association, indeed the equation, between Romilly and humanity or genuine feeling was one of the truly remarkable features of his career. According to an anonymous pamphlet published as a memorial in 1818, Romilly had earned a reputation for "the character of his mind, and the alike susceptibility of his heart"; his humanitarian interests seemed to transcend "party feeling" and embrace an "enthusiastic patriotism ever alive to the happiness of that community of which he formed a member." Romilly's suicide actually contributed to this image; he killed himself only a week after his wife's death, and—"a victim of sudden hopelessness"—he appeared even in this final act to display his susceptible heart and powerful feelings.[18]

Romilly may have been constructed as this kind of sentimental hero for his audience, but there is another and still more important line of argument that runs throughout his work and comes to define the central task of the Romantic campaign against the death penalty. What is inseparable from the opposition to capital punishment—indeed, what functions as a condition for that opposition—is a substantially revised understanding of what punishment is and how it operates. It is in this sense that Romilly's liability to attack on his dedication to French enlightenment "theory" becomes comprehensible, although it is mistaken. True, Romilly wrote an optimistic tract on the French Revolution, and also translated the Count de Mirabeau's *Considerations on the Order of Cincinnatus* (1785), a moderate republican criticism of the evils of aristocracy and nobility perpetuated by an American military "patriciate" of Cincinnatus.[19] But if Romilly may have admired Mirabeau's paeans to republican virtue, his work tends to be directed less consistently toward enlightenment philosophy and its preoccupation with the distribution of equal rights than toward a new designation of punishment's domain of operations—a domain aimed toward the benefit of individual subjects and at strengthening the legal and institutional means of securing it.

Romilly's specific aims could thus be understood as an attempt not only to humanize punishment but also to make it more effective. The death penalty, after all, not only offended an outraged humanity, but also exhibited an entirely ambiguous relationship to offenses. Madan offers a typical defense when he writes about punishment as if it were most important as a kind of staged image of the legal order's ubiquity and power. An audience viewing an execution "must now see, that certainty of punishment must await the guilty" (*TEJ* 30). But for a large number of offenders, such certainty—in cases of theft, forgery, and so on—seemed so vastly out of proportion to the crime that punishment could look more

18

like an unfortunate accident. Or, perhaps more to the point, those offenders were to be frightened into a vague respect for the shapeless and terrifying force of law: "The whole country feels a lasting benefit, in the security and protection which such an example of punitive justice has procured them" (*TEJ* 30).[20] Burke's instructions on how to conduct executions in his "Thoughts" take a similar direction, even though he pleads for a kind of mercy that Madan rejects. The purpose of capital punishment is not to punish the guilty but to impress the audience; thus his call for mercy for the rioters arises not out of any concern for criminals, but out of concern for the proper management of a suitably terrifying spectacle. Appropriately conducted, the penalty of death "fixes the attention and excites awe," whereas a great number of executions "rather resembles a massacre than a sober execution of the laws." The problem here, of course, is that the "massacre" is precisely what is legally ordained. Burke is arguing *against* an execution of "multitudes" of malefactors; thus reverence for the law needs to be achieved by curtailing its influences (*EBW* 6:247). Reverence, to put it another way, comes from clever staging, a lie that the government tells about the law. Since a mere "execution of the laws" would result in a massacre, the government properly choreographs executions in order to inspire respect for the very laws that are in fact being violated.

Public execution was thus an act that was either an incomprehensible accident (for the criminal) or a deception covering up a deep incoherence (for the legislator), and the anxiety generated over the control of the meaning of this spectacle speaks volumes about its actual unmanageability. Bernard Mandeville's celebrated critique of the conventional journey of the criminal from Newgate to the gallows viewed virtually every element of execution as a source of unrelieved disorder, from the drunken jeers of the condemned man to the crime-ridden mob.[21] (The shifting locations of the favored site of execution—from Smithfield to Tyburn to Newgate itself—supposedly quelled unrest but did little to change prevailing opinions about the chaos of such spectacles.) Blake's *Jerusalem* (1815–20), with its critique of Albion's "Fatal Tree" as a bloody and hypocritical continuation of primitive sacrifice, sustains the spirit of Mandeville's observation in the nineteenth century.[22] So do Sir Walter Scott's novels, which repeatedly remark upon the dangerous instability of execution as a spectacle—as in *The Heart of Midlothian* (1818), with its violent scene of Meg Murdockson's execution, followed by the murder of her daughter Madge Wildfire at the hands of an unruly crowd.[23] Many historians who have studied punishment in England and the continent (Foucault, V.A.C. Gattrell, and Thomas W. Laqueur among them[24]) have stressed this unpredictable and disorderly aspect of executions, and current arguments against the death penalty continue to emphasize its role as a "lethal theatre" appealing to a public's most uncivil emotions.[25] Closer to my purpose in this book, however—and what has received far less attention—is the complex logic informing the opposition to capital punishment, which in the handling of a whole range of reformers emerged not only as a humanitarian resistance but as a way of speaking to political subjects in a manner that combined new aims and methods with old.

First, against the notion that the awe-inspiring display of retribution would cause a deterrence of crime, new arguments about punishment make deterrence part of an essentially utilitarian understanding that punishment is effective only insofar as it is useful to those who are subjected to it. It is this utilitarian logic that joins the aim of deterrence to the aim of reforming the criminal. Instead of merely restraining the offender, that is, the revised form of punishment shifts attention to the efficacy or inefficacy of certain measures for the moral-political regeneration of the subject. Second, deterrence and reform are combined, uneasily and paradoxically, with a wholly new emphasis on the systematicity of punishment itself—punishment as a set of rules—and how such a system might appeal to the minds of the persons subjected to the punishments meted out by the law.

Philosophers of punishment have routinely attempted to distinguish between these sets of rationales and to defend one over the other—a "utilitarian" attention to the effects of punishment, or a "retributive" attention to the system of punishments "deserved" by the criminal. (In today's death-penalty discourse, opponents of capital punishment frequently stress punishment as utility, whereas supporters frequently stress punishment as retribution.[26]) But the revision of punishment I am tracing out in fact *does not separate one rationale from the other*: they are closely intertwined, nonidentical (in fact irreconcilable), yet mutually supporting.[27] It is a central claim of this book, furthermore, that the legacy of these intertwined rationales is visible and inescapable in our own present-day discussions of punishment's validity. Mentally handicapped persons, for example, seem (from a utilitarian perspective) to require us to prescribe different penalties that account for their different abilities in reasoning or judgment; at the same time, advocates for the handicapped insist that some system of penalties is necessary in order for them to navigate their lives as moral-political subjects. Yet even cases of criminals supposedly most deserving of capital punishment—for premeditated murder, for instance—show that the most fervent commitments to retribution are accompanied by at least second thoughts, if not an outright skepticism, about capital punishment's utility.[28] The skepticism about severe punishments only increases when the criminal—no matter how numerous or horrific the crimes may be—is too young or too old to benefit from sanctions. (The fairly recent struggle in the Chilean court system over how to punish Augusto Pinochet is a particularly powerful example of this problem.[29]) What remains a conflict in thought about punishment is not a confusion to be removed by further thinking, in other words. It is a conflict that in fact *constitutes* our thinking about punishment.

To return to Romilly, then: isn't it possible to view his celebrated humanitarian sympathies within the context of, and in fact as inseparable from, his devotion to the utilitarian effectiveness of punishments? Among the many revised ideas of punishment that Romilly gleans from the pages of Beccaria, William Blackstone, Thomas More, Montesquieu, and Samuel Pufendorf is the emphasis on the slightness of penalty in order to economize on the amount of pain applied to the accused.[30] This logic—in which pain is a social evil that needs to be reduced as far as possible in order to achieve the maximum benefit—supports the broader shift away from corporal punishment to fines, incarceration, and transportation (*OCL* 21).[31] Bentham—who both inspired Romilly's work and built upon it—is said to have claimed that if a fine of one shilling could prevent murder, then anything more would be "unjustifiable cruelty" (*HCL* 2:79). Paley, Bentham's own mentor, blithely suggests that a criminal might even be released rather than punished, if the release did not prevent the deterrence of future crimes (*PMP* 526). Such statements are only the most extreme versions of a general commitment to judging the success of punishment by its effects. In Romilly's view, arguing for uniformly reduced penalties means arguing, surprisingly, for greater efficiency in the execution of the law. Urging his audience in Parliament to "endeavor to invigorate the laws by relaxation," Romilly essentially suggests that a decrease in the amount of legally inflicted pain and suffering coincides with an increase in social security and integrity (*SSR* 1:354).

Oliver Goldsmith's Primrose anticipates this position when he wishes "that legislative power would ... direct the law rather to reformation than severity," at the same time that he insists that this would make punishments "formidable" rather than "familiar."[32] It is this position of utilitarian lenity that informs the scandalously light sentence on Michael Steno for his "foul affront" to the Doge in Byron's *Marino Faliero* (1821), inspiring the Doge's outrage and fatal vengeance.[33] And it becomes the guiding principle for Jane Austen's *Mansfield Park* (1818), discussed in Chapter 4, which depicts a fit between punishment and person so perfectly managed that sources of pain are crucial resources for Fanny Price's sense of who she is. We have ample cause at this point to reevaluate Romilly's reputation: he was considered not merely a man of sentiment, as I suggested above, but also a benevolent protector of the people—a "Friend of the Fatherless," an angelic agent of Providence helping to protect the defenseless from oppression (at the same time that revised penal reforms are designed to enhance the protection of property and facilitate bringing criminals to justice).[34]

Still more, this emphasis on punishment's effects in Romilly's writing helps to explain the position of *statistics* in his arguments and in the reformers' arguments generally. The carefully gathered and incessantly repeated figures showing how many crimes have been committed using one kind of penalty or another may seem like a pseudo-scientific attempt to analyze the national population under strictly rational principle. But statistics were revealing at a more general level for another reason: because the official statistic designates the political subject as the repository of the law's effectiveness—its utility—even while that subject achieves a newly dependent position with respect to the law. An unpredictable predictability, the political subject becomes, according to the new rationale of punishment, an uncertain but nonetheless crucial focus of legislative observation.[35]

This brings us to the second dimension of Romilly's opposition. For at the same time that he counters Madan's ossified traditionalism, he resists Paley's seemingly more generous approach to criminal law, in which judges might only infrequently apply the sentence of death. This distinction in views is a crucial one. Though Romilly is willing to agree that the feelings of judges who apply lighter sentences might in fact exhibit what is typically considered to be feelings of and for humanity, Paley's reasoning also leaves it open for magistrates to apply the law—a law known and believed by all to be inappropriate—with "arbitrary severity" (*OCL* 13). It permits, without check, the possibility of a law "continually shifting with the temper, and habits, and opinions of those by whom it is administered" (*OCL* 16). Illustrating his point with a series of identical cases, some of which had been punished with transportation and others with execution, he concludes only one thing: it is "cruel conduct" to put the fate of criminals in the hands of the "benignity of the magistrate" (*OCL* 18, 53).

Romilly's efforts, then, are equally targeted both toward making punishment more lenient and toward structuring the reservoir of lenient human "feeling" into a series of "formal statutes" that would significantly curtail the need for "judge-made" law. Deconstructive readings of the law frequently concentrate on the violence and force that arises from the fact that all law requires interpretation and is therefore "judge-made."[36] The work of reformers like Romilly, however, emphasizes that the problem with judge-made law is not that law needs to be interpreted, but that, once interpreted, the law is only irregularly enforced. In Romilly's view, the commitment to reducing penalties cannot be separated from the "absolute certainty" of their application (*OCL* 21)—an absolute certainty that seeks to reduce the power of a judge to decide whether or not a punishment should be applied. Further, the certainty of punishment participates in a more comprehensive impulse to name and identify crime. Although no man ever answers to the name of "murderer," William Hazlitt points out, "we reason and moralize only by names and classes" (*HW* 8:314). So potent is this aspect of punishment that Charles Lamb conjures up a satirical figure of an innocent man who receives a reprieve from the gallows but still cannot rid himself of the noose: a perfect image—anticipating Oscar Wilde's *The Ballad of Reading Gaol* (1898) and Franz Kafka's *In the Penal Colony* (1919)—of punishment as an indelible power that not only balances but even counteracts concerns about human utility.[37] Lamb's figure is obviously indebted to Coleridge's ancient mariner, whose obscure offense receives a punishment that is insistently rehearsed, as if to embody the reformer's ideal of the law's "firm and constant voice."[38] And it is precisely this aspect of penality that is of interest to Shelley, who (as I show in Chapter 5) attempts to vest a retributive penal power within the very text of his poetry.

Punishment widens in its scope, in Romilly's arguments, to include previously unacknowledged offenses; it also becomes more articulate in its discrimination between offenses through a series of gradations and variations of penalty. The effort to fashion punishments "proportioned to the offender's guilt" becomes central (*OCL* 22), thus burdening penalty with a new responsibility to speak about, or comment on, the crime that occasioned it. This was accepted doctrine from Montesquieu and Beccaria and was appropriated by British legal theorists like Blackstone, who declares that it is "absurd and impolitic to apply the same punishment to crimes of different malignity."[39] It was likewise intolerable to apply different punishments to similar crimes—as in the traditional practice of submitting nobility to beheading rather than hanging.[40]

This aspect of the reformers' arguments supplied welcome fodder for politicians—including the reformers themselves—to contrast their own commitments with revolutionary France and its use of the guillotine. Although the guillotine had initially symbolized equality and efficiency in punishment, the mechanism (as I discuss further in Chapter 3) eventually became an object of horror and revulsion, regarded as an instrument of uncontrolled and lethal revolutionary passion.[41] Byron's plan for the end of *Don Juan*, which involved sending his passionate hero to the hungry jaws of the guillotine, would thus have resulted in the tragic irony of having the sheer malevolence of law outdo any of the criminal's supposed offenses. The emphasis on proportion in the views of Romilly and his cohort nevertheless posed a troubling but consistent challenge to the first idea that punishments were to be slight, that they were to economize on suffering caused to the guilty. On the one hand, the first maxim suggested that even the greatest of crimes might be punished with substantially less severe penalties than death—maybe only a fine of a shilling. On the other

Chapter 1

hand, the second maxim suggested that penal law needed to be a system of understandable rules that instantiated moral-political conviction regarding the different shades of severity that characterize each crime.[42] It was thus difficult for even the most committed reformers of the day to imagine a system of penalties "slight" enough to exclude the death penalty. Blackstone was typical in his view that execution is "the completion of human punishment"; Romilly's campaigns were primarily directed toward eliminating theft and forgery as capital offenses; and the list could go on.[43] More common was the attempt to modify the death penalty itself, refining its meaning by removing executions from public view, or removing the doctrine of "corruption of blood," in which relatives of criminals were deprived of the criminal's rightfully acquired property.[44] There were, of course, those such as Henry Brougham, who eloquently argued against the death penalty for murder in 1831, and William Ewart, who in 1840 campaigned to eliminate capital punishment entirely. Although there was surprising support for Ewart's bill—ninety members of parliament supported it—it would not be until 1861 that capital offenses were reduced to four (murder, treason, piracy, and arson on dockyards and arsenals), and not until 1998 that they would be completely eliminated—a law of 1969 had cut murder and arson as capital.

The historical record, from one point of view, might simply show us that change happens slowly; current citizens of the United States (along with other nations) know this all too well. To add even more bleakness to the picture, we could look at any number of European nations where there is legal abolition of the death penalty but rising popular support for it. But from another point of view, the incremental changes in what is punishable by death (if anything) are the product of a negotiation between a commitment to economy or utility and a commitment to proportionate penalty or desert. The stakes involved in the elimination of capital punishment, in other words, are less accurately viewed as the triumph or defeat of goodness or humanitarianism and more accurately viewed in terms of the problematic I have been setting forth: as movements within the possible coordination of contending but inseparable commitments informing modern understandings of punishment.

Thus, while opposition to the widespread use of the death penalty served as the foundation for penal reform, penal reform simultaneously but ambivalently recovered the death penalty as one among a coherent series of punishments that met the equally pressing utilitarian demands of deterrence and individual reform. Once we see that Romantics and those following engaged in a common problematic rather than different philosophical positions, we can see why Ewart—despite his more particular differences in outlook—could regard himself as Romilly's heir, and could cite his mentor as the main inspiration for the complete abolition of capital punishment. We can also see why even the current American opposition to capital punishment often pays a similar debt by seeking out an "equivalent" to death, such as "life without parole," thus substituting one penalty for another while leaving the sense of a graduated and proportioned system of penalties intact. The death penalty's recovery and retention, distanced from the sacrificial rite critiqued in the pages of writers from Mandeville to Scott, amply demonstrate René Girard's claim that judicial violence both retains vengeance and reconfigures it by forging it "into a principle of abstract justice that all men are obliged to uphold and respect."[45]

The effect of this increasingly economized and rationalized mode of punishing is perhaps most easily visible in the new position that fear and terror assumes in the reformers' arguments, and this will be particularly relevant for my discussions of Wordsworth in Chapter 3 and the Gothic novel in Chapter 4. The death penalty is repeatedly understood as either an instrument of terror—a desire to instill a fear of authority in political subjects—or an ironic reversal of that terror. The two are inseparable. Either the gruesome penalties produce a shallow awe, or they merely encourage "compassion" for the criminal—a problem repeatedly noted by reformers and by today's theorists. Either way, such "exhibitions" lead to a "deterioration of moral feeling" (*SSR* 2:326) because the audience either is merely frightened by an alien force or utterly undermines that force.

Montesquieu's *L'Esprit des lois* (1748) claims that fear is only an instrument of despotic regimes and has no place in a democratic republic.[46] But Romilly, it might be said, heeds Hobbes's advice in *Leviathan* (1651), which declares, "Of all Passions, that which enclineth men least to break the Lawes, is Fear."[47] Indeed, while Romilly puts the greatest emphasis on the deterrence of crimes and the reform of the criminal, those goals are attained by a modified retributivism: punishment, he says, should operate "on society as terror" (*SSR* 1:49). Rather than merely exiling the terrors of the law, we might say that Romilly organizes or manages them. The subject's apprehensions are thus inspired not simply in order to encourage respect for authority, but so that they can be distributed throughout the law's penal sanctions, since they are associated with specific pains that follow from specific offenses. Whereas Romilly identifies public executions with a lack of coherence—a mere terrifying display so disconnected from the crime that the audience only witnesses a death and not a punishment (*OLP* 110)—the formalism of criminal law relinquishes the general sense of fear associated with capital punishment. In its place emerges a more determinate sense of "doom" that must befall those who perpetrate specific crimes (*OCL* 26), or a "dread" inspired by the contemplation of interconnected actions leading to the "certain consequence" of penalty (*OCL* 50).[48]

Chapter 1

Dreadful Reading

The two points I have mentioned so far—the economy of penalty playing off its certainty and graduation—entail a third element in Romilly's argument: an emphasis on law as a public text. Penal law as it was then practiced, after all, was frequently described by reformers not simply as cruel but as unreadable, either because it was an obsolete relic from the past or because it was a variable and transient human passion—the "temper, habits, and opinions"—in the person of the judge (*OCL* 16). To understand the problem of punishment on these terms is therefore to understand it not merely as an undesirable state of affairs but as a more profound crisis of meaning. Romilly thus approvingly quotes (or rather, slightly misquotes) Burke's "Thoughts" as it describes a state of sheer incomprehension that spectators feel when confronted with a mass execution: "A carnage at once as rather resembles a massacre, than a sober expectation [sic] of the laws" (*SSR* 2:327). Excessive punishment, Patrick Colquhoun claims, results in a kind of illegible language causing the "deflect[ion]" of the ends of punishment (*EBW* 6:131). Basil Montagu—a close friend of Wordsworth's whose son was cared for by the poet and his family—even claims that excessive application of the death sentence results in other forms of correction being completely drained of significance: "Transportation is laughed at, and imprisonment thought nothing of" (*BSP* 44).

Likewise, ineffectual and meaningless punishment—linked to its imprecision, violence, and excess—haunts a whole range of Romantic writing. Robert Southey's *Botany Bay Eclogues* (1794), for instance, shows the punishment of transportation to be a vacuum of meaning: a series of negations ("no cooling streamlet," "no joys domestic"), it is a punishment that only allows the characters to lament what they have lost in a barren waste without anything to mark the passage of time.[49] In the second, published ending of Godwin's *Caleb Williams* (1794), Caleb's tragic realization is that bringing Falkland to justice does not prove his innocence as much as it solidifies his guilt. As Falkland dies and Caleb calls himself Falkland's "murderer," it becomes clear that by attempting to punish one person, he has unleashed a host of unmanageable effects: doing justice has taken away the life of one person—Falkland—and the "character" of another—Caleb himself.[50]

James Montgomery's "The Pleasures of Imprisonment" (1797) provides an explicit contrast; in his rendering, imprisonment yields a completely legible text analogized to the writing of poetry. The speaker's imprisonment, that is, results in an orderly pattern of actions likened to the "the numbers of my song," and it also inspires him to view his fellow inmates as newly formed, fantastic identities: "felons" become "satyrs wild, with garlands crowned."⁵¹ Montgomery's poem enacts the work of the revised penal laws, whose increased visibility and legibility, Romilly claims, would yield a "regular, matured, and well digested system" (*OCL* 4–5). I cannot say whether Romilly intended to misquote Burke or not in the passage above, when he substitutes "expectation of the laws" for Burke's phrase "execution of the laws" in his account of the law's proper functions and applications (which are marred by capital punishment's "carnage"). But the change from "execution" to "expectation" is still striking. While Burke opposes executions in order merely to enforce the proper "execution" of law, Romilly opposes executions in order to emphasize (in a way Burke does not) the sense of a law providing the means for certain actions to follow in a recognizable syntax—allowing a "sober expectation"—from other actions. The syntax of the law would have its counterpart in the language of the judge, who should be required to say in a "formal sentence" what the punishment for a crime is and how the "sufferings and privations of the individual might be useful to society in deterring others from acting as he had done" (*OCL* 26). An emphasis of this kind on the law as form—used for the benefit of those who have not committed crimes (those in "expectation") and those who have (those subjected to "sufferings and privations")—allows Romilly to accommodate two of the main purposes of punishment according to the reformers' agenda: deterrence of future crimes, and individual reform. The act of reading a "formal sentence" itself, or of having that sentence "read" by the judge, frames actions in such a way as to make paths visible in prospect, assigning a legible meaning—a sign or series of signs—that serves as encouragement for future contemplation.⁵²

This analogy between punishment and text hardly disguises the fragility or uncertainty of punishment's effects on the political subject-reader. Indeed, at the foundation of all arguments about the reform of punishment is the assumption that punishments might mean different things to different people; that assumption might anticipate Elaine Scarry's account of the "unsharability" of pain, and Jacques Derrida's more sweeping view of the incalculability of all legal decision.⁵³ Thus, even as Bentham criticizes certain punishments for their lack of "equability" (*RP* 181)—their tendency to produce unequal effects in different persons—he must simultaneously concede that *any* punishment's "impression" on any subject is "susceptible of perhaps an indefinite variety of degrees" (*PML* 65). One of the many problems Bentham identifies in the penalty of death, for instance, is precisely its uncontrollable meaning. The mind's "elasticity and docility," its capability of "accommodating itself to situations which at first sight appeared intolerable," frustrate the effectiveness of death as a punishment that could appeal to the intellects of political subjects with any consistency (*RP* 185).

Chapter 1

Bentham is surprisingly eloquent on this subject of mental "elasticity," as Stephen Engelmann has shown in his account of the "rise to prominence of expectation and imagination" in Bentham's thought.[54] At the same time, the penal text itself comes to be viewed as a powerful product of the imagination that engages the imaginations of subjects. Although few would consider Bentham to be an ally of poets, his comments in the *Rationale of Punishment* (1830) tell a different story, and provide the most intriguing of suggestions as to why writers of imaginative literature might have been interested in the reform of penal law. On the one hand, Bentham openly sees the application of punishment simply as a violence or "evil" that is used to prevent another secondary or subsequent evil: "The delinquent is to be pelted with invectives," he writes, "and the legislator begins and casts the first stone" (*RP* 242). On the other hand, he views the reform of the penal law as a re-forming of violence through art. The legislator thus appears in his work first as a singer: "Here the legislator begins the song of obloquy, expecting that the people will follow in chorus" (*RP* 242). And only sentences later Bentham calls upon the aid of poets, echoing Sir William Eden's claim that "anciently the laws were composed in verse, which were frequently sung in public that men might remember them."[55] Harkening back to the classical age, when "poetry was invited to the aid of law," Bentham implores poets to lend their persuasive powers to the construction of new legislation that will replace the "barbarous language that disgraces our statute book" (*RP* 244–45).

If it seems at all surprising that the chief of utilitarian philosophers would have lauded poets in this way, it seems much less so when we realize that punishment is in fact consistently invested with power precisely insofar as it achieves the status of a full-fledged imaginative artifice. The penal law's authority, that is, consists of its capacity to appeal to the minds of subjects and give expression to a feeling that is only remotely or imperfectly acknowledged. If Romilly suggests that the law is to be consistent with the feelings of humanity, the feelings of humanity simultaneously need to achieve their shape through the law itself, which reinforces what Engelmann calls a "mental landscape" in the subject.[56] The founding paradox of the reformed penal law is that its effectiveness depends upon its uncertain foundation in popular manners, habits, or customs, even while those very manners, habits, and customs are insufficient in themselves. Because crimes do not necessarily produce evil consequences for the perpetrator, the law produces an "artificial consequence," as Bentham describes it, in the form of legally inflicted pain (*PML* 165).

For this reason, the reformed system of punishment by the end of the eighteenth century can be seen in a new relation to the moral-political subject, having become both imagined perfection of moral volition and also its source. Perhaps it is this relation that most clearly illustrates the costs of Foucault's characterization of late eighteenth-century penal reform as utterly empty formalism—"a play of representations and signs"—that "uselessly" operates upon the "mind" but not the "soul" of the individual.[57] In contrast to this, Foucault sets up a system of "discipline" that works not by "representations," but by "the body, time, everyday gestures and activities; the soul, too, but insofar as it is the seat of habits."[58] Punishment's unsettling exteriority to individual "habits" makes it a meaningless play of signs for Foucault, but—according to the way I have been tracing out the logic governing its operations—that exteriority is inseparable from its profound engagement with moral-political subjects. The systems of penalties that are foreign to the self are also intimate to its deliberations and decisions.

This is why that clarity in criminal law's writing appears, in the work of Romantic commentators, both within and outside of the agents subject to its rule. The "important influence" of penal law, John Wilson writes in an article on the death penalty in *Blackwoods*, is to give "clarity" to the "moral sense of the people." While acknowledging that terror is not in the laws but in "the minds of men," it is the role of the laws to "command these terrors" through the administration of justice.[59] Even while Sir James Fitzjames Stephen in his majestic *History of the Criminal Law of England* (1888) insists on a clear distinction between law and morality—criminal law was "narrower than morality" and itself subject to moral decision—he also insists upon the power of the former to shape the latter (*HCL* 2:78). In his most vivid formulation, he declares: "The sentence of the law is to the moral sentiment of the public in relation to any offense what a seal is to hot wax. It converts into a permanent final judgment what might otherwise be a transient sentiment." It thus compensates for human fallibility; a man's crimes may be unnoticed or forgotten, "but the fact that he has been convicted and punished as a thief stamps a mark upon him for life" (*HCL* 2:81).

Romanticism, Punishment, and the Space of Imagination

To close this chapter, I turn to Hazlitt's essay "On the Punishment of Death." The essay is interesting for us to consider because it initially opposes the reformers but ultimately, somewhat surreptitiously, agrees with them. Still more, it makes its reservations and approval hinge precisely on the subject of "imagination" and the degree to which reformers have or have not appealed to it. We could turn to any number of texts that explicitly connect imagination to the issue of punishment: in one of Mark Akenside's early examples of the imagination's power in *The Pleasures of Imagination* (1744), a village matron thrills her listeners with tales of crime and retribution, in which a robber hears his "death-bed call" and "unquiet souls" walk the earth to ease their guilt.⁶⁰

But Hazlitt's essay sets us on the right track for explaining the more profound ramifications of this common conjunction of terms. He first wrote it in 1812 and published it in a condensed form in *Fraser's Magazine* in 1831; Duncan Wu's recent publication of the manuscript version of the essay (actually a conflation of two fragments) is a helpful contribution toward understanding Hazlitt's views because of that version's somewhat more adventurous and extended arguments. The gist of Hazlitt's argument in his essay (my first quotes are from the early manuscript version) is that the death penalty has a specific instrumentality that the reformers have ignored; he thus argues against the reformers' utilitarian sympathies by saying that only the terrors of the punishment of death can be used to prevent perpetrators of "wanton aggressions of the rights of others & which proceed from hatred, cruelty &c." He states,

> Violence must be used to repel violence, the fear & indignation which is roused in necessary defence against a total disregard of all social ties must retort the injury & terror back on the heads of the aggressor in such a manner as to make them sensible of the consequences of their actions & to prevent them from triumphing in the impunity of their crimes.

In a sense, Hazlitt is simply arguing from the standpoint of retributive justice; more rigorous penalties should be applied to more extreme offenses. By the same token, he argues for a somewhat slighter penalty for "civil offenses": fraud might be punished by a fine, theft by hard labor.⁶¹

But the argument involves further complications that arise in relation to the way both versions of the essay place a particular stress on the activity of the "imagination" and the degree to which punishments appeal to or capture it. According to Hazlitt, the reformers' position confuses "imagination & the reason"; it substitutes the second for the first and, as a result, unleashes a whole series of misunderstandings, since the distinction between the two is the foundation for "all the sentiments & constitutions of mankind."⁶² In Hazlitt's view, the problem with Beccaria's argument is its false claim that the "continuance" of punishment over a long period of time has the "greatest effect upon the mind"; the problem with Bentham's is its similarly false claim that "imprisonment & hard labour could have a more profound impression on the minds of malefactors than death."⁶³

In terms resolutely attuned to the aesthetics of Burke, Hazlitt argues instead that the continuance of punishments only becomes habitual through repetition, and that "habit reconciles us to everything." To believe, as the reformers do, that punishment can be both slight and diffused over time "is to deny that there is any such faculty as the imagination in the human mind." To account for the imagination is to account for the power of death to excite a "horror" foreclosed by the reformers' resort to less horrifying penalties. Suffering, he argues, must be "accumulated & collected into a single point of time" so that it can strike the imagination "as one object: the mind is able to anticipate & grasp the whole of it at once."[64]

The insistence on death as a unique and novel occurrence, a concentrated moment of suffering, may at first seem plausible and even lend momentary support to Adela Pinch's claims about the close connection between Romantic aesthetics and violent corporal punishment.[65] Problems quickly emerge with this idea, however. The uniqueness and novelty is really reserved only for the one who is actually killed, and it is not clear what good the "impression" on the executed criminal's mind will do. For others who are not killed but only observe, moreover, it is not readily apparent that even the death penalty itself could be prevented from becoming so frequent an occurrence that it becomes habitual and its terrors diminished. Burke worries over precisely this point in his "Thoughts": a multitude of executions results only in an "overloaded and fatigued" sense of justice; "the laws thus lose their terror in the minds of the wicked, and their reverence in the minds of the virtuous" (*EBW* 6:247). Habit, from this perspective, threatens to infiltrate Hazlitt's logic so that it might corrupt the most sublime of all penalties and thus endanger the superstructure of the entire argument.

But we must also see that a contrary movement runs through the death-penalty essay, modifying the understanding of imagination set forth in the early pages and finally affirming the logic of penal reform that he initially opposes. Over the course of the argument, imagination becomes less consistently located in the mere application of a shattering application of power. The first complication in the initial view emerges in the claim that penalties are in fact said to come not simply from the imposition of force, but from the people to whom they apply: like a true reformer, Hazlitt comments that "in general all laws are bad, which are not seconded by the manners of the people." At the same time, though, this, too, is modified, for "laws are not in conformity with the manners of the people when they are not executed."[66] As he puts it in the revised version of the essay in *Frasiers*: "One end of punishment . . . is to satisfy [the] natural sense of justice in the public mind, and to strengthen the opinion of the community by its act" (*HW* 19:327). Hazlitt continues to locate the work of penalty in two sites: changes in manners and customs require that the laws keep pace with them, but it is clear that laws are not simply a reflection of manners but a substantial invention in their own right. Laws must produce punishments by attaching consequences to certain actions precisely because people's "manners" will not impose the punishments all by themselves. Some traditional crimes of "immorality or irreligion" are frowned upon by "society," moreover, but society cannot in turn demand legal punishment for those them.[67]

Punishment is therefore not simply a force with its own definition and not an emanation directly from the community. It is an expression of, and supplement to, the community's "natural sense of justice." In Hazlitt's words—not far from Bentham's account of artificial consequences, actually—punishment is an "aggravation of the natural consequences of things as is necessary to supply the deficiency of the natural or common sensibility to those consequences."[68] This is far from the idea of penalty as a thunderbolt striking a passive mind and forcing it to bow in submission. Hazlitt instead concludes that the imagination of the political subject engages with punishment's "aggravating" consequences—consequences that seem to be both natural and necessary, but also constructed precisely in order to be so. Indeed, only this more supple account of the imagination could explain Hazlitt's striking way of describing a murderer (the notorious Eugene Aram, tried and convicted fourteen years after the murder was committed) who forgets how to spell the word "murder": his "imagination was staggered," Hazlitt writes, from the struggle of reconciling his particular memory of the deed to the codified legal name—the "verbal admission"—of it (the misspelling is thus a sign of the staggering imagination) (*HW* 8:314). At the same time, the "aggravating consequences" are the work of the imaginative legislator, who constructs laws extending beyond "natural or common sensibility." Punishment emerges from the staggered imagination of the moral-political subject and in the imaginative constructions of the poet-legislator.

Hazlitt's essay ends up confirming the very reformist arguments he had at first opposed, and this becomes particularly clear in the later version of the essay. Now turning to "maxims" or rationales of punishment, he speaks finally of the concern for "economical" punishments just as the reformers do. He assesses the efficacy or inefficacy of punishment for those to whom it applies; the attention to effects in fact may demand that the severity of punishment be reduced in accordance with "public opinion" (*HW* 9:329). At the same time, Hazlitt insists upon the importance of "a gradation of punishments proportioned to the offense," and warns against attaching severe punishments to low degrees of guilt (*HW* 9:328). Like the arguments of reformers, then, Hazlitt's maxims do not add up to a theory—a theory about how the violence of the death penalty will deter crime. Instead, the theory is abandoned, and Hazlitt ultimately articulates punishment as a problem, a network of potentially contending directives.

It is hardly surprising that Hazlitt's 1821 essay on capital punishment for the *Edinburgh Review* offers virtually unqualified support for the reformers (*HW* 19:216–55). Still, there is a difference between Hazlitt's account and theirs, and it consists precisely in his attention to "imagination." That attention is useful because it prepares the way for discussing the place of literary works in the Romantic discourse of punishment, but this is not simply because it touches on a faculty of the mind long associated with Romantic works of art. Hazlitt's view of what the imagination is in fact declines to fulfill our expectations for imagination to reconcile opposites or resolve contradictions. As we have seen, he shifts imagination's definition, from an exclusive association with the logic of retribution (hence with a defense of the death penalty) in the first part of the essay, to a much more complex view that situates imaginative work in multiple locations. It is precisely this proliferation of locations that I think helps us to anticipate the arguments in Chapters 3 through 6 here. These literary works create imaginative renderings of punishment that inhabit a variety of vantage points: Austen's *Mansfield Park*, for instance, articulates punishment through character, while Shelley's poetry articulates punishment through the identification of his work with the operation of legal sanctions. In order to understand these works properly, we need to account for how they diverge in their tendency to privilege different aspects or rationales of penal reform; at the same time, we need to account for how these works actually complement one another and therefore offer varied illuminating perspectives on the same discursive and institutional space.

2

Uncertain Providence and Certain Punishment: Hannah More

> Guilt . . . gives rise, first, to individuality.
> Jean Genet, quoted by Jean-Paul Sartre, *Saint Genet: Actor and Martyr*, trans. Bernard Frechtman

In Chapter 1, I briefly suggested that the work of Samuel Romilly and other reformers met strenuous opposition from a number of different quarters. A more complete explanation of that opposition is in order here—not only because that opposition helps to clarify the logic of the reformist's argument, but also because it reveals the implications of that argument in a surprising and forceful way. This chapter concentrates on the didactic literature of Hannah More, whose work is both attracted to and repelled by the discourse of political reform. Her embattled but ultimately resistant posture toward the new rationales of punishment being defended in her day, I suggest, fuels the creative impulses in her own work. But that posture also does something else: its turbulent energies help to expose the religious, political, and aesthetic dimensions of those new rationales, and thus to suggest (albeit in negative terms) what attractions modern modes of punishment might hold for the writers of imaginative literature I discuss in the chapters that follow.

It must first be said, generally speaking, that didactic literature written for young men and women frequently defined itself through its rigorous and explicit positioning in relation to the philosophies of punishment that I discussed in the previous chapter. Still more specifically, it is possible to observe how that literature framed mechanisms of punishment—which had increasing amounts of power and authority attributed to them—as a support for social order and good government; consequently, to learn the rules of good conduct was to learn the law. Jeremy Bentham, for instance, imagined an orderly utilitarian society to be founded on the idea that learning the law was just as important as learning to read: "The principal instruction that government provides to its people is knowledge of its laws," he wrote in the third volume of the *Traités de legislation* (TL 3:151). Presumably a child would learn to read by learning the penal code itself.

It can come as no surprise that, early in his life, Bentham developed an enthusiasm for the works of Jean François Marmontel, whose strange and brilliant little *Contes Moreaux* he translated into English and published in 1777. Marmontel's young characters are repeatedly corrected in their progress through life by an expanded knowledge of the impact of their actions on the social good. In one of the most engaging and affecting of the tales, "The Shepherdess of the Alps," the young shepherdess Adelaide mourns over her dead husband, but is persuaded by a new lover Fenrose and his family to give herself over to new attachments. The point is not just to persuade her to fall in love again; both lover and parents ask her to consider "how many persons [she] will make unhappy" by refusing marriage. At that point her choice is clear. She chooses a new husband and new relations in order to avoid bringing a punitive misery on others and herself.[1]

The eagerness to have children learn the law quite plainly raises the issue of juvenile crime, precisely because (in this account) educability coincides with punishability. All of the writers in this book who depict or address children, in fact, see the child less in terms of a categorically different subject (as in nineteenth-century accounts of juvenile delinquency) than on a continuum with adults. The importance of Romanticism is thus to be found not in defining specific criminal identities but in defining punishment's pedagogical space, between the uncertain knowledge of the child-subject and the carefully calibrated sanctions of the teacher-legislator. The problem of the juvenile—the limits on her mental capacities—only serves to accentuate the lineaments of this pedagogical space precisely as a problematic, capable of being negotiated but never entirely solved.

Writers like Maria and Richard Lovell Edgeworth took Bentham's approach to heart, their *Practical Education* (1798) proclaims, "It is the business of education to prevent crimes, and to prevent all those habitual propensities which necessarily lead to their commission."[2] And a popular trend in the writing of literature for young women emerges in stories about saucy girls who are injured and publicly shamed, while they are also assured that their punishment is perfectly just.[3] But it must be said before going much further that the message imparted by the Edgeworths, Bentham, and Marmontel could hardly be called typical of didactic literature. From another perspective, society's modes of punishment seem quite clearly to challenge traditional religious rationales for social order, and it is the job of didactic literature to instill a proper respect for, and submission to, the ways of God. Both in conduct books and in the engaging fictions written for the consumption of youth by writers like More, we find played out a vivid drama in which mechanisms of earthly punishment compete for the reader's endorsement and attention with a Providential order that in turn supports "filial obedience" or "paternal authority."[4] Whereas the first option promises a knowable and rational system that aspires to guide a person's actions, the second teaches a more thoroughgoing obedience to divine direction; whereas one conveys the value of expected harms and benefits, the other communicates the futility of guiding one's actions based upon anything but the will of God or the directions of those who legitimately represent it.

My focus on More is not meant to imply that she is the only writer who exhibits the tensions between secular authority and the divine authority of Providence—far from it. Anna Laetitia Barbauld's *Hymns in Prose for Children* (1781), for instance, speaks to the child-reader as a "child of reason," capable (we hope) of protecting herself from whatever "improprieties" may come her way; but the hymns train reason toward the primary activity of obedience to, and praise of, God.[5] Or, in another well-known children's text of the period, Sarah Trimmer's stories about Mrs. Benson's children and the family of robins in *Fabulous Histories* (1786) constantly divide their attention between two goals that occasionally conflict. They cultivate a child's avoidance of "wanton cruelties" against animals and persons, yet they affirm a Providential order that justifies or even sanctifies some cruelties: they place animals—and certain people—at a "rank" below her reader, just as her reader is below God.[6] I focus on More, however, because her work—brilliant, devout, yet always courageously engaging with the questions that seemingly pose the most powerful challenge to devotion—deals with those conflicts in authority in unusually creative ways. In addition, the complex negotiations in her work achieve their resonance precisely through their wavering interest in, or distance from, the logic of penal reforms that are central to the discussions in this book.

Certainly V.A.C. Gattrell's enticing suggestion that More's writing intervenes within traditional practices in penal law—ritualized hangings, broadsides and ballads distributed by criminals, and the like—is relevant to the claims I make here. Distributing her pamphlets in prisons, More made her moral lessons operate as corrections of conventional literature that merely celebrated crime and proclaimed indifference to public law.[7] But even though her writings seemed cleverly pitched at those both inside and outside prisons, urging them to mend their ways, the precise nature of her message is sometimes unclear. Does she join reformers in urging her audience to guide their actions according to the scale of earthly rewards and punishments? Or does she reject such notions in favor of a more general and proper Christian submission?

When we look closely at More's writing on proper female conduct, her tales in the *Cheap Repository Tracts* (1795–98), and her novel *Coelebs in Search of a Wife* (1808), the questions often seem difficult to answer.

We realize that, at one level, More does indeed make the pedagogical aims of her work revolve around the validity of penal sanctions. These texts encourage readers to foresee the punishments—prison, transportation, death, and so on—that might arise as the predictable consequences of certain actions, and guide their own actions appropriately. This no easy task, to be sure: readers need to be instructed on how to steer clear of fraudulent systems of reward and punishment—endorsed by thieves and murderers—and govern their conduct in worldly affairs with the helpful warnings they have gleaned from More's works. But as much as she places faith at some point in these utterly secularized modes of punishment that are at the forefront of radical thinking during her day, she also must resist the threat—a threat that she makes explicit in her works as few authors do—that they pose to a proper submission to a Providential design. As important as it is to admonish her readers according to secular rationales, More encourages an occasionally contradictory humility and propriety, dissuading readers from imagining that they could know the ways of Providence and simply determine fate on their own. Only "the controlling hand of Providence" knows the future—only God knows the rewards and punishments in a future state—so the reader is encouraged to forswear the very level of understanding that these texts seem to embrace.[8]

Despite such tensions, critics have usually attempted to interpret More's work in more or less straightforward ways. Mary Poovey's *The Proper Lady and the Woman Writer* contextualizes eighteenth-century women's writing in the tradition of conduct literature, and sets up an interpretive paradigm in which authors either confirm or resist patriarchal order and self-control. For Poovey, More is the perfect avatar of conservative patriarchal values; other critics, like Elizabeth Jay and Elizabeth Kowaleski-Wallace, have reinforced that view by expanding on the role of Christianity as support for those values.[9] Few of these critics ignore the importance of More's evangelical activism or commitment to women's place in charitable work, yet others see these aspects of More's life and work as proof of her more progressive credentials. Dorice Elliott, Anne Mellor, and Mitzi Myers concur that her commitment to the advancement of women's position both within and outside the home makes her less a conservative ideologue than an active advocate for the "reformation of the middle classes."[10] Christine Krueger claims that even More's use of evangelical rhetoric cuts against the grain of traditional modes of authority among typical Anglican evangelicals by appropriating a male-centered rhetoric and therefore giving a "voice" to women's interests.[11]

Although they differ in striking ways, these critics share a great deal. Whether More's work is seen as narrowly conservative, more radical, or even revolutionary, readers explain it primarily in terms that view it as unproblematically ideological in one way or another. The only question that has been debated is simply what kind of ideology is being defended, not whether it defends, or how it defends, a more or less familiar ideology. My interest here is less focused on taking a side in this debate than on working at a somewhat more local level with the way More's texts enact struggles and tensions between competing areas of authority. Although some of these works offer relatively decisive resolutions to those struggles and tensions, I suggest that it is misleading to characterize them as narrowly endorsing one set of terms or values over another—action or submission, public or private, and so on.

What I argue instead in this chapter is that More's works consistently stage a struggle between secular and religious values that plays out most vividly as a showdown between two ways of estimating the status of legal punishments. Her works frequently endorse the logic of modern penal sanctions as a cornerstone for her own pedagogy—and even Providence itself operates according to the knowable and predictable mechanisms of a reformed criminal law. At the same time, her more theologically correct faith in an all-knowing but unknowable Providence leads More to demote the importance of those socially imposed sanctions. The point is not simply that these logics are balanced in her writing; it is rather that both directions of thought require attention, even when one is subordinated to the other. For only such attention can shed light on the costs and benefits of her allegiances and the hard work involved in bringing the conflicts in her writing to some form of resolution. Some texts—most notably those in the *Cheap Repository Tracts*—occasionally allow More's divided commitments to stay in a relatively symmetrical tension with each other; still others, like *Coelebs in Search of a Wife*—with which I end this chapter—more consistently view legal sanction as an initially compelling but ultimately misleading source of either moral or political authority. The novel thus entertains but dismisses the importance of worldly punishments, concluding that the values of "the world" and the world's "good opinion" are too discrepant from the values of "the Judge of quick and dead" to be used as a guide for human conduct.

Punishing Conduct: The *Cheap Repository Tracts*

It would be possible to add even more contrast to the interest I am taking in More's writing and the interest in the discourse of female modesty and self-control that I mentioned above. There are many instances of works contributing to this discourse, including John Gregory's *A Father's Legacy to His Daughters* (1744), with its stern injunctions to his female readers to cultivate "modesty" and "conscious virtue," which will arm them with the power to shun all manner of indelicacy and violence to the mind and body.¹² What such works imply is that women are to acquire a certain amount of knowledge—of music, art, languages, and so on—within proper bounds. As Hester Chapone's *Letters on the Improvement of the Mind, Addressed to a Young Lady* (1773) puts it, a woman is to seek after a "modest and proper use" of such knowledge, without any danger of "pedantry and presumption" that might lead to "envy in one sex and jealousy in the other."¹³ Even Wollstonecraft's *Thoughts on the Education of Daughters* (1788), which seeks to cultivate "sincerity" rather than the "imitations of affectation," nevertheless praises the virtue and consolation of a "cultivated mind."¹⁴

It is by no means the situation that the interest in punishment is utterly at odds with this literature of modesty, and Eliza Haywood's *Female Spectator* (1745) provides a case in point. In one well-known instance—amid admonitions to young women regarding the dangers of popular entertainments, improper marriages, and imbalanced passions—Haywood tells the tale of Erminia, seduced by a man at a masquerade. Her seducer, who repeatedly asks her to marry him afterward, spends (the narrator supposes, or wishes) the rest of his days in torment: "His own Thoughts must surely be the Avengers of his Crime, and make him more truly wretched than any exterior Punishment could do."¹⁵ This example is instructive, however, because of the unusual place that "Punishment" occupies in the narrative. Various puzzling and unanswerable questions arise as we read Haywood's text. We must wonder, for instance, what the author's intent is behind the suggestion that exterior punishment is insufficient for the seducer's crime. Are the torments of conscience to be preferred above it—and if so, why? What about Erminia? What does her example show the reader? Does she deserve her fate? Should women be content to punish themselves, as she does, by spending the rest of their lives not only in "Modesty" but in celibate retirement in the country?¹⁶ Why should she do so? Haywood suggests that the best that women can do is to try to avoid seducers—and maybe staying away from masquerade balls will help them do this—but the message is ambiguous at best.

Perhaps these questions arising from what Vivien Jones identifies as the issue of women's individual "morality and feeling" are unavoidable.¹⁷ Haywood, after all, is concerned primarily with the cultivation of female manners, not with the structure of authority that might demand or produce those manners. But it is precisely in this sense that we can observe a striking contrast between the questions arising in Haywood's writing and those arising in More's, which is specifically and vividly occupied with contrasting, and sometimes conflicting, sources of obedience external to the self. Consider, for example, a typical story from Hannah More's *Cheap Repository Tracts*—"Tawny Rachel," in which Rachel pretends to be a fortune-teller, tricking Mrs. Jenkins out of five guineas and young

Sally Evans out of an entire inheritance. The text is designed to serve two purposes, connected to two different vantage points on modern rationales of punishment, and they do not sit entirely easily with each other. First, the story punishes Sally for believing in Rachel: Rachel told her that it was her fate to marry Rachel's friend Robert, who is only interested in marrying her for her money. After she leaves her true love and marries Robert, Robert leaves her to die of a "broken heart"—a fitting warning, a "sad warning," to "all credulous girls."[18] The narrator at the end of the story warns us further *"not to have any thing to say to cheats, impostors, cunning women, fortune tellers, conjurers, and interpreters of dreams"* (4:162). We are not to be credulous in this way because credulity is both "foolish" and "sinful." It is foolish because fortune-tellers like Rachel are as ignorant as those whom they "pretend to teach." It is sinful because "it is prying into that futurity which God, in mercy as well as wisdom, hides from men" (4:162).

There is already a tension here, between the two alternatives of foolishness and sinfulness; the first implies that a poor decision has been made, whereas the second criticizes the very attempt to make such decisions. To be foolish is to seek advice about one's course of future action from the wrong people; to be sinful is to seek advice about one's course of future action at all. While it is indeed true that the narrative wishes to discourage any attempt to see into a futurity that God "hides from men," it turns out that this is actually a rather weak message in the story. Far more pervasive is the way that just punishments are applied to characters in order to serve as a "warning" to readers—readers who will be able to pry far enough into futurity to tell that certain actions will lead to proportionate and just punishments. Sally's punishment of death at the end of the story, for instance, does not merely demonstrate the inexplicability and unpredictability of God's ways. In fact, it can only serve as a "sad warning" to readers if they assume that predictable consequences would follow in a repeatable pattern from certain kinds of conduct.

The tension is actually even stronger given the text's insistence on providing a punishment for Rachel as well. This is the second purpose of the story. Rachel is sentenced to a year's imprisonment for stealing the five guineas from Mrs. Jenkins; she is then sentenced to transportation to Botany Bay for stealing a silver cup from Sally's home (4:161). More's text essentially confirms and abides by this regularity and predictability of the apparatus of punishment, and seems to admire it. In fact, while it might be said that Sally's punishment differs from Rachel's in that the first is a punishment by God and the second is a punishment by humans, it would actually be more accurate to say that the second provides a model for the first. It may be true that the punishment of death seems more than a bit extreme for Sally's offenses, but the point here is simply that this death (however cruel it may be) functions as a "warning" only because natural death can be interpreted as if it were intentionally inflicted. It can work as a deterrent, that is, only because it can be presumed to operate with the same certainty and regularity as the state's punishment of its criminals through systematic applications of the penal law. Sally's death is not simply an accident, and not simply a demonstration of God's unknowable plans for us, but a sentence of death imposed according to a predictable system of sanctions. Our taking heed of that system, More instructs, can keep us from harming both ourselves and others.

The example of "Tawny Rachel" thus exposes a vivid contrast between Haywood's work and More's. In the example from *The Female Spectator*, we are more likely to ask questions prompted by punishments that do not look like punishments (the seducer's avenging thoughts), or by punishments that have no relation to a crime (Erminia's suffering). In More's work, the problem is not that punishments themselves are uncertain, but that in all of their certainty and regularity, their relative *value* is uncertain. If the Providential perspective tells us that it is "sinful" to have faith in our ability to tell the future, it could hardly be "foolish" for us to refuse the tale's lessons as a guide for our future conduct. The tales encourage both humility toward God and confidence in the reader's reasoned appropriation and application of the tale's cautionary design.

It turns out, furthermore, that "Tawny Rachel" condenses in the most striking terms tensions that appear in a range of texts throughout the *Cheap Repository Tracts*. On the one hand, we can quickly see why Catherine Gallagher views More's writing as a recommendation for pure submission to the ways of an all-controlling Providence.[19] Characters in these tracts are routinely set up as atheistic or quasi-atheistic rationalists, who believe that Providence is sponsored only by "vulgar prejudices" in order to mask the reality of political "tyranny" (3:4), as the misguided hero of "The History of Mr. Fantom" puts it. Fantom's mistake, like many such erring characters in More's fiction, is to believe that the injustices of fortune can be corrected by means of human effort; More's tracts are therefore designed to show that such a position is both deluded and prideful: characters must learn that they cannot simply repair the ways of the world through the mere strength of their individual wills, bodies, or intellects.

On the other hand, More's clever pun on the name "Mr. Fantom"—which suggests that her character is haunted by the very illusions that he seeks to dispel—might imply that her own writing establishes a more secure footing than either reason or blind faith, reason's ghostly double. Indeed, the same tales that demote the use of vain predictions rely heavily on the possibility that the punishments characters experience as a result of their actions serve as lessons for readers of the works; such punishments serve as predictions that are adequate enough to guide future action. This

Chapter 2

is why so many sentences in More's writing sound like statute books: "A false witness shall not go unpunished, and he who speaketh lies shall perish," reads the heading to "The History of Diligent Dick" (which, although not written by More, was included in the tracts under her supervision).[20] For the same reason, Mrs. Simpson in "'Tis All for the Best" can be ridiculed for ignoring all of her hardships and injustices; her particular delusion is to believe that her sufferings are directed by the hand of God and that she is incapable of bettering her condition (3:251–72).

Obviously it could be argued that the lessons punishment conveys simply reinforce the will of Providence; the reader, furthermore, is to follow those lessons not only to avoid punishment but also to abide by divine laws. But this is hardly an acceptable conclusion to reach considering the regularity and clarity with which punishments seem to speak and appeal to the mind of the reader. Over and over, as in "Tawny Rachel," God himself seems to communicate through a pattern of ostensibly accidental actions and injuries that occur with so much regularity and proportion that they seem like rationally and intentionally inflicted penalties for bad conduct. In "Black Giles, the Poacher," for instance, Giles is punished for his thefts when a brick wall falls down upon him and kills him (4:145). And in "The History of Diligent Dick," the ways of Providence are "mysterious," but they also work according to a perfected logic of criminal law. After a chance meeting with his nephew, an uncle who once cheated him out of his inheritance is punished by dying "full of horror at the sins of his past life." Providence thus works as clever detective and stern judge; it brings "the most secret plots to light" and brings various forms of pain and death upon the guilty.[21] The list of such instances could go on. What becomes clear from them is that the organized mobilizations of apparently accidental injury and death work according to a fully understood Providential plan that tugs insistently against the belief that God's ways are not known to us and cannot be the focus of our rational planning.

These divided imperatives seep so far into More's tracts that characters themselves act as double agents, speaking for both proper religion and properly administered justice.[22] In one tale ("The Grand Assizes, or General Gaol Delivery"), the King is both an actual judge and a metaphorical representation of God (4:74–84); his secular offices, ostensibly limited to the sphere of human action, sit somewhat uneasily with his frequent quotations from the Bible and with his God-like power to see beyond the actions into the thoughts of his subjects. In another instance, the minister Mr. Wilson in "Black Giles, The Poacher" is the spokesperson for a religion that subordinates individual action to the power of Providence: "The ONE . . . who sees all things, and from whose eye no hole or corner can hide the sinner; for he is about our bed, and about our paths, and spieth out all our ways" (4:140). At the same time, he is the tale's representative of "upright justice," enforcing the very form of rational social order that the power of Providence might seem to demote in importance (4:124).

What, finally, is the result of the twinned injunctions of such narratives—to forgo vain and sinful attempts to plan our futures, yet to learn from the sanctions in the texts precisely in order to guide future action? Do the tales recommend obedience to God, whose ways are unknowable, so that only a general form of submission and contentment can be acceptable? Or do they recommend a more specific obedience to patterns of actions with predictable and recognizable consequences? It could very easily be said at this point that these tracts encourage a kind of divided subject that is the consequence of the divided vantage point on a system of rational rewards and punishments. The reader can (like the minister Mr. Wilson) occupy both sides of the issue in these texts, both believing and disbelieving in the ultimate power of Providence to determine human action in unpredictable ways, both emptied and full of expectations of predictable punishments that might emerge as the consequences of her actions. More's writing, then, cannot always be resolved only into a more or less straightforward inculcation of proper manners or individual conduct; what is more clearly the case is that conduct could be guided by contending sources of authority and contending modes of obedience.

Putting Punishment in Its Place

The tensions I have been describing can in many ways be defined in relation to the dissenting culture out of which More's work emerges—a culture that encourages a strong faith in God, while also encouraging independent exertion and improvement. Certainly this emphasis on both faith and works would explain why it is that worldly expectations and sanctions are not simply dismissed but receive a substantial amount of attention in More's writing, defended with rhetorical force and logical rigor. But we cannot let matters rest here, as if she were merely working out the principles of faith combined with the practical ordering of life, as described by Max Weber.[23] So far, I have been describing not only an ambivalence in More's writing but a tendency to favor legal sources of power and authority over religious ones, to such an extent that juridical law defines and explains the judgments of God. But this does not characterize the entire scope of her efforts, which frequently shift emphasis in the opposite direction. Without entirely banishing the force of legal authority from her writing, that is, she simultaneously mutes its force in favor of a Providential design that is unknowable, yet requires our submission.

In her *Strictures on the Modern System of Female Education* (1799), More thus finds a resolution to the tensions between legal and divine law by dissolving legal guilt into spiritual corruption. Legal punishment seems like an unnecessary addition to the broader impulse toward, or wish for, spiritual regeneration. Rather than hold to the centrality of legal guilt and punishment that we saw represented in the *Cheap Repository Tracts*, More consistently encourages her readers to accept their "natural corruption of the heart."[24] All sickness and evil in the world can be understood as evidence of sin (1:268–69), and thus crime and its consequent punishment loses all of its particularity. A "common depravity" characterizes all mankind and thus inspires a thoroughly generalized "fear," a "universal suspicion between man and man." The "prisons built, and laws enacted," furthermore, are simply evidence of this generalized fear dwelling in the breasts of all human beings (1:269–70). Thus the purpose of the *Strictures* is to reject the vanity of all external sources of value and concentrate entirely on "internal improvement" (1:x).

The attempt to reinterpret politics through religion moves the *Strictures*, even while it is directed toward the conduct of women in domestic environments, into a commentary on larger structures of moral-political authority. Indeed, one surprising effect of the argument is that it questions the apparently obvious purposes of criminal statutes and prisons: why do we have either laws or punishments if we are corrupt before breaking the law and corrupt after our punishment? Such questions continue to arise in this work's consistent attempt to undermine the status of both laws and the punishments they recommend. No longer endowed with the authoritative capacity it has in the tracts I discussed earlier, legal punishment has no authority on its own; it can only have a meaning within a Providential plan that cannot be completely known to us. Still more, that Providential plan may actually subvert or undermine the meanings imposed by conventional regimes of law.

If the fictional narratives in the *Tracts* seemed to provide a kind of blueprint for proper human action, More does something different here in the *Strictures*: narrative can show how the justice of human actions can be viewed and evaluated only in retrospect; such actions have absolutely no probative authority. More's account of the history of Henry VIII and Anne Boleyn, introduced to show how history needs to be converted into a "lesson of religion," provides one of the central examples of this way of thinking (1:198). At first glance, the history might seem to demonstrate a tyrant's profligacy and injustice; in More's view, however, it actually reveals a Providential purpose to assure the success of the Protestant Church in England. More thus deliberately chooses an example of a king whose injustices and tyranny cannot be denied, yet her point is not to use the example as a lesson to those who might rule more justly. She instead uses Henry VIII for the opposite reason: to show how we cannot look to the conventional institutions of human making to serve just purposes at this or at any moment during our lives. Instead, we can only learn from history a "distrust and diffidence in our own judgment" (1:210), a series of examples with no precepts. We can have no purpose for criminal law, then; if we took law as a guide, men would (like Henry VIII) murder their wives. All we can say is that law—whether we regard it as just or unjust—always provides proof of our general corruption but will ultimately be in accord with God's intentions for us at some point in the course of human history. People will be treated unjustly, but the Protestant Church will survive.

Although this ingenious line of argument is most fully drawn out in the *Strictures*, it is not entirely absent from the *Cheap Repository Tracts*; indeed, some of More's tales use this logic to resolve the tensions that I located in them earlier. Even as some of them hold up legal punishment as a means of both guiding and defining actions, still others have a way of more anxiously marginalizing punishment—or at least making legal punishment look secondary to spiritual regeneration. "Betty Brown, the St. Giles's Orange Girl" offers a case in point. Young Betty is duped by the usurious Mrs. Sponge, who has Betty sell oranges for her even while cheating her out of her profits and overcharging her for a squalid place to sleep in her lodgings. Betty's situation takes a turn for the better when she meets the genteel wife of "one of the justices of the new police" (4:107); the wife encourages her to live "independently" of Mrs. Sponge, from whom Betty has difficulty extricating herself until the justice himself intervenes. "He not only made [Mrs. Sponge] refund poor Betty's money, but committed her to prison for receiving stolen goods, and various other offenses" (4:111).

This aspect of the resolution is an important one, because it seems at first to give substantial credit to official apparatuses of criminal prosecution and punishment. How, the story makes us wonder, could Betty ever get on her feet without these mechanisms of punishment intervening on her behalf? How could she have escaped Mrs. Sponge if her tormentor had not been arrested and committed to prison? But the narrative also has ways of undercutting—or at least unsettling—this aspect of its own resolution. First of all, earlier in the text, Mrs. Sponge threatens to turn Betty over to the magistrates when she does not have enough money to pay her for rent (4:110). Betty manages to slip away before Mrs. Sponge can call the constable, but there is more than a suggestion here that the very authorities who end up saving Betty might have imprisoned her if things had turned out just a bit differently.

Still more, Betty's regeneration at the end of the story degrades the importance of punishment of any kind. Betty now thinks of herself as a "sinner," but a sinner who is spiritual rather than temporal, and in need of spiritual rather than temporal attention. Before, she thought sinners were "only to be found in the prisons, or in Botany Bay, or in those mournful carts which she had sometimes followed with her barrow, with the unthinking crowd to Tyburn" (4:112). As in many instances in More's writing, Betty rehearses the sanctions in order of their severity, as if to reinforce the virtues of penal rationality. But this rationality is an empty display: the point is that the crowd at the execution is "unthinking"—incapable, that is, of learning from the sanction set before them. (The fact that processions to Tyburn had been abolished in 1783 in favor of executions at Newgate only emphasizes the extent to which More's anachronism construes punishment—especially capital punishment—as though it were incapable of reform, incapable of extricating itself from its past irrationality and disorder.) Betty's insight, conversely, is simply to reject the sanctions of the everyday world. Her awareness that she "had been a swearer, a sabbath-breaker, and had lived without God in the world" (4:111–12) constitutes the most profound awareness of her wrongs. Her spiritual devotion at the end of the story is meant to show us that she is secure from any possibility of temporal wrongs as well—or at least that those wrongs are now more or less irrelevant.

A number of other stories convey a similar kind of logic, thus demoting—but not entirely eliminating—the importance of legal punishment as a way of influencing conduct or securing social order. In "The History of Mr. Fantom," the main character is a rationalist who devotes himself only to philosophical abstractions and revolutionary movements in far-flung places such as Poland and South America (3:17). Although I earlier suggested that this tale makes rationalism into a phantom in its main character—and seeks a more sure-footed truth than his misguided reason supplies—the truth the story offers is, finally, a religious truth. Fantom's friend Trueman offers a counterweight to the protagonist not simply by displaying his more practical human sympathies, but by making those sympathies privilege religion over law. He faults Fantom for not teaching religious principles to his servant William, and chastises his friend for not attending to the plight of Tom Saunders, a young man in town who has been put in debtors' prison "merely through the pressure of the times" (3:18). Prison in this case is a place of obviously unjust punishment for well-meaning people caught up in the "pressures of the times"; conventional sanctions seem all the more unjust considering Fantom's wish to ship his misbehaving servant off to "Botany Bay" or else have him "hanged" (3:34–35). If some stories make even God's punishments resemble the rationality of human sanctions, this instance makes all worldly punishments—whether prison, transportation, or hanging—both cruel and ineffectual.

This general structure of the plots I am now describing, in which the certainty of retribution takes a back seat to the uncertainty of a Providential plan, threatens to undo the authority of punishment as an intentional evil applied on account of a particular act. God has intentions, but exactly what He considers a punishing evil, and how He measures it, are futile speculations. This general structure, moreover, informs the delineation of specific sorts of characters that people More's narratives—characters that contrast with the devout yet rational Mr. Wilson in "Black Giles." As much as her work wants to set itself up as educational, and wants to make legal punishment operate as a pedagogical tool, there is still another way in which the reader of More's tracts encounters characters whose goodness or evil is utterly preordained and immune to modification. She repeatedly fashions utilitarian characters, for instance, who study the rationality of penal sanctions at the same time that such knowledge is comically drained of any effect. In "The Two Wealthy Farmers," Mr. Bragwell claims to follow the letter of the law but repeatedly breaks it and fails to impart it to his unruly family (3:113–15). By the same token, the tracts occasionally suggest that the goodness of More's good characters is not achieved through any expectation and avoidance of "terrors." Goodness or evil is simply an essence that is always discerned by the narrator and reader, dwelling underneath layers of false evidence or false accusation. In "Black Giles," for example—despite the tensions in that story I outlined earlier—the "good character" of Tom Price is predetermined, so that the false evidence of his theft of apples from the widow Brown's backyard tree seems unable to stick to him or convince others of his guilt. In More's view of things, good and bad character adheres with far greater tenacity to persons than the "appearances" that only contingently, sometimes falsely, define them (4:136).

Sublime Acquiescence: *Coelebs* in Search of Solutions

More's novel *Coelebs in Search of a Wife*—essentially a conduct book on how a young man should search for a mate, and how a young woman should style herself as such a mate—both incorporates the tensions between structures of authority and finds a particularly compelling and elaborate resolution to them. And, more than in any other work by her hand, the novel vividly demonstrates the aesthetic results of More's powerfully asserted resistance to the language and logic of penal-law reform. In one sense, the novel's concern with female education and conduct may seem to make it overtly didactic, encouraging its readers to follow the pattern of its virtuous main characters. Yet in another sense, I think that More's work adopts a rather complicated perspective on didacticism more generally. Its emphasis on right and wrong choices for producing earthly happiness is gradually obscured in the narrative's quest to produce a sense of human community that attempts to erase the importance of choices, and the consequences of such choices, altogether.

The entire novel essentially works as an odd allegory of Providential authority: two fathers plan a marriage between their children, Charles (who becomes the married "Coelebs" at the end of the novel) and Lucilla, but they leave their children to produce by consent the marriage that they had initially intended for them. We only learn about this Providential plan close to the end of the novel, though. More begins by having the hero's father die, followed shortly after by the death of his mother. Following the wishes of both parents that he should search for a wife, Charles goes to London and finds two able and well-connected guides in Sir John and Lady Belfield, who introduce him to a series of initially promising but ultimately inadequate prospective spouses. It is not until he ventures outside London and meets the incomparable Lucilla Stanley, daughter of his father's life-long friend, that he discovers his perfect mate—one who embodies all the womanly perfections of Milton's Eve and can therefore reproduce the "bliss of Paradise / Which has survived the fall."[25]

That Eve can be viewed in this novel as the paragon of female virtue is indeed surprising, and I will have more to say about this in a moment. Even at the level of plot, however, there are complexities that require comment. One dimension of the novel—in which the children merely act out their fathers' collective will—demonstrates that there is no force higher than Providential authority, and no greater virtue than resignation to it. The proper word for this resignation is "acquiescence." As Dr. Barlow, the rector of Mr. Stanley's parish and spokesperson for proper religious duty, instructs, mere "submission" is not all that is asked of the Christian. Submission applies only "to what we cannot help"; by implication, "submission" to God might entail reasoning through those actions that we conduct independent of God and those that we do not. Instead, "acquiescence is a more sublime kind of resignation. It is a conviction that the divine will is holy, just, and good" (1:135).

None of this can surprise us as a description of the novel's guiding principle, given the similar logic of resignation advocated by the *Strictures* and many of the *Cheap Repository Tracts*. Still, there is another dimension to the novel, and we might even say that it is this dimension that encourages us to keep reading. It is, after all, ostensibly a novel about Charles's "search" for a wife—which might seem to highlight his individual agency rather than his acquiescence. And the novel routinely puts choices of right and wrong conduct into the foreground, in order to criticize, based on a variety of standards, one course of action over another.

We would have to admit that Charles's search is not so much for a mate whom he loves or desires, but for a mate who demonstrates proper religious faith. His search for a wife, that is, repeatedly presents him with examples of women who do not show proper acquiescence: who value fashion over piety, or doctrine over simple faith, and thus neglect the lessons of "scriptural truth" (1:78). It might be said that the search for a wife is less a search than a continued demonstration of Charles's own attitude of acquiescence reflected in his unflagging search for it in another. Charles in this way enacts Barlow's principles: his suppression of the authority of legal and worldly wisdom in relation to an attitude of acquiescence. "Worldly morality is easily satisfied with itself," Barlow says. "It sits down contented with its own meager performances—with legal honesty, with bare weight justice. It seldom gives a particle 'that is not in the bond.' It is always making out its claim to doubtful indulgences; it litigates its every inch of contested enjoyment; and is so fearful of not getting enough, that it commonly takes more than its due" (2:403–4).

The reference here to *The Merchant of Venice* (1600) may seem straightforward enough; Barlow clearly wants to distance himself from a Shylock seeking after the exact terms of his bond. He stands for the spirit of general acquiescence over the letter of what is due. But just like the Shakespearean context itself, the novel is actually more complicated in its stance toward worldly institutions and values. After all, More often seems less interested in characters that are mere founts of religious wisdom and more interested in characters that shuttle between two worlds (as we saw in the *Tracts*). Dr. Barlow's position, while it may speak an authoritative truth about religion, cannot provide the blueprint for human character, and neither can Barlow himself. Or, at least, Charles cannot find in him a model worthy or capable of imitation. Mr. Stanley can, though. This is mainly because Stanley, rather than rigidly adhering to proper religious doctrine, sides alternately with the unworldly and the worldly, the religious and the secular. He criticizes the popular vogue for women to gather a "gay confusion of acquirements" rather than religious wisdom (1:340), but then again he cajoles Lady Aston to relax the very religious principles he elsewhere extols. Urging her to modify her treatment of her sluggish and uninquisitive daughters, he suggests that she "take them out of themselves" in order to enjoy the fruits of worldly knowledge and pleasure instead of indulging in religious melancholy (1:225).

There is still more to suggest that worldly wisdom is not entirely ignored or systematically subordinated to the novel's religious purposes. Even in Dr. Barlow's speech that I quoted earlier, there is a subtle irony. The very ability to claim that worldly morality treats itself to "doubtful indulgences" or "takes more than its due" implies that the unworldly requires worldly measurements for its program of critique: it calls, that is, for a preexisting worldly account of what is "due" to each person so that we can claim that someone has taken more than her fair share. Thus, the worldly morality that looks like Shakespeare's Shylock—keeping only to what is "in the bond"—cannot be supplanted by a transcendence of the maligned litigation but only by a repetition of it.

In addition, as in the *Cheap Repository Tracts*, More frequently represents the designs of Providence as if they operated with an impressive degree of regularity and systematicity. Providence, it might be said, does not always humble the intellect so much as it flatters the ambitions of utilitarian political reasoning. More populates her novel with disreputable characters who receive punishments that appear thoroughly just to any present spectator, not simply to the spectator endowed with the wisdom of hindsight. Mr. Tyrell is punished for his greed and "hollow" professions of faith by death at the end of the novel (2:365); in a somewhat odder instance, Mr. Stanley remarks upon the death of his only son, some years before, as punishment for pride: the parents loved him so "fondly," he explains, "that we might have forgotten who bestowed him" (1:141).

Odd indeed. That a parent's fondness might receive such a cruel rebuke in fact only begins to hint at the novel's persistent attempt to undo punishment's probative value. For it is ultimately impossible to overlook the way that *Coelebs* more consistently downplays the role of any rationale of reward and punishment in motivating the actions of its characters. The extended episode involving Lady Melbury and the Stokes family most clearly yet subtly defines More's position. The episode is so crucial to her moral and political vision that it nearly overshadows the marriage plot itself. At a fairly early point in the novel, during Charles's adventures in London, Lady Bab recommends that Lady Belfield and Charles patronize a young silk-flower maker, Fanny Stokes, who lives with her parents and assists them in making hats, lace, and other luxuries for fashionable London women. Fanny tells Lady Belfield and Charles about a debt of £700 that has driven her father into prison and her mother into a "paralytic fit"; the exact amount of the debt, she explains, is owed by a customer who has not paid her bills (1:148).

It later turns out that Lady Melbury is the cause of the Stokes's distress. Lady Melbury's character is already in question at this point, however, since we learn earlier in the novel about her inhumane, indeed homicidal, treatment of her maid. Earlier, she explains how her preoccupations with her millinery made her neglect the proper care of her "favourite maid," who became sick and died (1:153–54). It is at least consistent with her character, then, when Lady Melbury turns out to be the one responsible for the Stokes's debt and hence for Mr. Stokes's (and later Mrs. Stokes's) death. She is herself in debt for the same amount, but—once again preoccupied and self-absorbed—she can only think of her own predicament rather than that of the poverty-stricken Stokes family.

More's resolution to this subplot is startling and revealing, and there are two important stages in it. First, at a late moment in the novel, Lady

Melbury faces up to the magnitude of the injuries that she has caused—or some of them, at least—and we are told that she feels an appropriate "distress" as a consequence (2:437). Perhaps her sufferings strike us as a bit of a stretch: her "sense of want and woe" is supposedly that "of which a beggar can form no idea" (2:438). We may have some cause to wonder, that is, whether her feeling of pain here is entirely genuine and, if it is, whether her suffering is actually proportionate to the suffering she has caused. But the uncertainty that we may have about Lady Melbury's actual measure of want, woe, or pain turns out to be fairly irrelevant once we proceed into the second part of this subplot's resolution. At this point, the idea of retributive suffering or distress entirely disappears. Retreating with her aunt to Melbury Castle (surely an interesting choice for one whose distresses surpass a beggar's), Lady Melbury transforms her previous habits of "vanity" and "inconsiderateness" into practices of humility and charity (2:450). Offering proof of her altered ways, she takes in Fanny Stokes, employing her at the castle as governess for her children.

The Melbury plot perfectly demonstrates the position More wishes punishment to occupy in her moral-political thought. That Lady Melbury is responsible for her maid and is at least indirectly the cause of her death is ultimately left as a minor matter in the novel. We never hear about the servant again after the initial utterly shocking revelation of her death; that death is never the occasion for any of Lady Melbury's future remorse or reparation. Did More simply forget about this episode? Does her forgetting make her—the author—resemble Lady Melbury? In other words, is the maid—perhaps because of her class position—rendered unimportant in More's novel in a way that doubles and confirms Lady Melbury's neglect?

I tend to think that this is not really the author's oversight, but rather her pointed demonstration of an oversight at work in legal and institutional practices that leaves the lives of subordinate beings largely unnoticed. No one—no agent of the law, that is—intervenes on behalf of the "favourite maid," and no one punishes Lady Melbury for her negligence. If this were one of the *Cheap Repository Tracts*, More might have found a clever way to punish her: perhaps have her fall down the stairs of Melbury Castle, or even have the whole castle fall down on top of her. But the solution is different in this case. Here we have no attention to having punishments that fit their crimes. Lady Melbury's reform is sufficiently generalized so that no particular injuries need to be dealt with: all that is important is that vanity and inconsiderateness have been expunged. Earlier in the novel, Barlow asserts that "our Saviour does not describe criminality by the excess but by the spirit of the act," and Lady Melbury puts this into practice, correcting her criminality by correcting her "spirit" rather than any specific wrong or "excess" (1:272–73). The business of charitable giving, furthermore, is extended not simply to specific injured parties as compensation for loss (that would disqualify it as charity), but to wider populations that already include prior, present, and future victims of harmful actions. In other words, the lack of mention of the "favourite maid," an appellation that not only individualizes the maid but displays Lady Melbury's vanity (by flattering her power to raise the value of another person at her whim), is in fact proof that such vanity has been overcome by a thoroughly generalized benevolence.

It is within the context of the solution to its various plots that we could reconsider the importance of charity in the novel and in More's writing generally. Kevin Gilmartin argues that charitable enterprises represent one way that More focuses her energies on the domestic sphere, where she situates her wide-ranging and aggressive strategies for moral reform.[26] As Elliot argues, furthermore, More's notion of charity is not simply limited to work in the home but provides a new employment for women outside the home at the same time.[27] As a way of extending and revising these claims, I would add that the economy of charity has a direct way of addressing the economy of penality that is sometimes prominent and sometimes obscured in More's other writing. Thus charity encourages moral reform of a very specific and unusual kind. While it seems right to say that charity extends the home into the public realm, More's particular brand of charity virtually erases many of that public's familiar features.

More makes the following argument for us in *Coelebs*: "The wants of one part of the community [are] an exercise for the compassion of the other. As in different circumstances, the faults of one part of mankind are an exercise for the forbearance of the other" (2:67). Charity, that is, can be thought of as the opposite of retribution—charity is the forgiveness of fault. What is the impact of this reasoning? Certainly these attributes of charity and forgiveness constitute important facets of Lucilla's character and make her an appropriate wife for Charles. Her praise of Eve that I mentioned earlier both cuts against Milton's intentions in *Paradise Lost* (1674) and recovers an ancestral model for her version of domestic management and charitable giving. When Lucilla criticizes Milton for making Adam sorry for having to leave the presence of his maker and Eve sorry for having to leave the presence of her flowers, she is not simply criticizing him for making Eve look superficial (2:329). The point is that Lucilla, unlike Milton, views gardening as a version of charity and thus as a privileged version of the maker's own "forbearance" against sinning humankind. It could be further noted that the blooms of flowers—living and renewing remnants of Eden that convey perennial pleasures to humankind—come to look like perfect tokens of that divine mercy.

More particularly, the gardening that Lucilla practices and shares with poor women under her care leads the women's husbands away from the "public house" and back to the home (2:328). It thus has the ability to produce in all women a version of Milton's Eve, who strives, in More's quotation from *Paradise Lost* in the introductory chapter, "good works in her husband to promote" (1:2). But maybe even more important is the way that gardening in this instance performs the crucial function all at once of acknowledging, forgiving, and literally erasing the husband's fault. Besides offering a means of "forbearance" toward the erring husband, it also looks like an ingenious anticipation and prevention of future faults or injuries; it leads the husband away from the dangers associated with public houses and toward the routines of labor associated with cultivation and improvement.

Lucilla's charity might demonstrate the fact that More's novel is written for the gentry rather than middle-class readers: her characters seem at once dangerously liberated from the reach of criminal law (as in Lady Melbury's case) and raised up for careful scrutiny and regeneration. That new level of attention aimed at the upper classes might be said to supplement the actions of criminal justice in force against the lower orders. If the message of the *Tracts* is to obey the law, perhaps the message of *Coelebs* is to extend charity to those who will be harmed by the law's inaction. At the same time, however, charity takes on a much larger and more pervasive role in the novel. And it extends a skepticism about the purpose and legitimacy of law evident in many of the *Tracts*. Charity is assigned not simply to a single group of persons but to an entire society that might be cured by its salutary operations.

First of all, the charitable habits of gardening have a metaphorical significance in that they come to look very much like the habits of religious faith itself. As Mr. Stanhope informs Charles in a letter he sends him late in the novel, Lucilla's "right habits" in belief look like a pattern that keeps her from any temptation to "voluntarily renounce" her belief. There is no voluntary renunciation because voluntarism itself has been incorporated into the pattern of habit. The erring husband brought into the domestic fold is thus actually the double of Lucilla, who is herself kept from error by her right habit, just as the husband is kept from error by charitable action. Second, proper devotion and charitable action take on an almost limitless scope in their ability to absorb new members, who in turn become versions of each other. Right habits bring individuals into one continuous, undifferentiated movement or process, driving More's *Coelebs* toward the logic that Stanley Fish finds in Bunyan's *Pilgrim's Progress* (1678), where the importance of faith overrides and disqualifies all concern with "the pressure of temporal-spatial lines of cause and effect."[28] Such habits therefore stand as the antitype to all forms of criminal justice, providing security against both present and future wrongdoing and consequent punishments.

Chapter 2

The disadvantage to the strategy, it seems, is a disadvantage to More's work as a novel—at least if the genre can be said to privilege a "literal narrative" with a concern for "human efficacy."[29] Some disappointment is only to be expected once *Coelebs* abandons concerns of time and space and adopts a more archaic mode of theological argument laden with allegorical reference. So dedicated is the text to the philosophy of charity that Lucilla herself virtually becomes an allegorical figure, since she simply is reducible to the habits she advocates. That is, though her charity makes her attractive as a wife, it threatens her specificity as a rounded character with complex internal and external features.[30] Her character gradually looks like a repetition of preordained right beliefs and gestures. Still further, a range of other people who at first seem differentiated dissolve into such a pattern of beliefs and actions. Lady Melbury, whose particular character and actions the novel is so intent on erasing, ultimately looks like Lucilla, and so does the poor woman's husband. Charles knows that Lucilla is the right mate for him not because he chose her but because she, like him, has the "right habits." The list of replicated characters could continue. But then the advantage to the strategy (a moral or theological advantage rather than an aesthetic one) is that the vexed question about the status of punishment—should sanctions have a probative force, or should they be ignored in favor of a more general submission to divine will?—has been forcefully answered by dismissing punishment's relevance. There can be no need for punishment because there are no errors; there are no errors because there are no discernible characters left to commit them.

3

"Shuddering o'er the Grave":
Wordsworth, Poetry, and the Punishment of Death

> We fear a society of fearful people.
> Judith Shklar, "The Liberalism of Fear"

In the last chapter, I explored the ways in which Hannah More's writing engages in a rather complex relationship with the logic of penal reform. In much of her fiction, an attraction to that logic meets up with a powerful resistance to it. As the locus of attraction, punishment excites the energies of the imagination and defines the possible terrains for human action. As the locus of resistance, punishment stands as a threat to the wisdom of an all-knowing Providence and a possible threat to the social order sanctified by it. There is no simple solution to this tension, but rather a curious way of evacuating it by altering the very terms for writing about persons and their actions. In *Coelebs*, More rejects penality because she rejects criminality; by rejecting criminality, she essentially rejects any familiar idea of a self. Perhaps the only significant difference between More's writing and the mystical sacrificial violence so eloquently described by Georges Bataille is that More cleverly obscures the traces of the victims—the trail of dead bodies that Lady Melbury leaves in her wake—sacrificed in the project of spiritual cleansing.[1] By the end of the novel, the self is only part of one continuous and undisrupted divine action; reversing the logic of secularization—if secularization is understood simply as the humanization of divinity—More divinizes the human.

In this chapter, I turn to Wordsworth as a more typical example of the Romantic disposition toward a reformed penality, a poet who more fully embraces the connections between punishment and the literary imagination that More both acknowledges and seeks to put at bay. This is not to say that Wordsworth's views of punishment are by any means uncomplicated. Indeed, I will be arguing here that his interest in tying the power and authority of poetry to that of punishment involves a simultaneous and deeply paradoxical resistance and attraction to the penalty of death. Why and how this happens, I think, is central to understanding the place of the death penalty in the Romantic reforming imagination. Death, in More's texts, appears merely as one among many penalties that could ultimately be viewed as both "foolish" and "sinful" compared to God's infinite power and wisdom. But for Wordsworth, the death penalty takes on a new significance as the focal point for contending but inseparable modes of assigning value to punishment, and these are symptomatically expressed as contending but inseparable evaluations of capital punishment's validity. Both necessary and intolerable, the punishment of death in his writing stands at the pinnacle of a code of reasoned sanctions while destroying the life of the criminal and defeating the mental powers of the spectator in a scene of ghastly horror; the death penalty is thus constructed simultaneously as the locus of the imagination's inspiration and the cause of its degradation or destruction.

This chapter concentrates on two major poetic projects in which William Wordsworth explicitly focuses on the death penalty: *Salisbury Plain* (1793–94) and his much later *Sonnets upon the Punishment of Death* (1841). The two works take clearly different vantage points on the death penalty. The earlier work (and I extend my claims to revisions of the poem in *Adventures on Salisbury Plain* [1795] and *Guilt and Sorrow* [1842]) is designed as a work of reform, taking a principled opposition to the death penalty and other forms of legal murder, from the deaths of slaves in the colonies to the deaths of persons in foreign wars. The sonnets are unmistakably an endorsement of capital punishment, an instance of Wordsworth's later tendency to defend the very institutions he had earlier opposed. While I do want to analyze the divergent aims of these works, I also want to take account of their more intriguing and important convergence. This is because the earlier work, even with its radical commitments, cannot fully imagine a solution to the violent punishment it critiques; the later work, though it endorses the death penalty as a vivid source of terror that might frighten the political subject into submission, cannot support it without simultaneously insisting upon its archaism and (the poet wishes) its ultimate demise.

I thus want to modify arguments that others have made about these different ends of Wordsworth's career. Critics such as Enid Welsford have described the earlier protest poetry as a call for reform with "expectant hopefulness."[2] This hopefulness is attributed to Wordsworth's youthful and idealistic commitment to what Anne Janowitz calls "oppositional patriotism."[3] Like other radicals of his day, Stephen Gill argues, Wordsworth affirms "the integrity of human relationships . . . independent of all sanctions of law, authority and the state."[4] Wordsworth's later poetry, like the *Sonnets*, strikes most readers as a demonstration of the opposite—a betrayal of earlier "revolutionary ardors" and an unquestioning capitulation to the power of the state and the English Church.[5] What I suggest here, though, is that the opposition to legal murder in Wordsworth's writing coexists with, and cannot be extricated from, a commitment to it. In both early and later works, that is, the penalty of death operates as the grisly object of poetic attention for the poet's attempt to challenge the widespread and indiscriminate use of the death penalty. But this challenge is not a simple opposition to the juridical power over human life—the state's "breath" determining "the last alternative of Life or Death" (sonnet 5).[6] It is more accurately seen as an attempt, through the power of poetry, to appropriate and remold that power in a way that demonstrates the logic practiced by the Romantic penal reformers themselves: a logic that resists death while retaining it, combining lenience with severity by curtailing and limiting death's place within a graduated system of penalties. For the political reformer, the penalty of death threatens to result in a legal chaos requiring both "relax[ed]" and "invigorat[ed]" penalties. For the poet, the penalty of death threatens to result in a poetic chaos requiring his analogously relaxed and invigorated response. Wordsworth dismisses scenes of gothic bloodshed that can appeal only to those with "groveling mind[s]" (sonnet 9), while he emulates and celebrates the state's power to punish: the "awful rod" wielded by the "Law's firm hand" (sonnet 13).

Shades of Justice

Salisbury Plain takes on for itself the project of reform, and it is particularly complex because of its multiple and dissimilar targets: war, slavery, and punishment, with the first two collapsing at crucial moments into the third. (Wordsworth writes in a letter to Francis Wrangham that the object of the poem is partly "to expose the vices of the penal law and the calamities of war as they affect individuals."[7]) Adding still more complexity to the overt project of reform in the present is the series of ghostly reminders of terrors that the passage of time has not eradicated: reminders, that is, of the cultures of ancient Druids and early Christians, whose ritual killings are treated as phenomena in the ancient past, yet are ironically recapitulated in the harrowing ordeals of the present. The poem thus wishes upon itself a form of progress that seems (at least at first) to be undermined in other parts of the poem, where it is suggested that any apparent improvement upon the past might only repeat the past's injustices.

The poem opens with a traveler laboring with "painful step" (39) until at last he comes upon the ruins at Stonehenge from which he hears, or thinks he hears, voices accosting him; he then approaches the "lonely Spital" (122), where he finds a "female wanderer" (137) who recounts her story of loss and ruin: a father who has lost his land, a husband who goes to war and dies, along with her three children. In a powerful sense, Stonehenge and the lonely Spital provide the poem with a series of contrasting emblems of power and the sympathies associated with them—

even while these emblems begin to collapse into each other in a way that exerts pressure on the general narrative dependency on contrast. Stonehenge at first represents a part of the historical past: a violent heritage for modern forms of authority that can nonetheless be distinguished from them. The voice heard from the stones speaks of "priests and spectres grim and idols dire," of a "great flame" that "utters human moans," and of spectres rising from their tombs to haunt the "infernal gloom" on their ghostly steeds (93–99). Even while we are invited to view the voice as possibly a figment of the traveler's imagination ("He saw not, mocked as by a hideous dream" [101]), it functions as a crucial element in the poem's sustained efforts to tell a tale through distinctions between past and present. The "lonely Spital" seems to mark the next stage in the poem's historical allegory: "He came where, antient vows fulfilled, / Kind pious hands did to the Virgin build / A lonely Spital, the belated swain / From the night-terrors of that waste to shield" (121–24). But the "shield" from terror yields only a terrifying image in return. The very sound of the female wanderer's voice makes the traveler's hair rise in horror "to hear a voice that seemed to mourn in sorrow's throes" (135). Indeed, at this point in the poem, each alexandrine's metrical elongation—its addition of one more "painful step" in the shape of sorrow's throes (135), the heart assailed (144), and so on—acts as a formal equivalent to an agony extended through history. And although the continued voice of the female wanderer, a voice that proves itself to be "human," initially quells the man's terrified affect—"A human voice! And soon his terrors fled" (137)—the human voice actually confirms that the productions of humanity may not eliminate horrors but simply bring about new ones. While the female wanderer has sought retreat from the storms in the Spital, the place is reportedly haunted by the elements of a Gothic nightmare; her report of a man who lifted a stone, disclosing "the grim head of a new murdered corse" (153), all but reverses the poem's will to make the contrast of Druid and Christian into a progression from injustice to justice. Old stones are merely cover for new murder; the violent past is ironically repeated in the present.

There is a clear sense in which the parallelism in the poem does not simply allow the present to repeat the past, however—at least, if the poem itself can be regarded as a technology of the present. Indeed, the movement from ancient violence to a new murdered course also represents the way that the poem makes previous ages into an artful gloss. Druidical murders, just like the tale of the "Gigantic beings" and their "sacrificial altar" in stanzas 20–21, come to look like a necessary framework for interpreting the meaning of present events rather than merely a background for them. Even if druidical sacrifice is visible to the eyes of the reader as a clear case of murder, it may be comparatively less clear that the poem's ensuing scenes of war, slavery, and the execution of criminals are murder as well. The very articulation of immediate and discernible crime and suffering thus depends upon its poetic contiguity with sacrificial murders, and the formal maneuvers in the work coincide neither with an enlightened narrative of progress nor with a simple reversal of that progress. This formal contiguity reveals what is ordinarily and regularly concealed: the pervasive presence, in the reader's world, of legalized murder.

One way of putting this is that one allegorical framework critiques another. The projection of type into history through the discovery of repeated patterns of violence (a reverse form of Christian Biblical exegesis) critiques the projection of conceptual enlightenment into narrative (on the model of Greek interpretations of the "undersense" of Homer and Hesiod).[8] But we would also have to say here, I think, that allegory cannot be described merely in terms of its more traditional modes. Generally speaking, one of the primary aims of the poem is to produce new accounts of murder where they had not previously existed; the poet asks his readers to set up connections where there may be none immediately at hand, or to ferret out causes where there seem only to be disconnected effects. And the function of allegorical personification in particular is inseparable from this more basic and vital task of providing meaning amid the apparent chaos and randomness of death and bloodshed across the seas and at home in Britain. In the female vagrant's narrative—first published in the 1798 *Lyrical Ballads*—Wordsworth has his mournful speaker recount the tale of her husband's and children's deaths as natural deaths: "All perished, all in one remorseless year, / Husband and children one by one, by sword / And scourge of fiery fever" (320–22). But in another sense, they cannot be regarded as natural deaths. Indeed, the vagrant's words drift toward a different way of framing death: it is through the operation of a literary figure, the fever personified as "sword and scourge," that the seemingly random and natural event of a fever can look like an instrument of harm inflicted by human agents.[9]

Is it not in this sense—in the power of *Salisbury Plain* to assert causality, to attribute harm, and to seek justice—that Wordsworth's project pursues a version of poetic enlightening, and that this enlightening counters prevailing notions of enlightened politics *and* their critique? As if to confirm the earlier irony of past violence repeated in the present, the poem continues by explicitly framing the politics of the day as a false enlightenment doomed to repeat the past:

> Though from huge wickers paled with circling fire
> No longer horrid shrieks and dying cries
> To ears of Daemon-God in peals aspire,
> To Daemon-Gods a human sacrifice;

Chapter 3

> Though Treachery her sword no longer dyes
> In the cold blood of Truce, still, reason's ray,
> What does it more than while the tempests rise,
> With starless glooms and sounds of loud dismay,
> Reveal with still-born glimpse the terrors of our way?
> (424–32)

"Reason's ray" reveals only a world that contradicts reason's promise and threatens to undo its optimism; Andrea Henderson's claim that the enlightenment is "almost an enemy" to Wordsworth verges on understatement.[10] It is not simply that reason is betrayed by a world that is unreasonable, furthermore, but that the world inhabited and informed by reason does not differ dramatically from the world of archaic punishments (wickers paled with circling fire) and civil strife (treachery dyed in the blood of truce) that are supposedly things of the past. The only real difference is that the exponents of "reason's ray" both repeat a cycle of murders and mask the actuality of those murders. This enlightenment only leads to further "terrors," with a severely limited, rather than improved, vision: a "still-born glimpse," an immature and superficial form of knowing.

But, as I earlier suggested, the poem does not stop at this level of critique; instead, it proposes an alternative form of poetic enlightenment, and this continues to inform the arc of the entire work. It should first be noted here that the progress of the narrative, marching through a highly condensed progress of history (from Druids to Christians to modern secular government), plays off the progress or "proud career" of the sun rising in the east after the terrifying night on Salisbury Plain (398). The sun's proud career and the cluster of descriptions surrounding it serve two purposes: they comment on enlightenment's "still-born glimpse," and they provide a framework for the countervailing aesthetic work of the poem.

The sun operates within a completely abstract economy of light and darkness; it makes those things visible that are readily available to sight, but it is indifferent both to the actual humans who employ that sight and to what is seen. Simply put, the sun allows things to be seen but has little to do with seeing itself; it is therefore far removed from the suffering of human beings, who are seen and who do the seeing. One could say that all things in nature are similarly "Remote from man and storms of mortal care," but the sun has a privileged position here (357). This is because the highly conventional use of personification at such moments—simply applying human agency to nature—initially implies a parity between humans and the natural world; at the same time, the sun's way of imposing light on objects rather than exposing them, or of passing through the world without touching it, underlines the sheer artificiality of such conventions. The light of nature does not correspond to the world of humans, which is filled with actual sufferings. On the other hand, Wordsworth clearly expects the reader to see that this light, although "remote" from humans, is in fact *identical* to those enlightened rulers of his day who possess a certain kind of reason that remains indifferent to human suffering; humans are like nature—at least the sun—insofar as they remain resistant to, or care little for, humanity. The brilliant insight of the poem is to show how the extreme abstraction of nature analogically relates to a human consciousness that is equally abstracted from concerns of the human world.

Continuing to trace the poem's alternative to both enlightenment and its critique requires us to follow the implications of the sun's "proud career" a bit further. Wordsworth's strategy is not to identify the progress of the poem with the progress of the sun—the sun that only sheds light on people and things that are already available. Rather, it consistently takes note of patterns of light and shade. The morning sky filled with the sun's light still has discernible traces of "night's thin gloom" (396); the traveler's eye is "dimmed with Pity's tear" (400). The unfolding narrative exposes a series of shades and gradations of light; it thus yields a power or depth superior to that of the light that both illuminates and obscures those subtle shadings. Further, the poem more explicitly works its play of light and shade into a consistent poetic and political strategy, one that enlists the movements of narrative in the project of disclosing unseen objects and actions. Evidence now comes forth that has hitherto been hidden from view by the sun's light:

> For proof, if man thou lovest, turn thy eye
> On realms which least the cup of Misery taste.
> For want how many men and children die?
> How many at Oppression's portal placed
> Receive the scanty dole she cannot waste,
> And bless, as she has taught, her hand benign?
> How many by inhuman toil debased,
> Abject, obscure, and brute to earth incline
> Unrespited, forlorn of every spark divine?
> (433–41)

The "proof" that the poem offers, in other words, can be assimilated neither to the enlightened quest for empirically verifiable evidence nor to the mere subversion of that quest. Its proof will be made available through attention to darkness and shade: the reader is asked not to resort to common sense and visible examples of "Misery" but instead to examine the "realms which least the cup of Misery taste." Look where misery is less visible—"obscure," and thus less obvious to the eye—and you will find it. This is because those beings that require our attention—and that are at the center of the poem's enlightening strategies—are not only literally prowlers in the night, but also figuratively darkened, "forlorn of every spark divine."

There are two further interconnected poetic and political consequences of this orientation (or perhaps we might call it a disorientation, to distinguish it from the sun's orientation). First, the series of stanzas following the lines I just quoted above begin to reinvest the language of the work with a highly wrought and less conventional poetic language. Second, the same series of stanzas proceeds to identify unseen and previously unconsidered crimes inflicted on humanity, and to make the poem operate on behalf of a retributive justice that would offer proper punishment for those crimes. The work that poetic language accomplishes at this point is not indebted merely to allegorical uses of personification—the practice of calling natural objects or ideas by personal pronouns and endowing them with personal properties. We have already seen how Wordsworth works with the conventionality of the sun; "Misery" likewise falsifies the misery that stands at the center of the poem. As an alternative, the poem's figurative language now reinforces the vital quality that I earlier discussed in the context of the vagrant's narrative, by coagulating disconnected empirical agents into personified or quasi-personified abstractions.[11] It is not only in private life, we are told, that suffering appears. In fact, "nations" are involved in this cycle of suffering as well:

> The nations, though at home in bonds they drink
> The dregs of wretchedness, for empire strain,
> And crushed by their own fetters helpless sink,
> Move their galled limbs in fear and eye each silent link.
> (447–50)

The nations of which Wordsworth speaks become personified entities in order to raise the wretchedness they bring upon others—and the wretchedness they cause themselves—to a new level of legibility. The previously unattached actions of many persons within the nation now, through the help of a rhetorical figure, describe not only an actor but a victim as well, with galled limbs crushed by the very fetters they impose upon others.

Perhaps, in the broadest possible terms, the connection between figurative language and a resistance to "ocularcentrism" anticipates the philosophical privilege of the figural over the visual that Martin Jay ascribes to a certain strain of modern and postmodern thought.[12] But there is a moral-political dimension to this resistance; Ronald Dworkin's commentary in *Law's Empire* on the function of personification as a central legal strategy for conceiving of collectivities as moral agents—and determining judgments about the guilt or innocence of those agents—proves particularly relevant to Wordsworth's aim in this poem.[13] As this structure of highly wrought figures persists in the following stanzas, the primary result is that the poem (once again confirming the vagrant's narrative) makes death seem not merely random—not merely the unfortunate result of isolated or invisible actions. The agents and victims of death are collectivized within figures that expose the violent actions wrought by supposedly enlightened nations. It is the job of the poem, in other words, to make injustice apprehensible, and this injustice is crucially viewed as one form or another of violent punishment: the slave in stanza 52 bruised by the "cruel rod" of the "Tyrant" (463), the "virtuous" put to death with the "untimely stroke" of the sword in battle (506), the victim tortured by the Law's "iron scourge" or brought to "death's tremendous verge" (519, 522).

But it is at this point that more needs to be said about the humanitarian purposes of *Salisbury Plain*. For although Wordsworth is opposing the injustice of punishment, he is not simply opposing punishment in general; thus something more precise needs to be added to the suggestion of Karen Swann and Kurt Fosso that the poem aims to instill a desire for "social amelioration."[14] Part of Wordsworth's point in stanza 50, quoted earlier, was to suggest that nations engaging in unjust practices—cruelty toward slaves, cruelty in war, cruelty in violent punishments—merely bring further injustice upon themselves. I will have more to say in my last chapter about the highly specific relationship between slavery and punishment, and about the intimate link between abolitionist movements against the slave trade and the death penalty. For now, though, my main purpose is to suggest how important it is that Wordsworth expresses legalized murder not only as a cruel system but as an utterly self-destructive one: the use of galling fetters on others only fetters those who attempt to use them. The point here is one that penal reformers made repeatedly—excessive violence only breeds more excessive violence. Beccaria, for instance, took numerous occasions to caution his reader against the way that cruel punishments only created a hardening of criminals and general social disorder: "Impunity itself arises from the barbarity of punishments," he wrote.[15] Bentham confirms and refines this claim: any multiplication of punishments without strict reference to the crime "tends only to render the laws odious" to those ruled by them. It invites a disrespect for, and transgression of, the law (*RP* 80).

The Herculean Mace and the Imaginary Gibbeting

For Wordsworth, then, the point is not to reject punishment entirely, but to redefine its terms. Having directed his poetic energies against a variety of violent practices that they reinscribe as criminal—having used poetry as a means of describing guilt—he now embraces a new form of sanction.

Chapter 3

But what does the poem have to offer that would not simply be a repetition of excessive violence? What prevents it from merely restating the terrors of the Druids or the murders of the present? The poem does in fact assert a superior stance on the subject of punishment, although the terms in which that superior stance is framed are startling and disturbing:

> Heroes of Truth pursue your march, uptear
> Th'Oppressor's dungeon from its deepest base;
> High o'er the towers of Pride undaunted rear
> Resistless in your might the herculean mace
> Of Reason; let foul Error's monster race
> Dragged from their dens start at the light with pain
> And die; pursue your toils, till not a trace
> Be left on earth of Superstition's reign,
> Save that eternal pile which frowns on Sarum's plain.
> (541–49)

Certainly the language here must surprise us, partly because of the confidence in the "Reason" earlier subjected to criticism, and partly because of the return to conventional allegorical personifications earlier opened to skepticism—or even derision. But we need to notice at least one more characteristic of these final lines. For even as the power to harm is passed from the oppressor to the heroes summoned by the poet, the combined elements of the stanza nonetheless harness its violence to a retributive form of punishment that it asks the reader to see as just punishment.

To make the point clearer, a contrast could be made here with Wordsworth's characterization of the French Revolutionary display of force in *The Prelude* (1805). The "strong hand of outward violence" is only barely restrained beneath the surface of French politics in a manner that at first glance resembles the hand that is to rear the Herculean mace at the end of *Salisbury Plain*.[16] France later appears—in a still closer connection with the "Heroes of Truth"—as the "Herculean Commonwealth" that throttles "with an infant Godhead's might / The snakes about her cradle" (10.361–63). The connection here between *Salisbury Plain* and the Revolutionary books of *The Prelude* could perhaps be explained in one way by gauging Wordsworth's changing thoughts about the French Revolution. Forswearing his earlier sympathies, Wordsworth transfers language from one poem to another and thus pointedly deflates the triumphant tone of the first effort; Herculean "Reason" in *The Prelude* becomes oppression's cause rather than its cure. But there are still important ways in which the two poems actually frame the use of violence quite differently. First, the reference to Hercules in *The Prelude* casts France in terms that are mocking, or mock-heroic, rather than heroic: it is France's infancy that Wordsworth wishes to emphasize in the allusion. Infancy's might is instinctive and without thought. Like the infant Hercules, furthermore, the Commonwealth kills the snakes around "her" cradle, and the intriguing mix of genders here suggests something of a botched gender inversion. France is a woman attempting to act like a male god, while looking merely like a childish one in the process.

Second, and in keeping with the mock heroism, Wordsworth continually erases the distinction between agents and instruments of violence in the account of the French Revolution. Elaine Scarry sees this confusion as a fundamental strategy for making injury invisible in representations of war more generally;[17] in Wordsworth's articulation, the arm does not simply use violence but *is* violent; Revolutionary France does not simply grasp a Herculean mace but *is* (or wants to be) Herculean. The text is thoroughly consistent on this point, and other examples abound; no side in the conflict can provide an exit from the vicious cycle of attack and reprisal. The blighted young officer Beaupuy, for instance (once "Lord in many tender hearts, / Though heedless of such honours now" [9.145–46]), is strangely inhabited by his own weapon. While the "public News" is read, his sword is "haunted by his touch / Continually, like an uneasy place / In his own body" (9.162–64); he is simultaneously a chivalric hero and a mere tool of Revolutionary violence.

It might even be said that these separate instances enact the logic ascribed to the Revolution's official "implements of death," the guillotines mentioned by Wordsworth in Book 10 (10.375). Wordsworth gives a stunning poetic expression to the British penal reformers' fear of the French instrument of punishment. For the guillotine, while putting to death those like Madame Roland, whose "last words" give vent to the "agony" of France's forgotten "Liberty," is also significant as a killing machine that takes on the very attributes of the childish Hercules (10.53, 354, 349). The guillotine, in Wordsworth's terms, is manipulated by childish revolutionaries who are likened to impatient infants playing with a toy "wind-mill" that can't go fast enough; meanwhile, the machine itself accumulates the attributes of the tyrannical infant. "Ever thirsty," with "heinous appetites," the guillotine strangely mimics the infant god strangling the attacking serpents: "Head after head, and never heads enough / For those who bade them fall" (10.337, 339, 335–36).

The erasure of distinction between bodies and abstractions, bodies and things, obviously brings us into the realm of personification. That is, it brings us into the realm of a literary device in which things and ideas are endowed with the capacity to act as persons, and this brings us back to *Salisbury Plain*. Wordsworth uses personification in *Salisbury Plain*, as I demonstrated earlier, precisely in order to produce a sense of action and its consequences, to make legible what was previously obscured from a reader's falsely enlightened view: despite what he would have to say about the use of the poetic device later in his career, its restrained artfulness is essential to the poem's political vision. The point that Wordsworth wants to make by casting nations as tyrannical persons, furthermore, is not that nations believe themselves to be such persons, but that the reader is required to entertain that notion within the space of the poem; this in turn comes in aid of a possible relation of cause and effect. The situation is altogether different with *The Prelude*, where Wordsworth employs personification as a way of describing actual belief and practice, the mental and physical states of agents, rather than simply as a narrative device. The French Revolutionaries themselves, in other words, are led either by abstractions—acting as individuals in the name of "France"—or by their dangerous weapons, which substitute violence for deliberation. With political structures blending into persons and persons blending into instruments of violence, France can only seem in Wordsworth's reckoning like a vast scene of crime without visibly identified criminals or coherent penalties.

What is different, then, about the closing stanza of *Salisbury Plain*? While accepting the fact that Wordsworth musters violence in defense of his own poetic resolution, we also must realize how carefully and deliberately the language of retribution is now employed. At the same time that the imagery of "light" is appropriated here, the stanza's curious police action does not merely indulge in a repetition of the vocabulary of enlightened knowledge, but instead comports with the poem's artful attempts to submit criminality to public exposure.[18] It aims, moreover, to wield the "herculean mace" as an instrument (the decapitalized "h" emphasizes the place of Hercules only as a descriptive term) with measured purposes and effects. Having identified the "Oppressor" already as a murderer, it seeks to achieve a measure of the "justice" withheld from the victims in stanza 50: to make the oppressor pay for his crimes.

What emerges is, quite simply, a violence that is highly calculated, and thus in contrast not only to the French but also to the Spenserian tradition recalled in the stanza form. Spenser's Artegall, repeatedly identified in *The Faerie Queen* (1609) with Hercules, exercises a rough justice on his enemies that is always inseparable from his own physical "overruling might"; this proves the author's dictum: "Powre is the right hand of Iustice truly hight."[19] While violence is embraced victoriously in *Salisbury Plain*, this does not occur without a calculated distance. After all, the "Heroes of Truth" wield the instrument of Hercules, employing but not entirely identifying with his power. It is finally not the "herculean mace" that will kill the tyrant, moreover, and Wordsworth clearly wants us to recall that Hercules' mace, though as crucial to his iconography as his lion's skin, is not even his most dangerous weapon. In his battle with the lion and the hydra, his club proves to be less powerful than his hands.

For Wordsworth, too, the "herculean mace" is a deadly instrument that first threatens, then is withdrawn. It is, strangely, not any physical body but the "light" that will kill the offender—a light of exposure associated with the figurative work of the poem itself, rather than the shining indifference of the sun. And even this is not without its complexity: the oppressor will first "start" and then "die," as if to scramble our attempts to decide whether the death is a result of the poem's judicious punishment or the criminal's own guilt-ridden surprise.

Underwriting the humanitarian emphasis of the poem with a persistent but measured threat of retribution, Wordsworth sets forth in poetic terms what Judith Shklar more starkly identifies as the "liberalism of fear." "We fear a society of fearful people," Shklar asserts: so does Wordsworth. But the liberalism of fear is not a society cleansed of fear; it removes (again, quoting Shklar) "unlicensed acts of force . . . and habitual and pervasive acts of cruelty and torture," while allowing—we could also say encouraging and producing—"the natural and healthy fear that merely warns us of avoidable pain."[20] The reader of *Salisbury Plain*'s last stanza is one who fears oppression in order to reinscribe fear within its proper limits—a fear inspired by a clearly articulated and licensed threat of death, which the poem both endorses and carefully holds at bay. In *The Prelude*, this regulated fear helps to mark the distinction between the affect encouraged by Revolutionary terror and the affect adopted by the poet. Paris in the Revolution is a "place of fear" (10.80), as if violence is so inescapable that fear becomes a property of the place itself. The poet's fear, in contrast, is repeatedly connected to his imagination—a power of feeling fear from the expectation of future penalty for the Revolution's crimes. He is one of those whose "souls were sick with pain of what would be / Hereafter brought in charge against mankind" (10.366–67).

There is more to add here on the substantial alterations to the poem in the later version, *Adventures on Salisbury Plain*, and the eventually published version, *Guilt and Sorrow*; both, I think, add a commentary on the strategies I have just described through their divergences and convergences. *Adventures* and *Guilt and Sorrow* reorient the position of retributive justice so that a series of domestic dramas takes precedence over the historical and political concerns of the work (included in this series of dramas is the male wanderer's transformation into an escaped murderer). This much is certainly in agreement with the large number of critics who have commented on the later versions as a withdrawal from political polemic into an emphasis on the sympathetic identifications among the different characters in the poem.[21]

But there are some complications in this picture. It must be noted that the apparent conservatism of the later work—its shift from the political to the domestic—seems to coincide with a kind of leniency, an advocacy for a gentle rather than a violent reaction to criminality. In both revisions of the poem, we are told that the sailor, though a murderer, has undergone a kind of restoration; therefore the spectacle of punishment that he views on the wild waste of Salisbury Plain—a human body swinging in "a bare gibbet nigh"—appears as an excessive but meaningless display of force (*Adventures* 114; *Guilt and Sorrow* 78). Both poems thus sharply convey the sense that even without punishment, the murderer has undergone his own self-punishment and restoration: in the later poem's language, "no place to him could be / So lonely, but that thence might come a pang / Brought from without to inward misery" (*Guilt and Sorrow* 73–75). Meanwhile, the technologies of punishment appear in both versions of the poem to inspire "phantoms, horrible as vain" (*Adventures* 122; *Guilt and Sorrow* 85)—a horror that is "vain" because it is bereft of any purpose but to terrify.

The notion of these poems as a withdrawal from politics is also complicated by the continued prominence of violent punishment in both of these versions. *Adventures* closes with a description of the murdering sailor's execution, followed by a final commentary by the narrator:

> They left him hung on high in iron case,
> And dissolute men, unthinking and untaught,
> Planted their festive booths beneath his face;
> And to that spot, which idle thousands sought,
> Women and children were by fathers brought;
> And now some kindred sufferer driven, perchance,
> That way when into storm the sky is wrought,
> Upon his swinging corpse his eye may glance
> And drop, as he once dropp'd, in miserable trance.
> (820–28)

The purpose of the judicial murder and gibbeting of the sailor, like that of the gibbeting earlier in the poem, is unclear, as demonstrated by the mixed reactions to it. It inspires a "miserable trance" for those who suffer from misfortune; it goes completely unnoticed by "dissolute men, unthinking and untaught." Another, still more ambiguous effect of the execution and post-mortem punishment is the regular visiting of the "spot" by "fathers" leading "women and children." This passage surely anticipates another spot, described in the lines immediately following the "spots of time" passage from Book 11 of *The Prelude*: the site of a murderer's gibbeting is marked with a "monumental writing," maintained "by superstition of the neighborhood," encountered by the "faltering" young Wordsworth, and finally revisited in a series of "affecting incidents" recollected by the mature poet (11.295–300). *The Prelude* gives execution and gibbeting a privileged place in the poet's imagination, since the probative force of this particular punishment is honored by local belief, which is in turn celebrated by the lingering gaze of the poet. The alliance between the respect for the location of official killing and the poet's own voice helps to explain precisely what might be at stake in those lines about the father leading his family to the "spot" in *Adventures*. For even if Wordsworth's poem has implicitly criticized the death penalty up to this moment, it cannot name any form of "Justice" that would provide an alternative resolution. Indeed, even while the preceding stanza claims that the name of "Justice" has been "violated" by the killing of the murderer (819), the same stanza consecrates the very violence it questions: "Blest be for once the stroke which ends, tho' late, / The pangs which from thy halls of terror came" (817–18). Finally, then, this version of the poem critiques capital punishment, yet can only pray for a blessing upon it, urging us to view death not merely as the ending of a life but—more optimistically—as the termination of the murderer's "pangs."

In *Guilt and Sorrow*, the resolution at first seems different. Those in the city decide *not* to hang the murdering man, who has turned himself in to wait for his "doom" after he finds forgiveness in the last words of his dying wife:

> . . . no one on *his* form or face
> Could gaze, as on a show by idlers sought;
> No kindred sufferer, to his death-place brought
> By lawless curiosity or chance,
> When into storm the evening sky is wrought,
> Upon his swinging corse an eye can glance,
> And drop, as he once dropped, in miserable trance.
> (660–66)

A significant turn in the practice of gibbeting is surely relevant here: the last such event was to occur in 1832, even though much opposition had diminished its use far earlier. By the time this version of the poem appeared, in other words, the display of mercy ("His fate was pitied" [558]) reflected national sentiment and policy. Yet it is also the case that in the very gesture of leniency—a leniency that publicly credits the sailor for his contrition—the poem offers a compensatory display of force. For doesn't Wordsworth put a "form or face" in the place of the gibbet in this stanza? Though the phrase "no kindred sufferer" might at first seem to take the audience away from the spectacle of suffering, the lines nevertheless set it before us as readers: the "no" trails away from us as we read, and the "swinging corse" appears once again before the poem is allowed to close. If the dutiful father and family have now been erased from the stanza in *Guilt and Sorrow*, the dutiful poet nonetheless leads his readers to a scene of death that the stanza erases but inscribes into existence after each gesture of negation.

The point I am making here is not a deconstructive one—that Wordsworth's poem is somehow indeterminate and that the disappearing/appearing "corse" at the end of the stanza in *Guilt and Sorrow* therefore emblematizes a more general indeterminacy. Instead, I would acknowledge an uncertainty at this moment that is both highly specific and calculated: Wordsworth wants to distance himself from the power of death and evoke it at the same time; both *Salisbury Plain* and its later revisions remove and produce violence as part of their resolutions. The entire history of gibbeting is inseparable from Wordsworth's logic, moreover. Designed primarily as a way to display criminals by hanging them in chains after they were dead (although more than one instance was reported of a criminal gibbeted while alive), gibbeting—just like dissection—therefore offered a retributive value entirely dislodged from the experience of the offender. It functioned primarily as deterrence: a retribution anticipated in the mind of the political subject, adding "infamy" to death, an "addition" to the supposedly ultimate and unsurpassable penalty.[22] By appropriating the gibbet and extracting the criminal, the latest version of the poem not only rehearses the historical fact of gibbeting's demise as a practice, but also fixates on the aesthetics of the death penalty—not the moment of death, but the excessive trappings. Yet behind the aesthetics of the death penalty there is, after all, death. *Guilt and Sorrow* creates an aesthetic distance from death by fixating on an empty gibbet, but it ultimately raises the threatening specter of a corpse that might have filled it.

In addition to the history and policy attached to the death penalty, the range of legal and philosophical opinion on the subject is relevant to the argument I am making. I earlier noted how critics have linked Wordsworth's radical sympathies with the works of Godwin. Those critics accurately suggest that Wordsworth shares Godwin's political vantage point in early works like the Salisbury Plain poems, but they less accurately describe exactly what that vantage point is. Perhaps nothing better sums up Godwin's initial opinions in the *Enquiry Concerning Political Justice* (1793) than his confident assertion that a merely retributive purpose for punishment has no value whatsoever. Only an "untutored barbarism" would lead anyone to believe that punishment solely for its own sake could be legitimate. Instead, punishment can only be justified for utilitarian purposes, "for the prevention of future mischief."[23] But then two succeeding twists occur in Godwin's treatment of the issue. First, he undermines not only the retributive argument for punishment, but also a substantial portion of the utilitarian argument that he had reserved for it. Coercion cannot speak to the mind: it either degrades the powers of reason or causes the intellectual powers to recoil from the very example that coercive punishments are designed to set (642–48). Thus, if retribution is useless because we punish someone for an offense that is past and perhaps never to be repeated, prevention is also largely pointless. By supposing a repeated offense that has not yet occurred, prevention is "odious to an equitable mind" (655). Although it is not entirely abandoned as a rationale for punishment, prevention is narrowed down so far that only the purpose of "restraint"—merely keeping the criminal away from others—can be acceptable (670).

Second, however—even after insisting upon this, and reasserting that punishment is an offense to the "genius of the mind" (671)—Godwin begins to make increasingly expansive and comprehensive claims about punishment that tend to belie his initial intent to limit its force or effectiveness. For at this point, in his advocacy of how to manage punishment in a workable code, he begins to accommodate his arguments to the aims of other Romantic penal reformers. His attention to the adaptability of punishment to the "genuine sentiments of mankind" emphasizes punishment as an appeal to the very "genius" that it had seemed to violate; his emphasis on the predictability and certainty of sanctions likewise asserts punishment as a vital retributive apparatus, earlier dismissed as useless (671–73).

Godwin is certainly one of the most misunderstood of all Romantic writers (partly due to the fact that he often was misunderstood by others in his day, like Coleridge), and as a consequence the affiliation that Wordsworth had with him is also misunderstood. Godwin is not a writer advocating "an extreme form of decentralization or anarchy," as Marilyn Butler puts it.[24] His method is always to offer "extreme opinions"—Hazlitt's words (*HW* 11:17)—as critical interventions; but, like Wordsworth, Godwin critiques the workings of conventional sanctions with the intention of modifying them. Perhaps less well studied than Wordsworth's connection to Godwin is his connection to Godwin's friend Basil Montagu, the hapless father of young Basil (whom the Wordsworths took into their home to raise in 1795). Montagu, Sr. became one of Romilly's most fervent and outspoken supporters; he was active as a lawyer—obtaining reprieves for thieves sentenced to death—and as an author, editor, and publisher of works on the abolition of the death penalty.[25] If it is indeed true, as Stephen Gill writes, that the likes of Godwin and Montagu were providing "the intellectual stimulation [Wordsworth] was looking for," we can now look to those works in order to reconfigure a new way of understanding that stimulation.[26] Wordsworth's distant and hesitant embrace of the death penalty provides a poetic solution to an ongoing political negotiation, in which reformers sought to oppose the widespread use of corporal and capital penalties while simultaneously assigning them a new and limited use in a set of finely calibrated sanctions.

Chapter 3

Not for Weaker Minds: *Sonnets upon the Punishment of Death*

By the time Wordsworth was writing his *Sonnets upon the Punishment of Death* (1841), his political sympathies had in some ways changed. He no longer looked to reformers like Godwin or Romilly for inspiration; he was happier reading church histories and writing poems on "National Independence and Liberty." The sonnets I consider here may appear to reflect this trend by differing in significant ways from the treatment of penality found in *Salisbury Plain* and its revisions. Indeed, at times Wordsworth appears to celebrate the terrifying instruments of death that he earlier critiqued, and he critiques the limited, measured use of punishment advocated by the reformers he once admired.

This collection of sonnets is not by any means the first work of poetry to defend the death penalty; in somewhat more allegorical terms, Akenside's *Pleasures of the Imagination* (1744) celebrates how imagination "raises the majestic sword / Of public Power, from dark Ambition's reach, / To guard the sacred volume of the laws."[27] Imagination, that is, helps to sustain the monopoly of the state's right to kill. The uniqueness of Wordsworth's effort resides primarily in its apparently overt and strenuous apology. Yet even with this distinction, I argue that the work as a whole is not entirely decisive in this apology. Wordsworth is finally not able to view the application of judicial murder unequivocally as a right of the state or as an effective mode of deterring crimes; thus the sonnets ultimately converge in a crucial way with his earlier opposition to legal violence. If the Salisbury Plain poems show an opposition to judicial murder that must depend at least upon the threat of death, the later series lauds the punishment of death, but also strangely wishes for its disappearance.

The sonnet series first appeared in print in the *Quarterly Review* in 1841 with a commentary by Sir Henry Taylor, a politician, mediocre playwright, and fervent admirer of Wordsworth. He urged publishing the poems in this form because (Taylor claimed) the works could benefit from an "intervening prose" that would allow for "a more ready apprehension of their drift."[28] The article has two main purposes that require some explanation. It enthusiastically reviews Wordsworth's 1838 one-volume collection of sonnets, and it dramatically unveils the death-penalty sonnets before the public for the first time. Although there would appear to be no necessary obstacle to these two aims, the peculiar bent of the *Quarterly* article does not easily bring them together. This is primarily because the review portion of the piece praises the poet by anticipating Wordsworth's fame in the future, while the gloss on the sonnets worries over public recognition by boosting the poet's reputation in the present. It is not entirely clear, then—if the reader accepts Taylor's claim that Wordsworth does not write for his own age but "for posterity"—why the review would need to be written at all. If what really counts is a body of work that will endure, then why does the importance of the present work need to be impressed upon its current audience—an audience that, Taylor insists, has neither the intelligence nor the learning necessary to appreciate it?[29] All that can be said is that Taylor's "intervening" argumentative framework intrudes as a gratuitous, purposeless force—an attempt to impose upon the reader's mind the value of the works while emphasizing the futility of that project.

The confusion in fact informs the ways in which the correspondence between author and editor portrays the sonnets as if they both required and resisted Taylor's eager interventions. In one segment of this terse exchange, Wordsworth implores Taylor "to leave these Sonnets untouched in your Review"—a hint of a complaint about the way that Taylor's argumentation seems excessive in relation to its object, an attempt to exert an unnecessary level of coercion through the medium of the review.[30] Somewhat cryptically assuring Taylor in another letter that his work in the *Quarterly* will "materially promote the object you had in view," moreover, Wordsworth is led to say two things at once. He asserts his dependence upon Taylor—the "knowledge" in the sonnets, he assures him, will be "extended to many others, who may, for various reasons, have been disinclined to look into them." But he shrinks from the zealous promotion that the editor has offered by emphasizing that they are now being employed to further the success of an "object" that is Taylor's and not his.[31]

I mention these details—Wordsworth's acceptance of and separation from a violent, but perhaps pointless, intrusion on his work—primarily because they appear to be provoked by the logic of capital punishment that emerges in *Sonnets upon the Punishment of Death* itself. For the most important characteristic of Wordsworth's poetic stand on the legislative reforms that I discussed in Chapter 1, reforms that Taylor explicitly notes as the inspiration for the sonnets, is his utterly divided response to them. Wordsworth's defense of the death penalty openly battles with the penal reformers, while subtly endorsing their view of death as the most troubled of all penal sanctions. Perhaps this divided sense of purpose is not immediately obvious: to be sure, Wordsworth makes no secret in his letters on the sonnet collection that his sympathies lie on the side of the death penalty; he later lambastes his critics as "weak-minded humanitarians."[32] The publication of the sonnets themselves would seem to offer a rejoinder of sorts to weak-minded types like William Ewart, who rose to fame for his landmark, yet unsuccessful, motion for the total abolition of capital punishment in 1840.

But what are the specific characteristics of that rejoinder? Repeatedly, the effort to defend the death penalty depends upon the poet's description of, and appreciation for, the ability of the law's agents to conjure up supernatural machinery—"the statutes of Eternity" (sonnet 7), the "Hands" of God that "cannot judge amiss" (sonnet 11)—to enforce their authority. The punishment of death thus is described from the legislator's standpoint in sonnet 5 as an effort to inspire in the audience a simulation of the awe ordinarily reserved only for God:

> As all Authority in earth depends
> On Love and Fear, their several powers he blends,
> Copying with awe the one Paternal mind,
> Uncaught by processes in show humane,
> He feels how far the act would derogate
> From even the humblest functions of the State;
> If she, self-shorn of Majesty, ordain
> That never more shall hang upon her breath
> The last alternative of Life or Death.

The logic is odd, to say the least: the death penalty's inhumanity is made to seem consistent with a spiritual power copied from God and transferred to the "Majesty" of the state. Still, this hierarchical organization is repeated incessantly throughout the sonnets: the legislator produces sublime terrors, and the political subject is in turn filled with fear. Punishment on this account does not need any reference to a social good or social security, but only to a "fit retribution" (sonnet 8) that mimics the "Infinite Power" and "perfect Intelligence" of Providence (sonnet 10). The mind of the subject then is filled with correspondingly powerful emotions (shame, love, fear) and displays of emotion (heaves of the heart, shuddering, tears).

Wordsworth dramatically departs from Hannah More in this appeal to divine authority: if More eventually makes Providence discount the importance of any judicial punishment, Wordsworth strives in the sonnet above to make Providence into a certification of unrestrained violence. Thus he also dramatically departs from the account of retributive justice found in Sir Francis Bacon's essay "Of Revenge" (1627), to which he pays homage in sonnet 8. Although Wordsworth agrees with Bacon when he asserts the law's duty to prevent the "wild justice of revenge" from prevailing, Bacon sees no need to argue that princes follow the will of God. Bacon is less concerned with countering revenge with religion, and more concerned with countering private revenge with more open and public forms of revenge, which are considered "tolerable" or even "fortunate" for maintaining social order.[33]

Certainly this specific aspect of Wordsworth's defense of the death penalty may have appealed to his brother Christopher, who—as Archdeacon of Westminster—defends the death penalty some years later in a sermon on Genesis 9. (He dismisses God's protection of Cain in Genesis 4:15 as a "special dispensation.") God's words to Noah in verse 6 are the centerpiece of his argument: "Whoso sheddeth man's blood, by man shall his blood be shed, for in the image of God made he man." Man, the archdeacon explains, is God's own "viceregent" charged with the duty of "executing the divinely appointed penalty for . . . aggressions against the divine majesty, reflected in man, God's image and likeness."[34]

This aspect—the attempt to ennoble the death penalty by calling on a higher power—is also what usually defines the sonnet series as a whole for its most insightful twentieth-century readers. In Sharon Setzer's view, Wordsworth hypocritically appropriates an appeal to divine authority; he uses the poetic conventions of Petrarch, Spenser, and Milton only to further "a reified version of his own mind and what it is able to apprehend about the nature of perfection, eternity, and infinity."[35] William Galperin argues somewhat differently that the sheer conventionality of Wordsworth's gestures only shows the extent to which the poet has "relinquished his authority" to an utterly arbitrary source in a law made by humans and weakly vindicated by an appeal to God.[36] These views may differ on whether the late Wordsworth wins or loses from his appropriation of convention—whether the poet is a hypocrite or just a failure—but neither seriously questions the consistency or logical primacy of that appropriation.

The critics' assumptions receive some support from the ever-enthusiastic Taylor, who always speaks with great fervor about Wordsworth's rendering of the death penalty's purgative powers. He devotes an impressive portion of his review to an account of how the death penalty itself brings not just "fear" but "horror" into the minds of potential criminals; Wordsworth's rendering of the death penalty adds to that fear and horror, he writes, by acting as a deterrent. It inspires a "practical apprehension of the doom of death" by "investing the crime itself with the colouring of dark and terrible imaginations." Still more, Taylor defends all of this with a confidence in the poetry's ability to reinforce the death penalty's enactment of a higher purpose: the sonnets show how "God has devolved upon man a responsible agency" for administering the death penalty, which is itself an "instrument" of Providence.[37]

But Wordsworth himself does not display quite the same confidence in this aspect of the death penalty; in fact, on more than one occasion it is a cause of some uneasiness or embarrassment. The idea of rendering a person into an "instrument" of Providence, by at once involving and utterly occluding his or her "agency," would appear to repeat the logic Wordsworth critiqued in the French Revolutionaries, who believe themselves to be instruments and believe instruments to be inhabited by agency. Still more, though, don't the gruesome spectacles of death—the "colouring of dark and terrible imaginations"—resemble precisely the kind of excess that he associates with Gothic novels and popular theater in his earlier writing? Indeed, the punishment of death seems to furnish material not for those of higher intellects but for those of "vague will" (sonnet 4) or with a "groveling mind" (sonnet 9), terms that do more than merely suggest that Wordsworth might feel the need to demote, or at least compromise, the status of the punishment he ostensibly defends. Perhaps these are only the slightest indications why we might at least speculate that Wordsworth needs to defend himself—or his poetry— against the death penalty; following Taylor's commentary helps us to see even more explicitly why this might be the case.

Notice that Taylor sets up an implicit competition between the death penalty itself—the horrors of execution—and the horrors of poetry that strive to either match or outdo it. But poetry has a rather hard time in this battle. The very idea of celebrating the horrors of the death penalty puts poetry potentially in a secondary position in relation to the greater power of the gallows. Edmund Burke's *Philosophical Enquiry into the Origin of Our Ideas of the Sublime and Beautiful* (1757) comes to mind here, and may have come to Wordsworth's, too: Burke's memorable claim that an audience would abandon "the most sublime and affecting tragedy" in favor of an execution of "a state criminal of high rank" in a public square could hardly encourage a poet who wanted to write sonnets about hangings.[38] The sonnets themselves, to be sure, have contributed to their weakness—by turning the legislator (in sonnet 5 above) into a copier and the poet into a copier of a copier. Taylor only adds further emphasis to it: the death penalty is a kind of mimesis of God's terrors, and poetry is a mimesis of that mimesis. In his phrasing, the "imaginations" in poetry are "colouring" for the line and shading of something outside poetry— the horror of death—and the horror of death is presumably only the coloring for the horror of punishments beyond the grave. The death penalty therefore appeals to those of vague will and groveling minds, and it may well be the case that the sonnets themselves also appeal to those of vague will and groveling minds. The sonnets may not even succeed at this meager task, moreover, since such minds would be more satisfied with viewing an execution than with reading verse about it.

What can Wordsworth do? There is another sense of purpose in the sonnets that remains to be discussed in order to approach an answer to this question, a sense of purpose bearing directly on the positions of both the legislator and the poet, and frequently at odds with the logic of enforced terror I have discussed so far. If the legislator in the sonnets copies "with awe the one Paternal mind," it is also true that the legislator is involved in quite a different business: keeping intact the "humblest functions of the State" that the series repeatedly links to the issues of safety and security. As hostile to the rhetoric of penal reformers as Wordsworth claims to be, the language of his own work keeps drifting toward their position in surprising ways as it affirms punishment for the purposes of "firm safety" (sonnet 2) and "social order" (sonnet 7).[39] With that reasoning, he continually views the value of the punishment of death in terms of its ability to serve not as an incitement to "awe" but as one piece of a larger set of penalties that would cease to make sense if death were removed as the most extreme of them. Sonnet 6 thus speculates, for example, that removing the penalty of death would make other forms of penalty incoherent. Such a "laxity . . . could not but impair / *Your* power to punish crime, and so prevent"; death is the only way to make the "ancient" code of penalties "work for good."

Penitential Tears

Wordsworth subtly shifts from a defense of death as a mimesis of divine retribution, to an account that repeatedly connects a purely tactical sense of retributive justice to a devotion to public safety and security. It is not that one purpose reigns over another, but that the two play off each other, the need for "social good" weighing against retribution, whereas retribution is required for the coherence of social good. What is important for us to realize, then—and what critics of the sonnets ignore—is that the logic Wordsworth applies to the death penalty substantially weakens the reasons for its existence. It is no surprise that the sonnets are actually thoroughly consistent with Wordsworth's earlier Godwinian response to the death penalty as well as the reformers' arguments I mentioned in Chapter 1. For it is precisely on Wordsworth's grounds—according to which penalties might "work for good"—that the death penalty was vastly curtailed in the eighteenth century; it was precisely on those grounds, moreover, that the likes of Bentham opposed capital punishment *tout court* for its unprofitability to the public as well as its unequal effects on the convicted. It lacks "remissibility"—it cannot be revoked if a charge is mistaken; it also lacks variability—it cannot be increased or decreased in force (*RP* 181). Ewart would apply essentially the same reasoning in his own campaign against capital punishment, urging Parliament to repeal a penalty that had already proved to have no influence on crime, while strenuously arguing for "an efficient substitute" for it: something that would maintain the place of death within a graduated set of penalties.[40] It turns out that Wordsworth is not far from supporting the very argument he more overtly opposes.

Still more striking, I think, is the way that Wordsworth makes this political enterprise into a self-consciously poetic one: it is not (as I mentioned earlier) simply that he fears being read by people with "vague wills" and "groveling minds," but that he fears writing poetry that is equally vague and groveling. Taylor entirely ignores this in his appropriation of the sonnets as an unqualified and unproblematic endorsement of the punishment of death. Surely we must question exactly what is meant by the suggestion in the last of the sonnets in the series ("Apology") that the poet benefits from a relaxation of penalty: "The formal World relaxes her cold chain / For One who speaks in numbers; ampler scope / His utterance finds" (sonnet 14). This assertion that the poet deserves leniency from the conventional penalties of the "formal World" may at first seem like only a faint suggestion of his distance from the unyielding penalties he defends, as if poetic practice were directly at odds with the proclaimed subject of the poems. But this faint suggestion in fact extricates the poet's work from the merely derivative sublimity involved in imitating and celebrating conventional punishments and the terrors associated with them (as in Burke's model of the artificial execution outdone by the real one). Instead, Wordsworth's task—although few readers would call these sonnets "sublime"—at least aspires to a realm of invention with "ampler scope" than that found in the "formal World's" penalties.

In a series of instances, in fact, the subject of the poet's interest decisively swerves away from an interest in the death penalty. It is clearly the image of the penitent criminal—the criminal who has been effectively punished and does not need to be put to death—that attracts Wordsworth as a poet. The reader is requested time and again to envision, and sympathize with, a criminal enduring punishment: think of a criminal "locked in a dungeon" who "needs must eat the heart / Out of his own humanity" (sonnet 11); "see the condemned alone within his cell" (sonnet 12); consider the "pale Convict" (sonnet 13). It may seem obvious enough that all of these directions eventuate in the poet's request for the reader to endorse a punishment of death that will both end the convict's suffering and fortify the reader's "humanity" (sonnet 11). Nevertheless, what is peculiar here is that the sonnets repeatedly defend the penalty of death by entering the consciousness of the convict—a consciousness that exposes capital punishment as difficult to defend, whether politically or poetically. The sonnets, that is, dwell incessantly upon a reform of the convict's mind that renders punishment all but irrelevant; death, meanwhile, can only come as a penalty that ironically defeats the source of the poet's interest. The "penitential tear" (sonnet 10) that Wordsworth at first seems merely to ignore turns out to be the subject of all of these poems—it generates the poet's creativity and attracts the reader's corresponding attention. The poetic interest designated by and within the series therefore militates against the death penalty, even while more overtly coming to its defense. The basic structure of the work—sonnets extended into a series—reinforces this point. For even as the sonnets are extended into an "apology" asking for mercy beyond the appointed conclusion to the series, the sonnet form itself dramatizes the extenuating appeal of human emotion. As Adela Pinch has pointed out in relation to Charlotte Smith's *Elegaic Sonnets*, the sonnet structure (in both Smith's handling and Wordsworth's) is both an emblem of tradition and a vehicle for personal expression seeking "ampler scope" beyond the constraints of the "formal world."[41]

We are now able to consider one final link in this work that connects it in the most powerful way to the Salisbury Plain poems. Toward the end of his sonnet series, Wordsworth reaches an important resolution in the penultimate "Conclusion" sonnet, before the "Apology." He now gives voice to the hope that the death penalty defended so far in the series will eventually be rescinded. "Hopeful signs abound" indicating that such a future may in fact be in store for his readers:

> The social rights of man breathe purer air;
> Religion depends her preventive care;
> Then, Moved by needless fear of past abuse,
> Strike not from Law's firm hand that awful rod,
> But leave it thence to drop for lack of use:
> Oh, Speed the blessed hour, Almighty God!

The double vision at the end of the series is striking indeed. Wordsworth argues against a "needless fear" precisely in order to reinforce the healthy fear necessary for the public good and security. However, even while that fear must be maintained by the state's "awful rod," the poet weirdly makes death something that it is not: a mere euphemism, a "rod" or instrument of pain rather than of death. And he ultimately makes that rod into something that will not be required at all. Wordsworth's aim is thus to argue against any change in the penal code that might weaken the law's firm hand, but the claim exists alongside a conviction or wish that the instrument will become obsolete. Is this not a way of summarizing the full effect of the sonnet series more generally—a way of summarizing the sense of its thoroughly consistent and coherent vacillations? At the same time that the sonnets undoubtedly defend the punishment of death—I am not saying that this purpose is entirely shaken—Wordsworth consistently, albeit more covertly, undoes that purpose. He removes the violence that he seemingly defends.

At the endpoints of Wordsworth's career, then, lie inverted mirror images: assertions with counter-assertions cropping up in the background as ghostly outlines, as uncertain hopes or wishes. As the perfect flourish for this mirror-imaging of assertion and counter-assertion, Wordsworth gives his blessing both to the application of the death penalty in the earlier *Adventures* ("Blest be for once the stroke") and to the removal of that penalty in the sonnets ("Speed the blessed hour"). In the first instance, moreover, the "stroke" is death; in the second, the "strike" is exactly the opposite: the removal of the euphemistic instrument of death. We might phrase a summary of Wordsworth's career-long engagement with the death penalty, then, as "bless its stroke and its removal." The Salisbury Plain poems, I argued earlier, oppose the penalty of death at the same time that they reinforce it with a display of violence. The violence in *Salisbury Plain* and in the revisions of the poem is inseparable in Wordsworth's mind from its judiciousness. The *Sonnets upon the Punishment of Death* work according to a complementary inversion of this strategy. While the poet can defend the death penalty within a judicious system of punishments, he can only regard the horror of judicial murder itself as a threat to the poet's imagination and as an insult to his readership. The only way to secure the poetic purpose of the earlier poems is to invoke the display of retribution that they seem to undermine; the only way to secure the poetic purpose of the later sonnets is to unsettle their integrity as the unquestionable advocates of a penalty that only depletes the poet's power.

4

Jane Austen, the Romantic Novel, and the Importance of Being Wrong

> The pursuit of the incorrigible is one of the most venerable bugbears in the history of philosophy.
> J. L. Austin, *Sense and Sensibilia*

Jane Austen may seem like an unlikely choice for inclusion in this book's discussions: the drawing rooms and pruned gardens in *Mansfield Park* (1814), the novel with which I am primarily concerned in this chapter, seem far away from gibbets and paeans to the death penalty. But it is precisely this distance—a distance nonetheless accompanied by a confidence in the value of punishment—that solicits further examination. Austen's work occupies an important place among Romantic understandings of punishment because of its sophisticated evasions of legal violence that link it to more obvious critiques of capital punishment in works like *Frankenstein* (1818) and *Waverly* (1814), which I discuss at the end of the chapter. In Austen's fiction, the death penalty can be detected only in the margins, buried in dark hints and clever jokes. Beyond this implicit critique, however, lies *Mansfield Park*'s most remarkable feature: its unflagging effort to make punishments thoroughly answerable to a character's utility. Fanny is perpetually reforming herself by perpetually enduring sanctions. If Wordsworth's poetry looks to a day when the death penalty would cease "for lack of use," Austen rejects it entirely in *Mansfield Park*. This is not because punishment is banished from representation, but because it is as slight as it is pervasive. The novel makes sanctions into its most treasured resource for human value.

In *Mansfield Park*, Fanny Price leaves her aunts, uncle, and cousins with whom she has been staying at their estate, Mansfield Park, and returns to visit her considerably worse-off parents and siblings in Portsmouth. She is unpleasantly surprised by what she finds there. This is not the happy reunion she had hoped for—the relief from "fear," "restraint," and "reproach" from which she had suffered in the company of her wealthy relations.[1] Instead, she discovers that a return to her immediate family produces only further discomfort and anxiety—at best, only mixed "emotions of pain and pleasure" (318). Filled with "apprehension and flutter," alternately "shocked" and "fatigued" by the ceaseless bustle in her parents' home, she experiences emotions that are the very reverse of what she expected to feel among those nearest to her by birth; this in turn causes her to reconsider what they mean to her, and what she means to them (312, 320–21). A few chapters later, she is as anxious to leave her parents and siblings—to be "release[d]" from them with great relief—as she was to visit them (346).

On the one hand, the continuity between Fanny's painful emotions in both households, whether Mansfield or Portsmouth, is indeed striking. It causes us to wonder whether it is in fact possible for Fanny, orphaned from her family from the age of nine, to feel as if she belongs anywhere at all. On the other hand, the emotions that she feels when she visits her parents actually seem to have been inspired by very specific and interrelated features of her immediate family and their home—features that are remarkably different from those of the Mansfield household that she has left behind. First, Fanny finds that she is barely noticed by those whom she presumed dearest to her; they can only chatter in hermetic ways about her brother, his naval career, and the concerns of everyday life at home. Her sisters have "no advantage of manner in receiving her"; her father gruffly greets her, comments on her need to find a husband, and is then "inclined to forget her again" (315). Even her mother is quickly distracted by the latest news of the Thrush, the ship on which Fanny's brother William is to accept his commission (313). Second, Fanny takes note of the smallness and darkness of the rooms in the house—a parlor "so small that her first conviction was of its being only a passage-room to something better" (313), and a lack of candles that literally makes her disappear, "undistinguished in the dusk" (315). As the homecoming episode continues, it becomes more and more apparent that the conversation comes to proceed on analogy with the shape and lighting of domestic spaces; both serve as complementary causes and emblems of Fanny's inability to achieve distinction within the context of her own family. This is not just because Fanny is a visitor, moreover: even those members of the family most familiar to each other have oddly blurred identities, "drowned" or "swallowed up" in darkness and commotion (316–17). The homecoming chapters repeatedly enforce the sense that familiarity and intimacy not only make it difficult for the family group to accept new members, but also make it difficult for the intimate members themselves to be acknowledged meaningfully.

These interrelated features point out, I think, that what Fanny experiences is not so much a *repetition* of miserable conditions or painful emotions in two vastly different places. In fact, by leaving Mansfield to visit her family, she has traded one highly particularized form of pain and misery for another. At Portsmouth, she can only experience the pain of sheer exclusion and invisibility. At Mansfield, she experiences something like the opposite: a pain that derives from the impossibility of ever escaping unrelenting public notice, a distress that derives from the requirement to "harden [herself] to the idea of being worth looking at" (165). Simply put, at Mansfield, Fanny feels the kind of pain (here I mean not physical pain, but pain more broadly—following the *OED*'s definition—as any "distress") that precipitates from a virtually omnipresent pattern of judgments.[2] Thus, when she finally admits to herself that "Portsmouth was Portsmouth; Mansfield was home," she registers a preference not just for specific people, not just for a specific house, but for a specific kind of *pain* that vividly permeates her sense of appreciation for the house and its occupants (355). This preference is inseparable from the question of meaning: the pointless tautology of "Portsmouth was Portsmouth" echoes Fanny's invisibility in her family's house; "Mansfield was home" sets up a contrast through a triumphantly meaningful phrase. Indeed, Fanny wishes to return to the Bertrams' home not despite the difficulty she faced there, but because of it. For if Portsmouth had at first seemed appealing enough in its ability to offer joy free of care, Fanny—like the novel itself—ultimately articulates a preference for the "joyful cares" of Mansfield, to which she returns in chapter 46 (366).

The contrast I have described so far—a coincidence between pains or "cares" that actually turns out to be a contrast between them—helps us to understand the organization of the entire novel. Austen's work awards a special privilege to the pain that Fanny feels at Mansfield, and this positive value attached to "restraint" and "reproach" makes sense in the novel's logic because the series of chastisements and corrections from which Fanny must suffer has a curious way of constituting the very condition for her visibility as a character. It thus turns out that Fanny's sense of self is inseparable from the series of punishments that richly reward her with public acknowledgment—to such an extent that punishment seems like an invitation to the error that it might ostensibly be designed to prevent. We can hardly wonder, then, at Fanny's strongest character trait, which is to "cheat herself" of successes rather than merely attain them. Still more, Fanny's strategy is not just a personal disposition, but in fact a strategy taken up in *Mansfield Park*'s general structure of characterization. The novel renders errors in knowledge and conduct as objectives by and large to be cherished rather than avoided, since they serve as the very means through which *any* person might attain narrative distinction through a pattern of distinguishing corrections. This is why Fanny feels "distress" as a consequence of sufferings that are not her own, why other characters seem drained of visibility precisely because they seek to avoid punishment for the "sins" of others (85), and why the novel ultimately can provide its characters with no greater privilege than that of being exposed as publicly, conspicuously wrong. I ultimately want to suggest that to read the novel on these terms is to appreciate the contribution of Austen's fictional invention to the broader eighteenth- and nineteenth-century discourse on the reformed aims of punishment in modern British society. It is not that *Mansfield Park* represents agents or institutions of legal authority; rather, it provides a vivid fictional rendering of that discourse's intriguing tendency to equate a moral-political subjectivity with punishability—what would culminate in a certain modern philosophical construction of a "right to be punished," or (in another recent formulation) an alliance between "subjectivity" and "subjection."[3] Austen's novel, in other words, does not simply *reflect* a social process. At the most profound level, the construction of characters with reference to their errant actions—and the "just measure" of punishments they receive for them—both enact and reinforce the productive capacities of a new penal technology (386).

Mortifying Pleasure

It must be said at this point that my reading of the Portsmouth episode, and the painful emotions that Fanny experiences during it, continues to emphasize my departure in this book from a line of Foucauldian thought that has proved influential for accounts of eighteenth- and nineteenth-century novels generally. It also departs from a number of different accounts of *Mansfield Park*. First, I want to sustain the argument in this chapter against the way that Foucault dismisses the logic of Romantic penal reform (as I described in Chapter 1) as an empty sovereigntism; Austen's work considers punishing neither as a vestige of premodern society nor as an empty or powerless set of representations. Instead, punishing in Austen generally and in *Mansfield Park* in particular is a crucial resource for defining the boundaries of a person and his or her connections to the social world. It is in this sense, then, that Austen's emphasis on punishment differs from Foucault's account of "discipline," in which subjects internalize "habits of order and obedience."[4] In Austen, the emphasis on correction requires a persistent externalization of the individual's source of value, an externalization that is simultaneously felt as a decisive personal benefit.

Second, the argument that I am making departs in significant ways from a somewhat more obvious but nonetheless important set of claims that critics have made about *Mansfield Park*. In one sense, Fanny's disappointment with her homecoming discloses class differences between her more immediate family and her richer relatives at Mansfield. In contrast to her mother, Mrs. Price, both of Fanny's aunts—Lady Bertram and Mrs. Norris—managed to marry into privileged families and avoid such an "untoward choice" as that of a mere Lieutenant of the Marines (1). And it may seem that Fanny simply underscores a difference between financial resources in the two households when she observes to herself during the Portsmouth episode that her parents' home is "the very reverse of what she could have wished." With her newly refined aristocratic sensibilities (however inappropriate they may be for a young woman of her birth), she finds this home to be "the abode of noise, disorder, and impropriety" (322). The small, dark, and "scantily furnished" surroundings are not to her liking (321), and neither is the conduct of her family: she finds her father's "manners coarser than she had been prepared for" (322, punctuation altered); her mother is "injudiciously indulgent" with her children and shamefully "behind hand" in her housekeeping (323).

Fanny's estimations of the Price household might be taken as supports and examples of the arguments that many critics have made about the novel: it is often said to represent one of Austen's most traditional efforts in fiction, a work in which the hero champions conservative religious and political orientations upholding the twinned authorities of church and state. Although some recent critics have tended to place more emphasis on the subversive presence of Mary Crawford—and I will discuss such an interpretation later in this chapter—many more readers would tend to agree with some version of Marilyn Butler's view that it is "the most visibly ideological" of Austen's works, in which Fanny emerges as a quiet but forceful spokesperson for conservative, evangelical values.[5] Tony Tanner takes the novel to be an endorsement of "deference and obedience," for example.[6] Edward Said widens the scope to examine Austen's complicity with the hegemony of the British empire: Since the Mansfield estate is supported by its owner's plantations in Antigua, the novel "synchronizes domestic with international authority," defending the "productivity and regulated discipline" of both country estate and imperial domain.[7]

Katie Trumpener modifies this picture somewhat by arguing that *Mansfield Park* is not merely conservative but furthers the effort to reform the practices of landowners in Britain and slave owners abroad; it therefore endorses "a new breed of altruistic and nonpatriarchal paternalists."[8] Trumpener's intervention is indeed an important one because it has a way of describing the novel that is fortunately less dependent upon oppositions between conservative and radical; she perceptively shows that Austen's writing is less easy to categorize on these terms, since it reveals proclivities pointing in both directions. But what must be said about all of the accounts I have just mentioned, including Trumpener's, is that they tend to view the novel primarily as the defense of a class or group of persons (even if that group, as in Trumpener's account, is subtly defined) and their values. The argument that I am making about the novel involves a different argument about class; I am describing in more specific terms the tactical work that Austen makes class perform. The appreciable class difference at Mansfield Park, in other words, is important not merely because it stands for greater resources in property that people possess there; those resources enable a technique of social organization that lends persons and their actions a privileged form of legibility. What is at stake for Fanny is not more or greater possessions and not a higher class standing, but quite simply identity itself—her ability to be distinguished as a person. The Mansfield household provides not just a static emblem of upper-class taste or sensibility but a technology of classification. With her wealthier relations, she always knows where she stands.

Having said this, it is perhaps now more apparent why it is that, at the most general level, Fanny continually expresses seemingly contending but actually thoroughly complementary assessments of Mansfield Park's upper-class pleasures and the mortifications that relentlessly accompany those pleasures. Critics routinely forget to mention the second of these. She can, it is true, appreciate its comforts over the home of the Prices; she relishes telling her sister of "the people, the manners, the amusements, the ways of Mansfield Park," indulging not only Susan's "innate taste for the genteel and well-appointed," but also her own desire to expound on "so beloved a theme" (346). Still, it cannot be denied that the more pervasive ways of describing Mansfield Park have hardly been favorable: virtually every page of the novel set there seems to offer nothing other than "sameness and gloom," or—still worse—"threat," "terror," "misery," and so on (162, 296). The point that the reader must grasp is that the "manners" and "amusements" at the home of Fanny's wealthier relations are in fact not only inseparable from, but are constituted and supported by, the threat, terror, and misery she feels there. The impositions of pain are precisely what stand as the signs of the Bertram household's rigorous organization of personal actions and speech; Mansfield is above all a place where "all proceeded in a regular course of cheerful orderliness; every body had their due importance" (325). It is therefore crucial for us to see that scenes at Mansfield repeatedly make not simply Fanny's sought-after "peace and tranquility" but also her very identity inextricable from the censure and disapprobation of others; her pleasure in being recognized by others (and not feeling the pain of exclusion experienced with her Portsmouth relations) is inseparable from the pain deriving from her being inserted—receiving her "due importance"—within Mansfield's ordered system of punitive relationships.

This reading of the novel, I think, can at least begin to account for the way that Fanny's residence at Mansfield perpetually reminds her of her shortcomings rather than merely leaving her to enjoy the advantages of upper-class life. Indeed, virtually every sense in which Fanny is "worth looking at" or worthy of "notice and praise" (165, 166) is accompanied by a painful sense of her deficiencies. She is "ashamed of herself" and burdened with a "consciousness of misery" from her very first moments with the Bertram family (13). But what is even more surprising is that Fanny's senses of being "ignorant of many things" and "prodigiously stupid" (17) are not merely to be shrugged off through maturity but are to be carefully cultivated and sustained as a special mark of her position within the extended family group. Even the ball that Sir Thomas organizes at Mansfield later in the novel, supposedly for Fanny's own pleasure, is both an occasion for recognizing her importance in the family *and* an occasion for her to feel "happy cares" and "painful solicitude": indeed, "to her, the cares were sometimes almost beyond the happiness" (210). Whatever growth Fanny experiences in the novel from beginning to end does not remove the solicitude that seems inextricable from her happiness and self-assurance.

The early chapters are in fact worth lingering over because they provide striking examples of what it means for Fanny to become socialized through her contacts at Mansfield, and they install a kind of paradigm for other scenes to follow. In her geography lessons with the Bertram sisters, Fanny is quickly taken to task for not knowing the map of Europe, the location of Asia Minor, or the names of rivers in Russia; Maria and Julia chide her for imagining that the Isle of Wight is "*the Island*, as if there were no other island in the world" (17). These pedagogical scenarios may suggest that Fanny's movement through the novel must likewise involve a sense of social geography that is an extension of the natural geography she learns in her lessons. But it is equally important for us to see exactly how it is that Fanny's apparent stupidity—her conspicuous proclivity for absurd errors—emerges as a kind of *negative* knowledge endowed with a conspicuous advantage. It may at first seem as though Fanny simply lacks the Bertram women's "wonderful memories" for the proper names of geographical features (17). Still, what Fanny experiences at these moments, by experiencing gaps in the knowledge of names, is an acute sense of the geography of proper naming itself—the sense, that is, of finding a sequence of borders through a persistent series of blockages and missteps. In that way, the interconnection of boundaries makes geography less a matter of attaching proper names to proper places than a matter of syntactically relating one region to another. (Thus Fanny's claim that there is one island in the world might be taken as a mistaken belief that nonetheless opens up a whole field of opportunities for observing new distinctions and relations.) By way of contrast, the Bertram women's mastery of names of islands, rivers, and continents comes to look like a peculiar form of blindness in relation to Fanny's stupidity. For it is precisely through the experience of lacking geographical names for objects that she has demonstrated a superior sense of geographical relationships.

In so many words, Austen soon confirms the point I have been making about the peculiar value of this negative knowledge, when we are eventually told of the Bertram women that "with all their promising talents and early information," they are "entirely deficient in the less common acquirements of self-knowledge, generosity, and humility. In every thing but disposition, they were admirably taught" (18). The Bertram women, that is, have possession of a positive knowledge—a possession, it could be said, of cultural capital. But this is not, in the narrator's judgment, a form of "self-knowledge." Indeed, what is so striking about the very possibility of self-knowledge is that Austen disarticulates it from any form of self-possession; the very word "disposition" (surely one of the oddest words in the English language) means both "control" and "getting rid of" control, a removal or displacement of property or power.[9] The Bertram women thus have position but are lacking in dis-position. For knowing the self requires a consistent externalization of the self through continual reminders of the self's own lapses: the very sense of self-constitution depends upon a sustained and painful awareness of "ignorance" and "stupidity."

These pedagogical scenarios, rather than demonstrating a position of mistakenness from which the protagonist develops in order to attain a higher wisdom, function as a pattern for the remainder of *Mansfield Park*, a pattern according to which Fanny's sense of herself, and our own sense of her, repeatedly relies upon a sense of her inadequacies. Constantly reminded of her "foolishness and awkwardness" in the Bertram family group (23), she appears to us in every scene as "shame-faced" and conscious of her capacity to "disappoint" those around her (122). But at the same time, such inadequacy comes to provide the means of acquiring a value within the Mansfield environment: Fanny cannot disappoint anyone in Portsmouth because she cannot be noticed in the first place, because her more distant relations provide her with ever-renewed opportunities to stand corrected. Indeed, so consistent is this reasoning that the confirmation of error seems to be a reward in itself. Even when playing a game of cards, Fanny's ability to make the right move and win the game is subordinated to the pleasures of failing: if Henry Crawford were to help Fanny choose her cards, Edmund wryly comments, Fanny would not be "allowed to cheat herself as she wishes" (203). And the game of cards simply miniaturizes larger decisions that, even when felicitous, are most happily viewed as mistakes. Fanny's refusal of Henry's offer of marriage can be understood by Edmund as an example of "conduct" that, while "faultless," is still at fault: Edmund's indispensable value for Fanny is that he still wants to make her feel "mistaken," and "sorry" for a choice that is apparently correct (287–89). The point to be made over and over by such instances is not that Fanny does not measure up to a standard of correct behavior. It is rather that the feeling of not measuring up is precisely what gives Fanny a measure of her own self-worth.

Indeed, Fanny's sufferings become all the more recognizable as *opportunities* to suffer rather than simply unfortunate accidents, a source of a character's distinction rather than a violence or detriment to it.[10] Only this, I believe, can explain the pivotal role of Mrs. Norris in the novel. It is frequently the case that critics, so eager to see Austen's work as a dramatic conflict between Fanny and Mary Crawford, have little to say about Mrs. Norris. But we might instead go so far as to observe that Mrs. Norris (whose function is similar to that of Lady Catherine in *Pride and Prejudice* [1813]) is one of the novel's most sustained advocates of social invisibility, and that Fanny's very perspicuity as a person—that is, what makes it possible for us to have anything to say about her—depends upon her narrowly avoiding Mrs. Norris's attempts to blind the world to her existence. But the problem with Mrs. Norris is not that she makes Fanny feel pain for her errors in knowledge or manners; it is that she refuses to award her any such distinction. Mrs. Norris is not unkind to Fanny in any straightforward way; indeed, she insists repeatedly on making an especially generous "allowance" for error, on awarding her "pity" for her shortcomings (17). But her behavior combines mercy with negligence. Austen comically makes her care for Fanny utterly hollow; she offers assistance only to retract it, "refusing to do anything for a niece, whom she had been so forward to adopt" (27). And in repeated instances, Aunt Norris's inclination to pity Fanny is utterly inseparable from her inclination to deprive her of all occasions to be noticed or remarked upon. She insists that Fanny not assume that she has any social value in the company of others (183), that she has no business "putting [herself] forward, talking and giving [her] own opinion" (184), that she has no "purpose" at Mansfield (268), that she is "the lowest and last" wherever she is (184), and that she and everyone else "could do very well without [her]" (274). Mrs. Norris, in other words, occasionally provides a relief from pain, but this comes at the cost of being noticed; her willingness to excuse is inseparable from her unwillingness to register Fanny's significance within the family.

The Progress of Regress

The novel's way of sustaining Fanny's need and desire for correction, rather than merely allowing her to achieve correctness, might in fact imply that Austen has written a novel that is decidedly un-psychological, decidedly opposed to the design of many realist novels in which the movement of a character through time and space can be registered through accumulated mental reserves, from a position of corrigibility to a state beyond error—a movement, as J. L. Austin puts it somewhat surprisingly, toward "the incorrigible."[11] It is at this moment that we might pursue a more precise comparison between Austen's novel and two very different kinds of eighteenth-century predecessor, Samuel Richardson's *Pamela* (1740) and Elizabeth Inchbald's *A Simple Story* (1791). The very notion of character development as character correction is inextricable from a marriage plot in a whole tradition of writing in which marriage serves as the *telos* for personal development; it thus serves as a distinctively secular, domestic alternative to the maturity required for the epic quest or spiritual autobiography. Perhaps no military skill or heroic test of strength is needed for the marriage quest, but such a quest still requires demonstrations of fitness: marriage presumably calls for conformity to standards of virtue and thus the righting of wrongs, the correction of flaws. (The disappearance of all concern with error and correction at the end of More's *Coelebs*, as I explained in Chapter 2, is inseparable from its sudden shift in register to Christian allegory, and is precisely what compromises its status as a novel with distinct characters. Austen thus cleverly pokes fun at More and her circle of "evangelicals" in a letter by making revised opinion about the novel seem like the effect of a religious conversion: "Of course I shall be delighted when I read it, like other people, but till I do, I dislike it."[12])

But how correction is explicitly connected to marriage—whether marriage produces or is produced by virtuous characters—is itself a topic of debate in the world of fiction. In Richardson's novel, the protagonist must ultimately face the problem of how she can consent to marry Mr. B, a character consistently revealing a pattern of flawed behavior that might seem to threaten the integrity of any contract of marriage. The list of "proposals" or "honourable Intentions" that Mr. B draws up for Pamela toward the end of the first volume—proposals to keep Pamela as his mistress in return for financial support—offers the most explicit example of how Pamela's moral purity serves as a counterweight to Mr. B's attempts to seduce her.[13] In answer to each of Mr. B's numbered proposals in this contract, offering money, clothes, servants, and the possibility of marriage after "a Twelve-month's Cohabitation," she does not so much argue against the marriage but redefines it in order to secure the continuance of "Merit" and "Virtue" within it (167–68). The contract lays bare the need to have Mr. B's "Will" conform to Pamela's—the agreement not only reflects such a will but also is a kind of benchmark for it—so that he can put her "Doubt" about his character to rest (166, 187). That this code of conduct is negotiated contractually testifies to Pamela's "authority to define herself," as Nancy Armstrong has suggested, but it also testifies to the weakness of a contract that is only as powerful as those who live by it.[14]

In Inchbald's *A Simple Story*, the problem set forth in *Pamela*—how to make the moral error of one character consistent with the moral goodness of another—is neatly solved by the novel's abrupt shift from one generation to another. Miss Milner's insubordinate, improper conduct shows her to be an unfit partner in marriage to the inflexible Mr. Dorriforth. But instead of showing how the irreconcilable differences can be reconciled between the Lord and his Lady, Miss Milner dies at the beginning of the third volume (death being the best way out for the erring woman); the novel achieves a resolution simply by proceeding to the next generation. It moves on to a marriage between their daughter Matilda, conveniently cleansed of her mother's errors, and Dorriforth's nephew Harry Rushbrook, conveniently substituting "pity"—"the most pleasing passion that ever possessed a human heart"—for his uncle's unyielding and impatient opposition to his wife's frailties.[15] The religious politics of the novel are well served by this solution, too: the constant tension between Dorriforth's Catholicism and Miss Milner's freethinking Protestantism seems to find a solution in the next generation's secular sentimentalism that does away with religious controversy altogether. One might say that Inchbald's novel represents an ideal, possibly idealistic, solution to its problems that is in fact a skeptical attack on Richardson, since it is unable to view the marriage contract as a cure for the imperfect beings who enter into it. Those unfit for it will remain unfit; if Richardson shows that marriage can produce good behavior, Inchbald shows that only good behavior can produce marriage.

I will return in a more focused way to the subject of marriage later in this chapter. For the moment, though, I want to emphasize that Austen's novel, constructed though it may be as a marriage plot in which Fanny weds Edmund Bertram by the novel's end, repeatedly undermines the sense, evident in both Richardson and Inchbald, in which marriage must rely upon the arrival of these characters at a state of moral correctness. Indeed, the morality of the novel—if it can be said to have such a thing—may depend on the idea that error contributes to rather than detracts from personal worth. Austen thus avoids the alternatives of correcting character through marriage (Richardson) or correcting marriage through character (Inchbald); error is not a quality that must be excluded synchronically through the signing of a contract, or diachronically through the erasure of a generation. In fact, the pain that Fanny experiences from her faults and disappointments—from her negative knowledge—comes to be figured as a treasured form of personal gain. This is why, when we are told that "the vicissitudes of the human mind had not yet been exhausted by her" as she leaves Mansfield Park for Portsmouth, such "vicissitudes" seem like a resource of painful experience that is to be eagerly sought rather than avoided.[16] Whatever growth can be attributed to

Fanny in this novel, and whatever ways in which she shows herself to be a fit partner for Edmund at its conclusion, are attributable precisely to her experience of repeated externalized blockages: blockages that yield a sense of the self not simply as a *property*, since the mere sense of a property cannot yield "self-knowledge" in Austen's view, but (to borrow a term from Giorgio Agamben) as an *improperty*, an "event of an outside."[17]

I have been suggesting so far in a fairly general way that the coupling of error and punishment—Fanny's errors and the painful recognition of those errors—helps to explain Fanny's position throughout the novel, and her tendency to construe a locus of pain simultaneously as a locus of value. But I want to examine two frequently studied extended episodes from the novel—the visit to Sotherton and the performance of *Lovers' Vows*—to suggest how deeply the logic I have been describing informs those passages which attract the most critical notice. The novel immediately invests Sotherton Court, the estate of the Rushworth family, with a decisive significance by making it into a subject of debate among its protagonists. The visit to the estate is preceded by a discussion of "improvement" in landscape architecture; in the debate that emerges before the journey, Rushworth's zeal for improvement immediately contrasts with the apparently more moderate stance—according to one view, a stance of "nostalgic traditionalism"—taken by both Fanny and Edmund.[18] Fanny laments the removal of an avenue of trees; Edmund adds, in his distaste for the influence of an "improver," "I would rather have an inferior degree of beauty, of my own choice, and acquired progressively. I would rather abide by my own blunders than by his" (49). Edmund's comment does not in fact oppose improvement; "I have no doubt that it will be all done extremely well," he says (48). It registers a preference for gradual improvement rather than sudden change at the hands of an improver, and this opinion is all the more remarkable because it coincides with a wish to feel the force of "blunders," as if the very ability to experience the pleasure of improvement on his account might actually be dependent upon embracing one's mistakes or failures in the course of that improvement.

At this point, one of many contrasts arises between Mary's and Fanny's perspectives on improvement. Mary suggests that she would "be most thankful to any Mr. Repton who would undertake it, and give me as much beauty as he could for my money; and I should never look at it, till it was complete." Fanny, however, essentially agrees with Edmund when she proclaims, "It would be delightful to *me* to see the progress of it all" (49). The specific contrast here, between Mary's unwillingness and Fanny's delighted willingness to view progress through visible error and correction, becomes thematized during the visit to Sotherton itself. In this episode, Austen makes the more direct experience of landscape architecture provide an occasion for extending the struggle over the value of correction against the will to improve without having the opportunity to feel the painful recognition of blunders.

When Rushworth forgets the key to the gate that will allow the visitors across the "Ha Ha" to the knoll on the other side, he feels the distressing consequences of a particular kind of error—an error that derives from his not having planned ahead for a certain kind of action: "He had been very near thinking whether he should not bring the key; he was determined he would never come without the key again; but still this did not remove the present evil" (82). He responds by returning to retrieve the key; meanwhile, Maria Bertram and Henry Crawford (followed soon after by Julia Bertram) seem to commit a grave breach of decorum by refusing to wait for Rushworth's return. Instead, they proceed around the gate to continue their walk.

The episode is crucial on many levels. Austen cleverly foreshadows Maria's and Henry's elopement at this moment, and every detail—the gate, the trench, the key—is rather obviously saturated with sexual significance. But we do not have to ignore that level of reference in order also to see that the sequence of events shows how important it is for Fanny, "feeling all this to be wrong," and then "sorry for almost all that she had seen and heard," to suffer from the consequences of an error in judgment—even though, strictly speaking, the error is not even hers (84). Fanny eagerly embraces the painful consequences of Rushworth's error and every error that precipitates from it (Henry's, Maria's), and this directly contrasts with Julia's confident assertion that she is not "obliged to punish [herself] for [Maria's] sins" (85). Julia then proceeds to go around the gate rather than wait for the key; and the striking discrepancy here resides in Julia's desire to avoid punishment while Fanny passionately desires it and seeks it out.

To put it another way, the contrast is to be found in a difference of perspectives, not on internal but on external reasons—not, in other words, on the presence or absence of "sins" but on the acceptance or refusal of blame and consequent punishment (regardless of the moral deliberation or source of action).[19] For Fanny, landscape architecture—with its interconnected grammatical features of gates, trenches, organized vistas, planned shrubberies, and so forth—functions quite explicitly here as an opportunity to experience a blockage that functions as precisely the kind of punishment that Julia has avoided. Rushworth lacks the key to the gate, it might be said, in a way that corresponds to Fanny's lack of a name for any number of islands and rivers during her early lessons at Mansfield; the series of elements in the landscape garden operate on analogy to place names on a globe. In both instances, geography (of England, of a landscape garden) corresponds to a social geography. And in both instances, this is not because a character finds her way merely by accumulating knowledge. It is because in both instances, the pain that follows as a consequence of error provides a distinctive sense of interrelationship between persons and objects—a sense that is lost to those who seek only to cover up their errors and circumvent the pathways and borders of landscape architecture.

Lovers' Vows, Theatricality, and Privacy

The Sotherton episode, I am suggesting, repeatedly depicts Fanny in terms that emphasize not only her willingness to admit error, but also her *desire* for error—a desire so powerful that she says she is "sorry" even for the errant actions of others (86). What is at stake is thus not "habits of order and obedience" (to invoke Foucault once more), but the eagerness to recognize and abide by the consequences of straying from any such habits. The amateur theatrical performance of *Lovers' Vows* (a play by August von Kotzebue, adapted by Inchbald in 1798) at Mansfield is clearly connected to the Sotherton visit because it again provides Austen with what might seem like an opportunity to mobilize her characters in order to voice a conservative opposition to fashionable tastes (like those in landscaping) of her time. Yet, as we shall see, the issue of theater is not far from the subject of punishment that I have been discussing, and the episode therefore does more than simply voice a reactionary attack on popular entertainment. It is certainly true that this incident in the novel, in which the young residents of the Bertram household stage a performance of the Kotzebue/Inchbald play during Sir Thomas's absence, makes the desire for theater seem decidedly improper. Leo Bersani's compelling and influential suggestion on this issue is that the home theatricals emblematize a "moral deficiency" at war with Fanny's "asceticism," a deficiency caused by the theater's capacity to provide fictive words and personalities for real characters.[20]

As helpful as this reading may be in demarcating the centrality of the episode—precisely because it seems to emblematize a certain way in which Austen is thinking about character—I would still suggest that Austen's opposition to theater in the episode is in no way a simple indulgence of the conventional prejudices that Bersani describes. It is true that when the subject of putting on a theatrical performance is raised, Edmund indeed objects to it because it would lack "decorum" and would involve "taking liberties with my Father's house in his absence" (106–7). But what is particularly interesting here is that Edmund does not object to *theater itself* as immoral. After all, he is a professed admirer of theater, of "real acting, good harden'd real acting," and he finds occasion to proclaim his interest in it. He objects because, rather than "good" and "real" acting, it is "private," and therefore evades the scrutiny and judgment of others (104–5). Tom Bertram, by contrast, wants to put on the performance precisely *because* it is private—"We want no audience, no publicity," he insists (105).

The relationship between theater and privacy becomes all the more apparent when the discussions of the theatrical continue. Perhaps at first glance, following Bersani's lead, it might seem as if the real threat that theater poses is that it produces publicly immodest roles for privately modest women: this, at least, would be one way of explaining Fanny's belief that the parts are "unfit" for "any woman of modesty" (115). But the further sequence of events and conversations shows that the problem with theater is not that it provides destructively deceptive fictions, but rather (in this instance of it) that it represents an implosion of fiction into human emotion; the novel's characters manipulate theatrical parts to allow themselves to express their private—and *already* immodest—feelings. Theater therefore takes on a merely instrumental value as a way of mimicking the attitudes that persons already prejudicially possess in advance of reading or examining plays that are possibilities for performing. This is why a whole range of dramas from Shakespeare to Sheridan are rejected by the troupe of amateur actors: they are too "ranting" or otherwise inappropriate for the characters who will take on the roles. The actors simply want a play that will "suit them all"; the characters search for theater not as a fictional experience but as a reflection of their current states of feeling and desiring (111). The peculiar thing about the amateur theatrical is not that it is fictional, but that it is not fictional enough: it only functions as a transparent screen for the expression of private emotion.

If theater seems like a private indulgence in this way, it is so in yet another interesting way. For even as the play operates as a kind of outing of private emotion, the actors themselves seem inclined to shield their expressions from any public consequences. Though the amateur characters assume that they will be judged by the most intimate audiences—so that they "do not expect perfection" and can thus make "every allowance" for bad acting—Edmund is far more aware of the fact that the words spoken in the midst of a private theatrical might have an audience unconfined to the stage or even to the Bertram household (122). Edmund's eventual decision to act the role of Anhalt in the drama—despite the apparent inconsistency in his behavior—is an attempt to protect the "privacy" of the Bertram household precisely because he assumes a connection between the household and the public world from which it requires protection. Embedded in the very possibility of acting, for him, is the possibility of uncontrollable consequences erupting from acting.

Chapter 4

The very specific significance of *Lovers' Vows* cannot be ignored here. In many ways, the play seems thoroughly consistent with Inchbald's *A Simple Story*, and Austen's novel thus responds to both of Inchbald's works in a similar fashion. Austen knew the play well, and it is likely, as Jonathan Wordsworth suggests, that she "assumes that her audience does so too."[21] It is tempting to see the main problem of the play as a problem of excessive erotic frankness and a lack of proper subordination to paternal authority. Inchbald claims in her preface to the play to have transformed Kotzebue's drama to make it more appropriate to the English stage, yet Amelia's character still boldly exposes her love for Anhalt and speaks "plainly" of her desire to her father (41–43). But what must surely have struck Austen about *Lovers' Vows* is not that Amelia's pursuit of happiness is immodest or immoral; in both *Lovers' Vows* and *A Simple Story*, Inchbald is concerned to identify proper and improper sentiment as if it could exist independent of the actions and reactions of others. The exact opposite of Fanny, Amelia in the play is a character who assumes infinite forgiveness for her own actions because personal feeling overrides all obligation: "In [my father's] passion he will call me 'undutiful,' " she admits, knowing that her father will disapprove of her choice, "but he will soon recollect himself, and resume his usual smiles, saying 'Well, well, if he love you, and you love him, in the name of heaven, let it be' " (43). She urges the same kind of lenience toward others, and she proves her sentimental credentials through her "pity" for Frederick after he has tried to kill her father (47).

The erasure of error through allowance and forgiveness—an avoidance of error that is also an indifference to it—constitutes Inchbald's highly significant contribution to theater and to the novel, but it also constitutes an important line of demarcation in relation to Austen's fictional strategies. Surely nothing appears to recommend Fanny more during the *Lovers' Vows* episode in *Mansfield Park* than the fact that she not only declines to act, she "cannot act" (122). And her inability to act is so inflexible that the mere fact of the theatrical's privacy only further encourages her in this conviction. Although this certainly confirms the suspicions of critics like Tanner, who emphasize Fanny's immobility and stasis, readers of the novel have given scant attention to the fact that Fanny's refusal to act onstage is accompanied by her persistent feeling that she has acted anyway.[22] This is not because Fanny views herself as a theatrical actor (as David Marshall contends), but because she feels implicated in, and constructs a relation to, the *action* of acting in a way that most of the actors in the stage performance do not.[23] Removed as she is from the acting downstairs when Edmund comes to visit her in her private chamber, Fanny still cannot be protected from feeling affected by the acting of others and somehow engaged in it. She cannot, that is, indulge in the luxury of the privacy that she seems to have provided for herself, since she finds herself losing all "composure" and feeling that "it was all misery *now*" (130). Later, when we are told that "she could not feel that she had done wrong herself," this can hardly protect her from feeling a kind of distress that would imply that she actually did do wrong. She is "disquieted in every other way," and Edmund's own actions continue to make her feel "wretched" (132). Fanny's activity of reading in this scene, moreover—Edmund finds her studying Macartney's *Embassy to China*—provides yet another development of her early geography lessons at Mansfield (130). While reading Macartney brings her into a virtual proximity with territories that may seem distant, the episode similarly shows how Fanny's actual removal from the other members of the household does not keep her from feeling like part of the group. Her apparent privacy in her room is actually permeated with public awareness. She supplements a material distance in the household with a sense of virtual proximity; actions that are not her own nevertheless inspire a painful consciousness of wrongdoing.

It turns out that Fanny's feelings at this moment complement Edmund's own precarious predicament. It may be tempting to interpret Edmund's eagerness to condemn the theatrical even while acting in it as plain and simple hypocrisy, a poorly disguised attempt to indulge his desire for Mary Crawford by playing the part of Amelia's lover. But Fanny's peculiar propensity to feel the effects of actions from which she has apparently removed herself finds an analogy in Edmund's own behavior. Edmund's actions would seem to emblematize the very impossibility of removing himself from other actors in the household that Fanny inwardly feels. Edmund does not so much act *against* his denunciations of theater, but *according* to them, both acting and accepting the blame for acting. Sir Thomas's sudden arrival at Mansfield at the end of the first volume causes the other characters to try to avoid feelings of guilt (like Tom, who blames the acting "infection" on his friend Mr. Yates [154], or like Mrs. Norris, who tries her best to deny all responsibility and praise her own "*general* attention to the interest and comfort of his family" [158]). But it causes Fanny nearly to faint with "dread," and it causes Edmund to solicit, rather than avoid, the punishment that now might seem inevitable: "We have all been more or less to blame," he tells his father (157). Reflecting on the incident later in the novel, Edmund insists on the wrongness of all involved—"We were all wrong together"—but also on the specific wrongness in his own actions—"but none so wrong as myself" (290). His claim that Fanny is exempt from wrongdoing, moreover, can hardly diminish our appreciation for the fact that Fanny does not remove herself from such blaming as much as she imitates and competes with Edmund in his desire to appropriate it for himself.

Chapter 4

The Distribution of Retribution

In the Sotherton and *Lovers' Vows* episodes, Edmund and Fanny seem to achieve a kind of validation in the narrative insofar as they advocate error and mistakenness—not merely to be overcome and corrected, but as an inverted or negative knowledge and virtue. The fact that Fanny and Edmund achieve this position in the novel, a position of error among erring characters, crystallizes a further (and perhaps initially perplexing) feature of Austen's punitive imagination. It should not escape our notice that erring characters not only are shown to be wrong but are shown to be wrong repeatedly by characters who are themselves profoundly flawed or mistaken in judgment. When Fanny fears "doing wrong" by resisting Henry's suit, for instance, that sense of wrong derives precisely from Edmund's corrective measure directing her to "give the smile that . . . was asked for" by continuing to encourage him (289). To put it simply, her sense of error derives from a correction that is itself shown to be utterly mistaken advice. This is an instance of a general paradigm. As in *Pride and Prejudice*, in which both Darcy and Elizabeth correct each other even though both are mistaken in thought and action, the ability to point out error in this novel is not reserved for those with superior knowledge, any more than having knowledge exonerates one from feeling that one is mistaken.[24] In fact, it would be more accurate to say that the reverse is true. Austen arranges her characters according to a narrative *distribution* of error, a distribution that continually subordinates the importance of the metaphysical origin of correction to the set of corrections itself. Or, to put it another way, what Austen privileges is not a standard of correctness from which to judge error, but opportunities for error that will occasion or solicit correction. She awards certain characters, like Fanny and Edmund, a central or privileged position, but this is not because such characters provide a higher moral ground than others. It is because they both demonstrate and embrace the correction that forms the very condition for their individuality as social beings within the world of the novel.

If I am describing a logic at work in "the world of the novel," moreover, it is a logic that is not unique to Austen's writing but that participates in a mode of thought in the world of political theory of her day on the subject of punishment. For it became precisely the claim of reformers in the late eighteenth century to view punishment not as a rare exception occasionally applied to perpetrators of a range of offenses from petty theft to murder, but as a system inseparable from the rights of the political subject. Opponents of violent punishments from the pillory to the death penalty did not simply object to their cruelty; they repeatedly showed that the injustice of such punishments coincided precisely with their infrequency, as if the injustice to persons consisted in their being deprived of punishment. Although criminals were sentenced to death, for example, statistics cited by the likes of Samuel Romilly and Basil Montagu showed that the sentence was only rarely put into practice. The result for criminals, Romilly argued, was "frequent impunity. . . [which] encouraged offenders to repeat their crimes"; the result for the British public was a "deterioration of moral feeling" and a "reproach against our national character" (*SSR* 1:49, 2:326, 1:431). The criminal offender, simply put, was a socially undistinguished being.

In contrast, programs for reform, minutely calibrating the severity of punishment according to the severity of the offense, were continually shaped in order to make punishment more widely distributed among a national population. To be a political subject, that is, coincided with the possibility of penalty, with a "sober expectation of the laws" (*SSR* 1:327). No longer a merely random act of violence attached to a field of improperly articulated offenses, punishment would uphold—and would be upheld by—the political subject's most profound sense of self. Romilly thus designed his own reforms to "impose a cheerful obligation upon every person to assist in the exercise of public justice" (*SSR* 1:354). According to Basil Montagu, abolishing the death penalty and arranging a more calibrated set of punishments could be seen as the a sign of intellectual advancement—"the love of acquiring and the love of diffusing knowledge."[25] It could also seem like the occasion for inciting that advancement by encouraging all persons, through "the habit of weighing consequences," to view themselves as potential subjects of punishment (*BSP* 36).

Austen's novels as a whole provide fictional enactments of the political discourse of penal reform. There are no courts of law to be found there, no judicial sentences—as much as characters like Sir Thomas may seem to resemble magistrates. Still, Austen's fiction launches a response at two main complementary registers. First, the death penalty hovers in the background of her novels at the level of oblique reference, implicitly acknowledging and distancing her work from rituals of execution and the literature (the legions of eighteenth-century biographies, autobiographies, and novels about criminals) associated with them.[26] In *Sense and Sensibility* (1811), for instance, Mrs. Ferrars emerges as the tyrannical judge who executes and pardons at will. Edward's "crime and annihilation" is followed by his return to her favor—his "resuscitation," allowing him "once more to live"—and her corresponding "annihilation" of Robert.[27] *Pride and Prejudice*'s Mr. Collins, who claims that Lydia would be better off dead than disgraced by eloping with Wickham, is not far from Mrs. Ferrars; in *Mansfield Park*, moreover, Mrs. Norris, though she does not kill anyone, is, as I suggested earlier, the novel's most visible advocate of social death.[28] That threat of social death is the most visible counterpart to the murderous underside of Sir Thomas's plantation in Antigua—the counterpart, that is, to the reality of the slave's actual death at the master's will.[29] And surely we must not ignore the highest compliment that Austen can pay to any character in her novels, namely, a character's ability to be "mortified," to experience a pain that both recalls and significantly reduces the penalty implied by the word's more ancient meaning: to be "put to death."[30]

These muffled references in the novels are accompanied, and even illuminated, by an incident in Austen's family history. Austen's aunt, Mrs. Leigh Perrot, was tried for larceny after she was accused of stealing lace from a shop in Bath in 1799.[31] The crime, not capable of reduction by Benefit of Clergy (in which the offender had a sentence reduced simply by proving the ability to read), was punishable by death. I mention this not simply to prove that the death penalty loomed large in Austen's mind; in fact, Aunt Perrot received a verdict of "Not Guilty," and even with a charge of guilty, opportunities for a stay of execution (among those of her standing) were numerous.[32] The point is rather that the case vividly demonstrates how the sheer number of capital offenses encouraged judges and juries not to impose the death penalty, with the result that the operation of the death penalty, while it aimed to inspire awe and terror, was also consistent with a blindness to, or disregard of, criminal action.

This brings us to the second, more conspicuous way in which Austen's works address the issue of criminal-law reform. Aunt Perrot brushes with death only to receive the blessing of acquittal due to those of her class; Austen's writing acts as a formal revision of that logic. It makes the acquisition of public personhood dependent not upon release from penalty but upon penalty's beneficial regularity and perspicuity—an account of correction set forth in thoroughly utilitarian terms. Characters in their collective corrective judgments and openness to correction enforce the narrative logic of the novel into which they are written; meanwhile, the celebrated "free indirect style" of the narrative voice itself resists either reduction into a knowing voice of the magistrate (as in Trollope's novels) or incorporation into a single morally superior character (as in *Pamela*). The result is that the regular series of corrections that come from everywhere collectively affirms, while never equaling or challenging, the view from nowhere that is the hallmark of what D. A. Miller identifies as "Austen Style."[33] That hallmark is not, as John Bender argues, established merely by making characters transparent through narrative. In Bender's account, Foucault's view of Bentham's "Panopticon" is analogized to narration insofar as institutional order renders its subjects visible only to expose their sympathetic replication of that order as discipline.[34] Frances Ferguson is more accurate in her view that individuals in Austen's fiction "would cease to be individuals . . . if they ever coincided with the communal stance" instantiated in free indirect style.[35] Austen's "style" is thus felt through the decisive ability of the retributive narrator of *Pride and Prejudice* to convict Bingley and Darcy for their faults, before they, or we, fully grasp those faults or their implications.[36] Likewise, in *Mansfield Park*, the superiority of Fanny and Edmund in the author's eyes can be found precisely in the extent to which they themselves find, and accept, fault—even while the narrator reigns supremely, judging the imperfections of seemingly perfect days (90), or pronouncing on the essence of mortal happiness as "very much . . . finely chequered" (226).

It is, of course, Fanny and Edmund who are most assiduously devoted to the "habit of weighing consequences" in *Mansfield Park*, and more can be said about why and how that habit demonstrates their fitness for each other and their privilege as individual characters within the realm of Austen's narrative point of view. These are the issues—marriage, and the position of these characters within the novel's point of view—to which I want to turn in the closing pages of this chapter. I argue, then, that we must see how marriage in this novel can only be fully appreciated according to a certain lack of idealism that represents a departure from the tradition of the marriage novel that I mentioned earlier. That tradition had tended to assume that marriage required that erring characters be either corrected or eliminated altogether. But there is a degree to which the very notion of marriage in Austen's novels sustains and supports error—as if the parties to the contract continually required the distinguishing marks of correction. Particularly relevant to this issue is one of the oddest, but most emblematic, passages in *Mansfield Park*—one that appears close to its conclusion, where we are treated to a particularly wrenching account of what Fanny's engagement and marriage to Henry *might* have looked like:

> Could he have been satisfied with the conquest of one amiable woman's affections, could he have found sufficient exultation in overcoming the reluctance, in working himself into the esteem and tenderness of Fanny Price, there would have been every probability of success and felicity for him. His affection had already done something. Her influence over him, had already given him some influence over her. Would he have deserved more, there can be no doubt that more would have been obtained; especially when that marriage had taken place, which would have given him the assistance of her conscience in subduing her first inclination, and brought them very often together. (385)

Austen's casuistry at this moment—she asks us to consider the possibility of Henry marrying Fanny "within a reasonable period from Edmund's marrying Mary"—proposes futures for both Fanny and Edmund that would involve them in marriages entailing choices that, in many ways, would be simply "wrong" choices. The last suggestion here, that his "influence" and her "conscience" would have "brought them very often together," offers only a slender escape route from an otherwise unhappy and unsympathetic union. Whereas Austen has asked the reader to imagine discord within matrimony, the Baron in *Lovers' Vows*, in contrast, claims something quite different: "Matrimony, without concord, is like a duetto badly performed; for that reason, nature, the great composer of all harmony, has ordained, that, when bodies are allied, hearts should be in perfect union."[37] (Mary earlier quotes Anhalt's similar words to Fanny: "When two sympathetic hearts meet in the marriage state, matrimony may be called a happy life" [297].) Austen's narrative voice asserts that Fanny would have been married to a person who, "without concord," has repeatedly articulated ideas and inclinations opposed to hers, pursued courses of action that are repugnant to her; yet that voice extends a certain generosity to Henry until the last. His "public punishment" is made to look compatible with "virtue": "That punishment, the public punishment of disgrace, should in a just measure attend *his* share of the offense, is, we know, not one of the barriers, which society gives to virtue" (386). Edmund, likewise, would have married a woman equally at odds with him, one with "a mind led astray and bewildered, and without any suspicion of being so; darkened, yet fancying itself light" (304). Both possibilities for matrimony would seem to bear out Edmund's earlier suggestion that "unlike" temperaments and "opposition" between partners is conducive to marital happiness (289).

Although many critics have tended to agree with Lionel Trilling's sense of the novel's desire to "establish, in fixity and enclosure, a refuge from the dangers of openness and chance," the remarkable feature of the casuistry at this moment in the text is not just that Fanny and Edmund have avoided these futures and therefore avoided the dangers of marriages to flawed characters.[38] We misunderstand Austen's novel if we believe that the erring behavior of Henry and Mary is in itself the cause of their unfitness as partners. The point of the passage above, I think, is to show that marriages between characters flawed according to any standard of judgment are not impossible. While we may at first find some wryness in Austen's suggestion that "society" is not inclined to make "punishment" a barrier to "virtue" (as if to distance Austen's voice from that of "society"), the most striking aspect of the claim is that (in Austen's view) punishment is not only *not* a barrier to "virtue," it practically *constitutes* such virtue. The problem with Henry and Mary, then, is not, as Claudia Johnson would have it, that they perpetrate "acts of immodesty" or that they "subvert the law of the father";[39] nor is it that they are led "astray and bewildered"—adjectives that might easily be applied to Fanny and Edmund themselves. The problem is that they routinely attempt to deny or cover up traces of the very errors that Fanny and Edmund appear to embrace, so that they can avoid all "public punishment." Henry, for instance, does not want to accept the amateur theatrical as a mistake but sees it as a harmless indulgence plagued by bad luck (188). And this is only a prelude to his way of addressing his elopement with Maria; he repeatedly attempts "to keep Fanny and the Bertrams from a knowledge of what was passing" (386). Mary, likewise, advocates that the wrong be forgotten or suppressed, constituting, as Edmund puts it, "a compliance, a compromise, an acquiescence in the continuance of the sin" (378). "It was the detection, not the offense which she reprobated," Edmund explains to Fanny (375). Through covering and acquiescence, Henry and Mary constitute a danger not because of their wrongs but because of their desire to escape from them at any cost; their pursuit of an unassailable, "incorrigible" position is precisely what renders them impossible choices for marriage. Although Edmund is able to imagine a marriage with "some difference in . . . opinions, on points too of some moment," the "difference" exposed by the desire to hide error from view is the only truly intolerable difference.

Maybe even more striking than the glimpse of legitimate marriages between seemingly inappropriate partners is the rationale for Fanny's and Edmund's marriage: a union that is perplexing mainly because it has so little to do with a sympathetic union as it is described in novels of affective marriage or in *Lovers' Vows*. So difficult is it for the novel to serve up any account of affective relationship between the two—a progress of internal compatibility or sympathy—that we are laconically told how it is only "natural" that Edmund's affections turn from Mary to Fanny, within an amount of time that is also "quite natural" (387). The absence of explanation is in fact a consequence of the novel's formal priorities. Indeed, it would be possible to go so far as to say that Fanny and Edmund are united not through affection but through a joined moral-political reasoning: their combined appreciation for, and susceptibility to, the coupling of error and punishment. Roland Barthes, with a typically elegant stroke of wit, suggests that one element of the lover's repertoire of signs is a sense of wrongdoing to the other: "Any fissure within Devotion is a fault."[40] His point, of course, is that the lover desires the fissure that, through the vigilance of guilt, will amply prove devotion's strength; we might stretch the claim to suit Austen's case by saying that a sense of wrongdoing to *anyone* is not simply a sign of love but the privileged basis for it.

Reading Distress

To observe the union of Fanny and Edmund as a matter of privileged logic rather than a matter of affectivity can prepare us to see just what it might mean to view these characters—especially Fanny Price herself—as targets of interest for Austen's point of view as a writer. Even though the critics

Chapter 4

I mentioned earlier in this chapter more or less openly suggest that Fanny and Edmund are magnets for Austen's sympathy because of their high moral standing in the author's eyes, actually the opposite is true. These characters in fact rigorously deny the possibility of a certain traditional moral or religious mode of authority. Meanwhile, no characters in the novel seem busier in their attempts to produce an appearance of proper behavior than Henry and Mary. The positions of Fanny and Edmund attract Austen's interest not because of their moral correctness but because their investment in the perspicuity of error continually lends support to what can only be called an investment in the tissue of narrative itself. Fanny and Edmund, in their embrace of error and penalty, turn out to be advocates, that is, of the very possibility of stating in narrative terms that something has happened. Fanny's impulse to be "sorry" for the wrong actions of others in the Sotherton episode, for example, derives from her impulse to expose the visibility of fault and participate in it; it is thus inseparable from her impulse to narrate events: to "communicate what had passed" to Mr. Rushworth once he arrives (85). By contrast, the threat continually presented by the Crawfords, in this episode and everywhere else, is not reducible to the far less considerable threat of moral corruption. By asking for silent "compliance" or by hiding "knowledge" from others, the real threat they offer is something more profound from the standpoint of authorship—the subversion of narrative potential, the undoing of the very possibility of writing a novel.

In this respect, *Mansfield Park* stands as the culmination of Austen's abiding interest in blame. *Sense and Sensibility* secures "appropriate punishment" and "proper submission" for its characters; *Pride and Prejudice* makes Darcy and Elizabeth compete with each other for the cherished prize of guilt for having contributed to Wickham's elopement with Lydia—while Miss Bingley insists that Darcy cannot be blamed for anything.[41] *Emma* continues the trend with its central character defined through her pervasive "blunders" and "blindness," made all the more poignant by her sustained belief that she has simply been misunderstood.[42] Repeating and inverting the doctrine of original sin, Austen assumes fault to be so central to personhood that she jokingly congratulates her brother in one letter for the birth of a son whose "native fault" will "give birth / To the best blessing, conscious Worth."[43]

But we must go still further to see how *Mansfield Park* makes the exposure of error—an exposure in alliance with the logic of narration itself—repeatedly coincide with the practice of reading. I earlier pointed out that Fanny avoids theater only to turn to the rigors of reading in her room, and that this reading, though it seems to be conducted in private, makes Fanny seem like an advocate of a more profound linking of the self to regions beyond the privacy of the home. To conceive of reading on these terms is to produce the strongest possible contrast with the Benefit of Clergy that (as I mentioned earlier) allowed proof of reading ability to excuse criminals from punishment or reduce their sentences. Statutes providing for clergyable offenses, dating back to the fifteenth century, were gradually overturned in the early decades of the nineteenth (the most significant changes occurring in 1827); thus Austen's fiction emerges at a moment in which such statutes were held in particular disfavor. Her work frames a profound and decisive contrast to the place of reading in the logic governing the Benefit of Clergy. While that logic sees reading as the guarantee of a release from legal obligation, Austen sees reading—including the reading in which her audience engages—as a demonstration of obligation. This reasoning continues in *Mansfield Park* as Edmund spars with Henry over the subject of reading aloud, once again rehabilitating the distinction between reading and theatricality. Henry reads from the volume of Shakespeare that Fanny has been reading to Lady Bertram, with a felicity that "was truly dramatic" and that "brought all his acting before [Fanny] again," but it is soon revealed that Henry has not even read the play—*Henry VIII*—that he is reading aloud (279). He has only seen it "acted" and admits that his exposure to Shakespeare is merely through a vaguely defined "instinct": "Shakespeare one gets acquainted with without knowing how. It is part of an Englishman's constitution" (280).

Henry insists on the validity of his "dramatic" performance at the expense of a complete reading, a validity that resembles an "instinct" or biological instance of the "Englishman's constitution" (280). Edmund cleverly compliments the reading, eventually diminishing the importance of its dramatic effect: "To know [Shakespeare] in bits and scraps, is common enough, to know him pretty thoroughly, is perhaps, not uncommon, but to read him well aloud, is no everyday talent" (279). Edmund is at first willing to pay Henry the "honour" of praising his success at reading "aloud." But the conversation eventually exposes a distinction between one kind of reading and another—reading "aloud" theatrically, and reading for knowledge of the text (279). Whereas Edmund praises the "art of reading" (280), Henry's appreciation for reading repeatedly coincides with the "common" talent of appreciating mere "bits and scraps" of works learned through osmosis: "I am not always so attentive as I ought to be," he admits (281).

This emphasis on reading has certainly not escaped the notice of critics.[44] But the contribution I would make here is that Austen does not make reading into a private act that is compared to theater's publicity. Indeed, the opposite is the case. Each instance in the novel in which theater is contrasted with reading makes theater seem like an especially private act, an intimate and impassioned correspondence between the sympathies of the actor and the role that he or she plays. By contrast, reading a text

Chapter 4

is identified repeatedly with a heightened sense of public accountability. Fanny's reading accompanies her aroused sense of the wrongness of the private theatrical; Edmund praises reading precisely in order to associate reading with the ability to find fault. He thus points to the "blunders" and "failures" in the current practices of reading aloud in contemporary school systems, and praises reading practices in contemporary congregations—where a large proportion of the people are trained to "judge and criticize" (280–81). Throughout the discussion of reading, Henry's breezy confidence in his own inattentiveness to reading seems like the perfect demonstration of his inattentiveness to his errors or his desire to render them secret or invisible; Edmund's embrace of reading provides a contrasting demonstration of his love for the public, conspicuous display of error.

Perhaps another way of framing the point that I have just made is that, if the embrace of error in the novel repeatedly signals a heightened awareness of a social geography, it also signals a heightened awareness of textual geography: the account of Fanny's reading practices suggests that she is trained to read the very novel into which she is written. One of Austen's closing gestures in *Mansfield Park* helps to make this entire set of connections particularly vivid. When Fanny is summoned back to Mansfield by a letter from Edmund, she feels a distinct pleasure in that letter. The letter requests her return to the Bertram household in order to participate in its hardships; she is able to feel happiness in "sharing the distress even of those whose distress she thought of most" (366). The link between distress and happiness now seems plausible enough, given the argument that I have been making about the novel, and this link continues until the last chapter, where we are told that Mansfield Park's "tolerable comfort" is inseparable from a range of punishments, from Sir Thomas's feelings of "disappointment and regret" over his daughters' conduct to the "mutual punishment" of Maria's and Mrs. Norris's solitary confinement (380).

But there is something else that is important about Fanny's return to Mansfield: her sister Susan accompanies her. The most striking way in which Fanny shows her superiority in reading when she visits her family at Portsmouth is not by reading books but by distinguishing differences between persons, demonstrated by her gathering "a better knowledge of Susan, and a hope of being of service to her" (328). This "knowledge," or what we might call a reading of the Portsmouth household, has a way of supplementing the darkness and utter unreadability that I first mentioned in this chapter. It also of necessity consists of a detailed observation of Susan's errors in household management. Fanny sees that Susan sees that much is "wrong at home," and that she wants to "set it right"; she in turn observes Susan's tendency to "err in the method of reform" with her reliance on "unassisted reason" (328). Fanny's gestures of reading are nothing less than a triumphant process of distinction through the remarking of error. To find error in Susan is precisely to invest her with special value; like Fanny herself, Susan is distinguished—she is awarded a privileged position in the family—because of the errors that Fanny sees in her. Still more, even while Fanny seems to be offering her younger sister the benefits of her maturity, those benefits come primarily in the form of Fanny's appropriation of mistakenness for herself. She takes on a form of responsibility for Susan's errors, as if she were implicated in them or indirectly the cause of them, and she actively invests herself in the need for such errors to be corrected.

The solution for these errors, however, is not for Fanny to correct Susan—to tell her the right way to manage a household (even though we might expect her to be able to do so). Rather, the solution, so thoroughly consistent with the rigor of Austen's logic, is for Fanny to take Susan with her to Mansfield, where she—like Fanny herself—will feel stirred by the pleasures of "anxiety" and "dread" that are themselves the sign of being distinguished (368). The pain that comes from having her errors detected and corrected will be her cherished reward. If this particular version of anxiety and dread is absent from Portsmouth, so is the visibility of personal conduct. The severe distresses, which are themselves the occasion for the pleasures of personal distinction, can never be felt there. It thus turns out that a return to Mansfield Park is not merely a return to a place that is a property owned by the Price's wealthier relations. It is a return to a place, like a novel, where personal properties become visible.

The Gothic, the Historical Novel, and the Problem of Exception

Now that we can see how thoroughly a utilitarian logic of sanction pervades Austen's novel, we can also see how closely related it is to more explicit critiques of the death penalty found in both the Gothic novel and the historical novels of Walter Scott. If Austen's fiction wills the death penalty into the faintest presence, glimpsed only in hints and insinuations, the Gothic makes the death penalty into a persistent threat that motivates its plots. Ann Radcliffe's *The Italian*, as I mentioned in Chapter 1, mocks the logic of Madan's defense of the death penalty by putting the words of that defense in the mouth of the villain Schedoni. In contrast to this, the virtuous heroes of the novel, Ellena and Vivaldi, continually experience guilt even for bringing villains to justice, so fearful are they of "[bearing] witness against the life of a fellow being."[45] It turns out that a whole range of Gothic villains speaks the language of the death penalty: they do not merely kill but talk of killing in the interest of justice. In James Hogg's *The Private Memoirs and Confessions of a Justified Sinner* (1824), Gil-Martin's "great work of reformation by blood" is likened to the death penalty when Wringhim tells him that his "ideas of retribution are too sanguine, and too arbitrary for the laws of this country."[46] Wringhim's comment is utterly ironic, though; the novel represents law itself—its violence, its incorporation of false evidence, and so on—as Gil-Martin's identical twin.

Mary Shelley's *Frankenstein* (1818) offers an even more intricately patterned version of this logic. It is Shelley's monster who becomes the death penalty's double: he becomes executioner and apologist for executions, and his conduct ends up exposing the monstrosity of the legal system. In Shelley's novel, Victor's creation causes numerous deaths that are, Victor says, "the victims to my unhallowed arts."[47] But even though Victor blames himself for these deaths, the monster himself has a large role in demonstrating the unyielding brutality of the punishment of death as an instrument of retributive justice.

There was in fact a great deal of talk about the death penalty and its abolition in 1816, when the Shelleys joined Byron and Polidori at Villa Diodati on Lake Geneva for the most famous round of ghost stories ever told. (As Mary Shelley reports in the 1831 introduction to the *Standard Novels* edition of *Frankenstein*, this was the incitement to her own work.) Polidori had published his essay on the death penalty in the same year, and Percy Shelley had written his essay on the death penalty the year before. In Geneva itself, moreover, Jean-Jacques de Sellon, founder of the first society for international peace, launched his celebrated campaign for the death penalty's abolition. *Frankenstein*'s setting in Geneva is certainly significant because the little "republic" (289), home of Rousseau, sets the stage for a commentary on the pitfalls of enlightened political and scientific reasoning. But I suggest that it is also significant for a less obvious reason. Geneva occupied a prominent position in the history of enlightened thought, even as it retained death-penalty statutes that had come under increasingly public and articulate scrutiny. It thus heightened and dramatized contrasts that were present in England itself.

The context of the death-penalty debate is relevant even for Mary Shelley's account—once more reading from the introduction—of Polidori's ghost story,

> about a skull-headed lady who was so punished for peeping through a keyhole—what to see I forget—something very shocking and wrong of course; but when she was reduced to a worse condition than the renowned Tom of Coventry, he did not know what to do with her and was obliged to dispatch her to the tomb of the Capulets, the only place for which she was fitted. (262)

The narrative obviously gives a particularly comic example of the bad storytelling of "poor Polidori" (262). Mary Shelley's story is better, but it is important to see that at least one reason why is that it reformulates the sources of terror. Polidori's failed narrative is about a "skull-headed lady" who is funnier than she is scary; the punishments she suffers—blinding, then burial—are not only absurd (how do you blind a ghost or keep it buried?), but have the look of mere afterthoughts tacked on to an already shabby premise. Punishments in Shelley's tale are not the afterthoughts they are in Polidori's: they instead take center stage, inseparable as a source of terror from the monstrosity of Frankenstein's creation.

I think it is important, then, that the monster's murders are linked to legal murder: he not only kills people, but also causes Justine to be falsely accused of William's murder and then put to death. The details surrounding the false accusation are crucial: she confesses to the crime, but her confession is essentially a mistake—a confession that is a "lie" for the sake of "absolution" rather than an admission of legal guilt (350). The horrifying way in which Justine's intent becomes suppressed in the mechanisms of justice—which otherwise convict her on the basis of circumstantial evidence—cannot be altered by anyone's commitment to her innocence: none of Elizabeth's or Victor's efforts can reverse the decision, and Justine is thus "punished on the scaffold as a murderess" (352). The monster himself therefore comes to emblematize (in both his body and his actions) the monstrosity of death as a legal penalty. His murder of William—not to mention other innocent people—looks like the imprecise and irremissible form of revenge upon Victor that is accomplished by Justine's execution on the scaffold. The monster vengefully and violently punishes a relation of the injurer rather than the injured; the law vengefully and violently punishes one connected to the crime rather than the criminal.

The pattern of death and false accusation is repeated later in the novel when Victor himself is threatened with the death penalty for the murder of Clerval (450). What these instances show is not simply that the monster perpetrates specific crimes, or that Victor seems quite right in taking the blame for those crimes, but that the monster's crimes repeat the brutality of law. The monster's murders—frequently explained by him as acts of "revenge" (403, 405, 407, 409)—provide "atonement" (411) for Frankenstein's offenses against him; the monster's own actions thus resemble the vengeful and sacramental violence of Geneva's bloody code. By the same token, Victor's question about Justine—"Who is safe, if she be convicted of crime?"—is a reaction to the insurmountable force of law, but it also sounds like it could be a reaction to the monster himself, who vengefully takes away the lives of innocent victims connected to Victor in order to pay back his negligent creator (342). So closely bound are the monster's murders and judicial murders that the body of the monster and the body of law sentencing its "victims" to death look like versions of each other: inflexible and cumbersome patchworks (similar to Madan's understanding of what the criminal law should actually be) incapable of modification and deaf to all intercession.

The Gothic novel thus magnifies the terrors of the death penalty, to which Austen's novels refer only obliquely, but the point I want to make is that characters like Mrs. Ferrars in *Sense and Sensibility* and Mrs. Norris in *Mansfield Park* are metaphorical executioners who need to be connected to figures like Schedoni, Gil-Martin, and Frankenstein's monster, who are inseparable from the Gothic novel's critique of traditional English (and more broadly European) standards of criminal justice. In Scott's fiction, the Gothic violence of the death penalty and other corporal punishments continues. Violence and vengeance in his novels become associated not with a demonized character, as in the Gothic, but with a distant past, or with a world of chivalric romance against which the very writing of the "real history" in the historical novel defines itself.[48] This logic emphasizes the precise degree to which Scott's historical novels depend upon an ideology of progress.[49] For his novels repeatedly draw attention to the way that their own ability to recognize the contributions of individuals to their historical moment stands in direct contrast to the violence and disorder of legal killing in past ages. In other words, the historical novel attends to persons in history only by extricating itself from, and advancing beyond, the history it describes.

There are two important features of this progressive standpoint. First, Scott continually awards privileged vantage points on "real history" to specific characters in his novels. In *Waverly*, for instance, the Scottish Highlanders are both regressive adherents of an "undoubting fanaticism" (1:224) and advocates of violence and unjust punishment: they constantly take umbrage at small slights and exact revenge for trivial offenses. Their valor and ancient customs, that is, are inseparable from their illegality, their adherence to a code in which criminals are gentlemen and vengeance bears no relation to injury. This is why Highland characters like Fergus combine fervent clan attachments with little else in the way of loyalty or obligation: Fergus seems willing to sacrifice his life for his cause, but quickly abandons that cause when the outlook for success is bleak; he is strangely indifferent to Edward's "feeling" for Colonel Talbot or his family.

Colonel Talbot, meanwhile, shows a contrasting respect for the rewards and penalties that derive from multiple obligations; when he is captured, he at first refuses to be released, preferring to suffer the "indirect and consequential" punishments for his actions (1:341). It is precisely this level of obligation to others—Talbot's ability to see himself connected to, and implicated in, multiple actions that extend beyond his sphere of immediate attention—that constitutes his distance from the Highland world of romance, with its characters focused on a single "event" or "cause" (1:173).

Thus, while in one sense all characters live in history, only specific characters have a progressive awareness of "real history." It is this "history" to which Edward finally attends when he pays sufficient regard to his "feelings" for his familial relations (1:311). Talbot tells him that his actions are putting his uncle in danger, and thus Waverly begins to feel a sense of obligation as powerful as Talbot's; he acts on feelings for those to whom he is most indebted, and who are most indebted to him.

The point here is not that Scott simply endorses an abstract legalism. Talbot is finally released from the Highlanders after obtaining a "parole of honour" (1:342); Waverly later learns that Talbot has in turn risked his career to obtain a pardon for him. The point is rather that both law and pardon are motivated by utilitarian considerations: the degree to which obligations and sanctions do or do not provide an individual or social benefit. But now we must address a second dimension of Scott's characterizations. The situation for Fergus is different; he cannot be pardoned. Talbot assures Waverly that "interference" in Fergus's execution will be "unavailing"; but, if the assurance hardly satisfies, his justification for having Fergus killed is ambivalent, to say the least. His justification, that is, contains an implicit complaint against the system of justice that he apparently supports: while "Justice" demands "some penalty of those who had wrapped the whole nation in fear and in mourning," Talbot also construes Fergus not merely as the recipient of a fair penalty, but as Justice's "victim" or "martyr," a casualty of a sacrificial rite (1:418). Fergus's own sentiments before he is executed continue to paint a disparaging picture of English criminal law and of its cruel and gruesome penalty of death and public exposure of "the senseless head" (1:430).

The ambivalent, wavering position of Talbot—an endorsement of capital punishment compromised by a complaint against it—finds an echo in the narrative voice, which marks its historical separation from Talbot's perspective as a progressive separation. Whereas Talbot ultimately confirms the justice of state killing merely because of the luck of the draw—"The dice have gone against him"—the narrator hurries in with further commentary on this defense: "Such was the reasoning of those times. . . . Let us devoutly hope that . . . we shall never see the scenes, or hold the sentiments, that were general in Britain Sixty Years since" (1:419). *Waverly* thus establishes a historical vantage point not only by marking historical difference, but also by making privileged characters into anticipations of the progressive critique of capital punishment. Those who demand (or wish) that persons achieve exceptions to the law, it turns out, do not act against or outside the law; the possibility of pardoning, from the novelist's perspective, continually arises from an interest in achieving a measure of lenience that is now—"Sixty Years since"—part of English law itself and incorporated into the narrator's own perspective. In anticipation of Jacques Derrida's link between the pardon and "the possibility of the progress of the law,"[50] the narrator's additional commentary shows how individual characters, while seeking an exception to the law, actually have a better, more progressive, version of the law in mind.[51] Romilly—whose reforms Scott supported[52]—suggested essentially the same thing (as I explained in Chapter 1) when he claimed that frequent pardons indicated a need to make law more lenient. Scott's general support for Romilly's reforms echoes, then, in this particular fictional logic. Exception to the law, for Scott, is lawful (in contrast to the account of exceptions in the work of Agamben[53])—a perspective that is finally demonstrated by the way the narrative voice both confirms and perfects the characters' progressive critique of capital punishment.

The progressive perspective in Waverly's privileged characters and in the narrator—between a critique of capital punishment and an endorsement of it—stands close to the heart of Scott's moral-political vision as he pursues it beyond the novels. In repeated instances in his journals, he argues against the archaic practice of using the corpses of criminals for anatomical research, even swearing to "fight knee-deep to prevent or punish such an exposure."[54] Even more interesting is the way that he seldom avoids making an excuse for those subjected to the punishment; he provides detailed and sympathetic criminal histories, making each one a way of stacking the scale of human value against the severe punishments that the criminals are to receive.[55] In one case, Scott supports the punishment of death for a poisoner supposedly because she "deserves" it; at the same time, he wishes for some other legal solution with the "benefit" of "saving her life."[56]

Still, despite this level of critique, Scott—like Wordsworth and many Romantic penal reformers—cannot dispense with the death penalty entirely. A long passage in the journals, for instance, speaks out eloquently in favor of capital punishment, since only "severity" can be used "to reform a corrupted nation"; thus "gentleness" cannot be employed until there is sufficient proof of a society's "mastery by terror."[57] Indeed, the progressive standpoint that Scott adopts here and in his novels would be best described as a utilitarian critique of the death penalty combined with a hesitant and limited acceptance of it. That standpoint, we have already seen in *Waverly*, condemns the law of high treason and its "horrible accompaniments" (1:418); it also criticizes those, like Talbot, who support that law. But the critique is not aimed at *all* capital punishments, which even among reformers (as I explained in Chapter 1) continued to be retained within a reformed system of lenient and efficient laws. Although English law finally put an end to the disemboweling and quartering of traitors, the progress claimed by the narrator has resulted only in a diminution rather than a disappearance of violent punishment; hanging and decapitating remained a penalty in Scott's day.⁵⁸

The fictional logic in which pardons, exceptions, and complaints critique conventional law while anticipating a lenient but orderly system of modern penalties appears in a wide range of Scott's writing. In *The Heart of Midlothian* (1818), the queen's intercession obtained by Jeanie Deans at the end of her pilgrimage to London saves her sister from execution for child murder (7:379–91). But the extralegal solution is legal from the progressive position of the narrator. As Scott's note 7 on "child murder" explains, the "severe" law forming the basis for the novel's conflict—a law that exacts the death penalty for the crime even without "direct proof"—was replaced in 1803 by another more "lenient" but still severe law requiring banishment. The pardon that Effie ultimately receives from the king does not release her from penalty but requires her to be banished from Scotland for fourteen years; thus the exception to the law is consistent with its progressive revision (7:399–408). In *The Fortunes of Nigel* (1822), set during the reign of James I, the place of exceptions in relation to the law's progressive reform is even more pronounced and clearly connected to the aesthetic work of historical fiction. The mishaps of the novel's hero, Nigel Olifaunt, take a particularly bleak turn when he engages in a duel within the precincts of the king's lands, an offense that automatically lands him in "Star Chamber business" (14:187). Both Margaret Ramsay (who has fallen in love with him) and the Templars seek to rescue Nigel from the Star Chamber's "severe and arbitrary proceedings" (14:187). Margaret's plea to her mentor, Lady Hermione, to work for his release is particularly illuminating in this regard, since her request demands listening to the "heart" over the "cruel" laws of the land; the heart is "the echo of the voice from Heaven within us" (14:226).

Lady Hermione does indeed petition the king, who, after a complicated series of maneuvers, issues a "warrant of mercy" for Nigel's release (14:403). But at the same time, the very condition of seeking mercy seems virtually indistinguishable from a submission to the rigors of the penal law itself. Scott makes Nigel and his advocates, even in their plea for mercy, embrace a still more rigorous form of penalty. Nigel is repeatedly shown mulling over the narratives of punished criminals or poring over the melancholy scrawls of prisoners. Even while meditating on an escape from the terrors of the Star Chamber, his "youthful imagination" inflicts upon him the dread and eventual pain of his penalty. Anticipating the punishment of dismemberment, he fears it as "more ghastly than death itself," and "his wrist tingled as if already under the blade of the dismembering knife" (14:187–88). Nothing better characterizes Nigel, then, than his persistent enactment (like Romilly in his *Memoirs*) of the sufferings he attempts to avoid. Indeed, the reasoning applies not only to Nigel, but to Lady Hermione as well. Her willingness to plead to the king is already qualified by her respect for the law that places her under the king's protection; but still more intriguing is her merciless repetition of the painful narrative of her clandestine marriage and persecution, as if to provide a periodic punishment for herself. Her own telling of her story makes her feel "like a criminal on the scaffold" (14:239), as if she were as anxious to pay for crimes that are not hers as she is to be exonerated. We can only conclude, finally, that Hermione and Nigel, both agent and recipient of mercy, need to be guarded against the law by a merciful intervention, even while they seek out a punitive pain that restores and sustains them.

In the preface to the novel, Scott essentially suggests that the combination of lenience and rigor in the law is at one with the reformed aesthetic perspective of historical fiction. The narrative involves characters exhibiting "ancient manners" while involved in "incidents of a marvellous and improbable character." Yet at the same time, his characters do not simply practice ancient manners, but embody the "great variety of shading and delineation" associated with those living in "the newer and more improved period, of which the world has but lately received the light" (14:ix). The very possibility of writing a historical novel, in other words, arises from the novel's realist strategies of rendering fine distinctions in character; these strategies are in turn inseparable from the advances in English law, with its lenient reduction of penalties with graduated "shading and delineation" in proportion to offenses. The dependence of the novel's priorities on the "light" of English progress becomes the formal equivalent of the novel's progressive denunciation of James I's "extravagance," "fanaticism," and "depravity"; these stand in contrast to a more modern "philanthropy and good breeding; both of which ... depend upon the regard paid by each individual to the interest as well as the feelings of others" (14:ix).

Unlike Austen's heroes, the heroes of the Waverly novels (like the heroes of Gothic novels) resist or take exception to conventional punishments. This is the difference that history makes in Scott's historical novels, for legal violence is one of the crucial features that both distinguishes his sense of the past and requires the narrative distance of the present. This difference, however, disguises a deeper affinity: exceptions to legal violence in Scott arise only in order to reinforce the claims of utility on the functioning of penal law. For, like Austen's heroes, Scott's become fictionalized embodiments of the reformers' efforts to make penal law more directly attentive to the benefits that punishments confer upon human life. The numerous examples of exceptions to the law in Scott's novels enable his privileged characters to articulate a demand for reform—a demand for the kind of distinguishing correction that Austen's protagonists constantly honor and receive. For Scott's characters, this demand can be met consistently only in the revised structures of law and literary representation that typify the narrator's—not the characters'—historical moment.

5

Coleridge, Shelley, and the Poetics of Conscience

> My conscience hath a thousand several tongues,
> And every tongue brings in a several tale,
> And every tale condemns me for a villain.
> Richard, in William Shakespeare, *Richard III*

In his *Essays on the Principles of Morality and Natural Religion* (1751), Lord Kames speaks eloquently in the first essay ("Of Our Attachment to Objects of Distress") about the vulgarity of public executions. The problem is not quite the usual one pointed out by other writers of his day who criticize capital punishment because it leads to unruly, uncivilized behavior. Instead, his complaint—applicable not merely to public executions but to executions of any kind[1]—is quite simply that we cannot easily feel sympathy with anyone who is being hanged. We do not know what it's like to be hanged, and no one who has been executed can tell us about it, the frequently published accounts of criminals narrowly escaping death at the gallows notwithstanding.[2]

Indeed, reports of survivors like "Half-Hanged Meg" Dickson, believed dead after her 1728 hanging until she awoke in her coffin on the way to her grave, actually reinforce the view of death not as simply beyond experience, but as more fundamentally resistant to meaning. True, such narratives sensationally offer personal experiences of a sort; the 1651 account of Ann Green, hanged for child murder but then "revived," is exemplary in its tantalizing promise to display the "manner of her suffering."[3] Strictly speaking, though, the accounts of Dickson and Green are not the "suffering" of death; they are everything *but* death. They therefore testify to the failure of death to function as a penalty for the bodies upon which it acts, and the failure of death to mean anything for the reader—except as something avoided, and therefore undefined.

In Kames's view, not knowing what it's like to be hanged means that it is impossible for any of us to claim that we could feel a pain approximating that of the criminal being executed. Still more important, and reasoning further from this, it is impossible for us to have any discussion of what the *consequences* of our deaths might be for us. Without such sympathy, we can achieve "no degree of self-approbation" from seeing or contemplating such an execution—a self-approbation that, Kames suggests, is the reward for having contributed, through a mutually felt sympathy, to the "security and happiness of mankind" (29, 13). The problem with executions, in other words, is not that they lead to unrest, but that they appeal only to those led "by the present instinct," without any feeling of connection to, or responsibility for, the felicity of others (29).

This objection to execution is indeed a distinctive one that might be contrasted with Adam Smith's *The Theory of Moral Sentiments* (1759). Smith also values the expression of shared sympathies, but does so precisely in order to support the death penalty. An audience of men will "readily . . . sympathize with the natural resentment of the injured," he writes, "and the offender becomes the object of their hatred and indignation."[4] So powerful is that resentment—the kind subjected to Nietzsche's critique over a hundred years later—that we sympathize even with "an odious person, when he is injured by those to whom he has given no provocation."[5] Smith sees sympathy as shared feeling; the death penalty is effective simply as an inevitable result of a "natural" propensity to sympathize with injured parties. There is always enough resentment to go around. The effects of death—since death is important as a necessary expression of "natural" resentment—are not important for Smith; for Kames, they are, and this is why he must oppose execution. Kames understands sympathy not as sharing someone's feeling—what he calls "present instinct"—but as a more general sense of the interrelated ingredients procuring our "security and happiness." Death must fail as punishment, on these terms, for death's sheer unknowability makes it impossible to say definitively how it has contributed to anyone's security or happiness.

If we press on further, we realize that the opposition to executions is only a small, though integral, part of Kames's interwoven discussions in the subsequent essays. For in the second, "Of the Foundation and Principles of the Law of Nature," he makes it clear that his position on the death penalty is inseparable from his account of the workings of conscience. While he argues that our notions of obligation are ultimately dependent upon the will of God, he insists that it is our conscience that makes that will real to us—presumably by reflecting on the security and happiness of others. "Upon the commission of certain crimes," for instance, we feel the "remorse of conscience"; this "remorse of conscience" is fundamentally different from public punishment because it emerges from a private act of the mind, in the "imagination" (64, 65). But it is not *merely* private, for this would again seal us off from the sympathy that Kames mentions earlier; it is a "dread of merited punishment" that acts upon the imagination in such a way as to perfect the operations of merited punishment that may not be socially available. Even when the law does not inflict a penalty, the one with remorse of conscience feels that "every extraordinary misfortune is considered as a punishment purposely inflicted for the crime committed" (65). Conscience is thus not a rejection of, or alternative to, legal punishment; it ratifies and intensifies punishment's forces.

Kames's complex view (anticipated by Shakespeare's Richard III) shuttles between two prominent and often separate philosophical views of conscience: one that consigns it to private opinion against the law (as in Hobbes's *Leviathan* [1651]), and one identifying conscience with law itself (as in Pufendorf's *The Whole Duty of Man* [1691]).[6] And it is the mobile, multidimensional aspect of conscience—its tendency to span over a range of alternatives, turning itself inside out and outside in—that connects Kames's representation of it to Romantic penal reform. As I briefly suggested in Chapter 1, the discourse of penal reform occasionally appears to speak through the voice of conscience and thus—in Madan's terms—in opposition to the smooth and mechanical application of the Bloody Code. But in a still more revealing way, the reformer's appeal to conscience could only secure its legitimacy by externalizing itself as law, conspicuously rendering itself as a supporting element in a comprehensive system of "merited" penalties. Playing a central role in the conception of Romantic penality, conscience protests in favor of a lenient reform of existing penalties, at the same time that it enforces an even stricter adherence to penalty as such.[7]

Kames's account begins my discussion not only because it usefully compresses a long history of thought on conscience, but also because it explicitly claims an association between conscience and the "imagination," an association central to the Romantic poetry I discuss in this chapter. If Kames prefigures a Romantic account of conscience by exposing its dependence upon poetry's imaginative resources, Romantic poetry itself repeatedly focuses its own displays of imaginative power on a negotiation between internal meditation and external punishment. Certainly the numerous instances of gibbets and gallows in poetry of the late eighteenth and early nineteenth centuries demonstrate the general relationship I am attempting to describe. From the wanderer's pangs in *Salisbury Plain* to the chastening gibbet mast episode in *The Prelude*, the articulations of punishment are not merely static representations of the law's power; they provide insights into the imaginative involvement between the subject and penal sanctions. I mentioned in Chapter 3 that Wordsworth takes a poetic interest in the probative authority of the gibbet mast in Book 11, and follows the "superstition of the neighbourhood" in doing so, but we could add still more to that account (11.297). For even if the poet imitates that superstitious regard, his own meditations and cherished "spots" effectively substitute for it. His experiences of scenery compose a "visionary dreariness," and his experience of his father's death can seem like a "chastisement" to his desires and ambitions (11.311, 370). The poet, in other words, achieves such alacrity at imagining connections between empirically disconnected elements, between causes and effects, that he can invent punishments for himself even when legal sanctions do not seem readily at hand.

The list could go on of different modes of representing conscience, from lesser-known instances like Joseph Fawcett's portrayal of a "conscience-goaded wretch" haunted by his own mind's "intruding terrors," to better-known examples like *The Prelude* and George Crabbe's Peter Grimes.[8] But if we examine these texts more closely, we see that what conscience means in relation to penal apparatuses differs slightly in each one. In Fawcett, conscience is a punishment so unique to the self that it results in nothing less than a flat denial of all external existence; the guilt-ridden traveler cannot even notice nature's "sweet retreat."[9] In Wordsworth, as we have seen, nature itself looks like its own system of penalties. And in Crabbe, the sense of guilt is barely distinguishable from the imposition of social norms: the resemblance between "Grimes" and "crimes" makes the criminal's own name anticipate and publicly register his actions; his guilt is inseparable from the demands of "the People" for confession and repentance.[10]

As in Kames, such examples collectively show how poetic representations of conscience achieve a surprising flexibility, capable of demonstrating and reinforcing different rationales of punishment that form Romanticism's complex legacy. Conscience might be easier to describe, then, less as a singular entity than as a plural set of interrelated conscience-formations in which the term—along with others I associate with it—takes on different but complementary significations or associations, from the meditative frame of mind in the moral subject to the rigorous operation of the retributive rule. In the following pages, I examine two poets, Coleridge and Shelley, in greater detail, precisely in order to pursue the range of conscience's multiple attachments and to demonstrate the relevance of those attachments to the subject of Romantic penality.

In his drama *Osorio* (1797)—rejected by Sheridan at Covent Garden but later revised, accepted, and successfully staged as *Remorse* (1813)—Coleridge, like Kames, places the highest value on a self-punishment that avoids the violence, cruelty, and vulgarity of public punishment. But it is also clear that "remorse," a "punishment that cleanses souls," cannot simply reside in the soul but needs to be transformed into legible incitements to suffering that can be consumed both by the criminal and by those who seek to condemn him. In *The Triumph of Life* (1822), Shelley takes this externalization of moral reasoning still further, utterly dislodging conscience from any individual and identifying it with the author's work. In this last great effort in Shelley's career—actually the endpoint of a carefully cultivated relationship between conscience and poetic creation—his tyrants and misguided philosophers do not in fact display their remorse, since they have none. Instead, they are subjected to a process of scorning and shaming that is imposed first by nature but finally by the poem itself. If the poetry of remorse in Coleridge solicits conscience in support of a humane form of punishment, Shelley's poetry of shame makes verse itself scandalously appropriate and leads it to exercise conscience's power.[11]

Osorio, Remorse, and the Ethics of Fear

The plot of Coleridge's *Osorio* is fairly simple. Albert returns to his family disguised as a Moor—threatened by agents of the Inquisition—to confront his brother Osorio, who had attempted to kill him (with hired murderers) and woo Albert's still-faithful lover Maria. Simple as it is, though, the play produces something of a theatrical puzzle. Remorse is the state of mind that Albert wishes to see inspired in his brother; but even if remorse seems like the exemplary state of conscience, witnessing someone's remorse is not always, and perhaps not ever, satisfying. We do not necessarily like the way that people say they are sorry. Remorse demands a theatrical representation that weakens its authority, yet this hardly dissuades Coleridge from freighting remorse with tremendous dramatic pressure. On the one hand, then, this crucial emotion functions as the play's keystone in its opposition to oppressive forms of Inquisitorial religious and political authority enforced by "the rack," the "black dungeon," and the "fire of faggots" (2.232).[12] This is apparently because remorse is an internal movement of the mind that cannot be solicited from sources of external power any more than it can be expressed through a personal assurance or confession of its veracity. Far deeper than this, it is, Albert says, a unique form of "punishment that cleanses hearts" (1.328).

In one sense, this quality of remorse confirms what William Jewett identifies as *Osorio*'s more general and thoroughly Protestant hostility to the power of external images over belief and conduct.[13] Remorse is still a "punishment," however, and is consistently understood on those terms; it is an alternative to punishment, yet it expresses itself as a commitment to the external sanction it is initially designed to supplant.[14] We must attend, then, to the ways in which Coleridge's remorseful conscience does not simply withdraw into a mute self. It makes itself articulate, but in the strangest of ways: not by confessing contrition, but by pointing to a legible series of words and images that serves as its terrifying inspiration.[15] This is to say that the attempt to express an internal state issues in an effort to describe a prior motivation for that state in the form of an external threat. When we find the wronged brother Albert struggling to persuade Osorio at the end of the play to "call up one pang of true remorse" (5.197), we encounter the vocative terminology central to the remorseful conscience: it makes itself "true" by way of a calling or naming. A pang, by definition both a "pain" and a "resonant sound,"[16] is feeling made publicly and aesthetically available through its outside—hence the important distinction between a pang of true remorse and the "secret pangs" that Maria dismissively associates with the hypocrisy of monastic life and confessional institutions (4.301). What is crucial about Coleridge's poetic and political vision in this play—and what makes it a particularly interesting focus for the discussions I have been tracing in this book—is that conscience is an antidote to the spectacular and unjust punishments associated with political and religious tyranny; at the same time, true remorse can make itself known to itself and to others by steadfastly clinging to the sources of the pain and terror that, rather than simply avoiding, it claims to merit.[17]

Before continuing here with a more involved reading of the play, we should acknowledge the last act's explicit connections to the discourse of penal reform—connections that show how Coleridge's interest in guilt and remorse (which Kenneth Burke some years ago saw as a common ground between *Osorio* and the "The Rime of the Ancient Mariner" [1798]) is not only metaphysical but also political.[18] What is important in this last scene is not just Osorio's confessing that he had ordered his brother to be killed; we also see a carefully negotiated resolution that settles the question of what his penalty should be for this offense (not to mention his killing of Ferdinand, one of his hired murderers, in Act 4). Maria wishes to save Osorio, the man who hired murderers to kill his brother, from the punishment of death. She insists that the other characters "must not murder him" (5.295), but rather should impose a milder penalty. (Earlier in the play, Albert also rejects death as a proper penalty for explicitly utilitarian reasons: his death would simply inflict suffering on both his father and Maria [2.68–77]).

This suggestion may seem like a humane one, and it certainly falls in line with the ways in which Coleridge criticizes the violence and inhumanity of legal punishments in his day.[19] But the decision to avoid punishing by death does not necessarily avoid violence and cruelty. At least something of this kind is suggested when Alhadra—wife of Ferdinand—disagrees with the plan, and wonders whether allowing Osorio to live would in fact be more severe than death. Should they permit him to "waste away / With inward wounds, and like the spirit of chaos / To wander on disquietly thro' the earth, / Cursing all lovely things?" By this reasoning, the choice of life seems more like "deep revenge" than death (5.295–99).

Osorio is, in fact, allowed to live. But it becomes clear that Maria's and Alhadra's accounts of that revised penalty—one emphasizing its mildness, the other emphasizing its cruelty—do not contradict but in fact modify and constitute each other. The punishment of allowing Osorio to live is both more tolerant and more severe. Refusing to inflict a vengeful murder upon Osorio accomplishes two aims. First, there is a benefit to lenience that can be felt by both Alhadra and Maria: the public—most notably women in the public—will not have to "behold the ugliness of death" (5.302). Second, however, such mercy does not simply eliminate punishment; it inflicts its own kind of violence. The "forgiveness," like that extended to Cain, is a "curse" (5.252). (It is quite likely that Byron's *Cain* was inspired by Coleridge, although it is the later version of the play that he read and praised.[20])

The closing scene accompanies other moments in the play that also echo accounts of punishment common among reformers: Alhadra's view of poor prison conditions producing violence rather than reform (1.207–26), or Albert's soliloquy on his dungeon cell's loathsome conditions and corrupting influences, first published as "The Dungeon" in *Lyrical Ballads* (5.107–36). But what is especially relevant about these instances is the way that the interest in punishment is more generally informed by local articulations of the remorseful conscience. In the closing scene, for instance, notice the specific terms framing the logic through which the penalty of death gives way to a punishment suffered in the workings of Osorio's own mind: the "inward wounds" provide a "revenge" greater than any penalty. Yet notice, too, how that inward movement is itself set forth as injuries or "wounds" inflicted by external instruments of pain—"wormwood" and "gall" (5.297, 304). Like the "pang" I mentioned earlier, this form of expression operates in a carefully constructed logic, according to which remorse alternates between an inward reflection and a persistent attribution of a punishing externality, a punishing power that is linked not simply to a private psychology but to the possibility for collective, visible, and systematic order.[21] It is hardly surprising, from that vantage point, that both wormwood and gall are defined not only as sources of pain and irritation, but also as sources of bitter *taste*, emphasizing the aesthetic dimensions of inward wounding.

To see how this works even more broadly in the play, we can piece together Albert's curious role in it. From his earliest lines, when Albert recalls the moment in which he comes face-to-face with his brother's hired murderers, he remembers exhorting them by speaking of "virtues" that are simultaneously "dead in no man" but need to be summoned by "looks and most impassion'd words" (1.296–97). In a fairly straightforward sense, the looks and impassioned words are Albert's, yet Albert himself seems oddly detached from them, as if the possibility of recognizing one's deepest sense of guilt depended upon a set of utterly exchangeable expressions. This becomes especially clear in a striking series of metaphors, when Albert continues to recount his anxious prayer that "Remorse might fasten on their hearts, / And cling, with poisonous tooth, inextricable / As the gored lion's bite" (1.319–21). Produced neither by Albert nor by those in whom he wishes to inspire it, remorse becomes a quasi-personified entity. Thus, as in Wordsworth's negotiation of personification in *Salisbury Plain*, remorse's status as an agency without agent—eerily lurking outside the play's characters—provides a condensed account of just punishment itself.

As a consequence, it is not altogether clear that Albert, by wishing to solicit a "pang" of remorse, actually wants to extract a confession of Osorio's attempted crime. In fact, it is not altogether clear whether Albert expects proof of remorse at all, or whether he is contented with summoning terrifying images to inspire it. This much might be suggested by the most celebrated scene of the play, in Act 3 (the "incantation scene," as Coleridge called it), when Albert arranges for a painting—painted by Albert himself—of his "assassination."[22] It is to "rouse a fiery whirlwind in his conscience" (2.326), because the image of the fictive consequences of his actions are represented before him. Yet this artifice is even further extended when Albert continues by depicting himself as a vengeful spirit—a ghost once again uprooted from Albert himself—returning from the dead to inflict a punishment that is severe and inescapable: "What if his spirit / Re-entered its cold corse, and came upon thee, / With many a stab from many a murderer's poniard . . . / . . . and with one look / Hurl thee beyond all power of penitence?" (3.80–86).

In this way, the scenario in *Osorio* both touches upon and departs from its most obvious predecessor, *Hamlet* (1600). In Shakespeare's play, conscience becomes visible as an internal emotion theatrically expressed in Claudius's gestures and speech. The inaccessible moral work of the mind is finally made available first by narratively representing historical truth (the play performed by the traveling actors); this in turn elicits the body's involuntary confession.[23] In *Osorio*, Coleridge's interest is not in turning the inside out, rendering internal states suddenly visible; surely this has something to do with his anxiety over the "miserably undramatic" quality of the scene.[24] The painting, of course, does not represent what actually happened; still more, it is suggested here that Osorio has not even seen—or at least entirely absorbed—the painting displayed before him, since he is in a "state of stupor" and later needs to have the details of the picture explained to him. The confusion and difficulty of the task, however, is precisely the point: conscience is continually represented both as internal and uniquely fit to the movements of the mind, and as an alienation of the mind, a submission to an artificial and inflexible construction.

It is true that "guilt" is something that at least might seem to be legible to characters as if the interior were cryptically written on the face: Maria thus speaks of a "mystery" perceptible in Osorio, "And guilt doth lurk behind it"; "remorse" in this account is obscured by other emotions—"rage ... scorn, and stupid fear"—that must be cleared away (4.259, 261). But it is more consistently the case that remorse can be located only by pointing to a threatening force outside the conscience-guided agent. Albert's presence for Osorio is not itself a direct threat, I have been trying to suggest; his role is to provide Osorio with occasions or prompts for the activity of conscience—his words inspiring "fear and wonder" that "crush [his] rage, / And turn it to a motionless distraction" (5.184–86). And the most convincing glimmerings of remorse that Osorio himself can supply occur not with the passing "gust of the soul" in Act 1, but with the implicit chastisement of "a desolate widow's curse" or "an orphan's tear" (5.204–5).

It is not sufficient for the guilty man to feel guilt, or to experience threatening incitements to it. Coleridge consistently engages his characters in the dynamics of remorse even when it would make more sense for their consciences to be clear. Even beyond Osorio himself, that is, the clear conscience takes visible and audible shape as an incitement to pain or death. Although Maria is supposedly "innocent" of having allowed Osorio to court and marry her, for instance, her constancy is inseparable from the "horrible" fear of having her husband return to find "a brother's infant / Smile at him" from her arms (1.49–50). Albert is sure that, if she had been unfaithful, "she would have died, / Died in her sins—perchance, by her own hands" (1.323–24), making innocence inseparable from a conviction that the spectacle of her sins might have furnished a sufficient power to punish her, even with death.

Ferdinand's conscience, furthermore, demonstrates what we hear from Albert's report in Act 1; he refuses to carry out the murder when inspired by a "look and a voice which overaw'd me" (2.84). And his credentials continue to be enforced in the play: his capacity to feel "fear" is not the "cowardice" that Osorio calls it (4.37). His fearful affect—passages on the subject in Act 4 are heavily glossed in MSII, a copy retained after the play was sent to Sheridan—is one of Coleridge's most complete visions of a developed moral-political imagination. Shrinking from the influence of "beings that live, yet not for the eye" (Ferdinand's words that Coleridge added in *Remorse*), he demonstrates a capacity to feel "haunted" by a "guilt" imposed by the forces of darkness.[25]

And then there is Albert. It is not the case that Albert simply wants to inspire guilt in his brother; he seeks means to inspire remorse so compelling that they produce terrors even for himself. If it is true, as he suggests, that Osorio's depravity is like a narcotic—a "strange solution / ... to satisfy thy fears, / And drug them to unnatural sleep," Albert demonstrates that fear—fear of retribution even when he has not committed crimes—can be a powerful guard against that depravity. In the last act, Albert declines to drink from a goblet containing poison that Osorio has given him; self-preservation is subordinated to a fear that extends even to an insect on the wall that might drink the poison: "Saw I that insect on this goblet's brink, / I would remove it with an eager terror" (5.168–69). It is not the case here that Albert simply reveals his love for all living creatures (therefore avoiding the fate of the ancient mariner). The speech contrasts with Osorio's in Act 3, which confidently asserts that, since forms of life are replaceable, all are "strange alike" and all are "predestined rottenness." To kill one therefore cannot be a "crime" any more than it can inspire "guilt" (3.212–19). Whereas Osorio would essentially suggest that wrongful actions against others might avoid painful consequences, Albert's terror (like Ferdinand's in Act 4) testifies to his sense of a possible retribution for allowing a living creature, endowed with "will" and seeking its own "pleasurable ends," to die. Albert's love for human and animal life is expressed as fear of punishment.

The movement of conscience I have been describing—its resistance to and reinstatement of external punishment—continues to shape the last speech of the play, delivered by Alhadra. Before proceeding to that, however, we should contrast the earlier version of the play to the later *Remorse*, which changes not only this speech but other features of the play's conclusion as well. The revision is a significant one; rather than have the characters allow Osorio to live, Coleridge has Alhadra (Teresa in *Remorse)* stab Osorio (Ordonio) to avenge the death of her husband. Albert (Alvar) has the last words in this version, recommending forgiveness for Alhadra/Teresa, since "delights" in this world should not be "unalloyed with grief." As Julie Carlson notes, Alhadra/Teresa becomes a troubling Orientalist's fantasy of the vengeful Moor, but she is simultaneously made less troubling by being recuperated into a vision of a God whose kindness is mixed with vengeance.[26] The stabbing of Osorio/Ordonio is ultimately accepted as the work of the "arm of avenging Heaven"—a transparent embodiment of God's will; thus *Remorse* recommends an acceptance of violence as a feature of God's government. Whatever stand against capital punishment might have appeared in the earlier version of the play now seems to have been evacuated, or at least severely weakened, by the suggestion that violence must simply be accepted.

I think there is much evidence to suggest that at no point in Coleridge's life could he have preferred the resolution to *Remorse* on terms that were either doctrinal or poetic. (The simple accord of God's vengeance with our own vengeance too clearly risks accusations of fanaticism—of a kind that "pensive Sara" answers with a "mild reproof" in the "The Eolian Harp" [(1796), 1, 49].) It is more likely that the implicit dangers of fanaticism residing within the conclusion of the revised play—even though they seem to cut against the grain of his writing in *The Friend*, the *Lay Sermons*, and elsewhere—made good theater. The high drama and confident (though questionable) resolution would have compensated for the shaky incantation scene. The concluding lines that Alhadra speaks in the earlier version, however, are more in line both with Coleridge's politics and with his broader poetic practices. The final gesture is important because Alhadra, inclining toward vengeance elsewhere in the play, now imbibes Osorio's own "self-accusing spirit"; she speaks here both of a certain kind of power and of a certain kind of "song" that puts that spirit into aesthetic practice:

> That point
> In misery which makes the oppressed man
> Regardless of his own life, makes him too
> Lord of the oppressor's! Know I an hundred men
> Despairing, but not palsied by despair,
> This arm should shake the kingdoms of this world;
> The deep foundations of iniquity
> Should sink away, earth groaning from beneath them;
> The strong holds of the cruel men should fall,
> Their temples and their mountainous towers should fall;
> Till desolation seem'd a beautiful thing,
> And all that were and had the spirit of life
> Sang a new song to him who had gone forth
> Conquering and still to conquer!
> (5.308–21)

The "new song" is an endorsement of social order rather than a theatrical display of violence, as in *Remorse*; Alhadra throughout this speech reinforces the lenient but inflexible penalty applied to Osorio in the last act. The misery and desolation of which she speaks simply must be accepted, because no punishment done to another—no matter how severe—can restore a loss of life. This level of acceptance, however, is of value not for the purpose of consolation, as though it surreptitiously sanctioned acts of violence. The oppressed man instead becomes the model for a new kind of sociability, a new relation to others, that rejects vengeance and violence. Meanwhile, Alhadra, though regardless of her own life, becomes the lord and conqueror of those like Osorio who have been the cause of her misery. The triumph achieved at the end of the play, then, is not a triumph involving a display of violent authority; it rejects conventional penalties in favor of a lenience achieved by abandoning one's demand for personal satisfaction for loss. But at the same time, this triumph is marked by an unyielding punitive power over "cruel men." Combining both lenience and severity, it is a triumph of Coleridge's vision of justice.

Shelley, Penality, and Poetic Legislation

I spoke of *Osorio*'s last act as a miniaturized discussion about, and solution to, the issue of capital punishment, but Shelley takes a much more explicit stand in his "Essay on the Punishment of Death" (1815?); he also establishes a powerful and surprising set of connections between punishment and works of art. Although the essay was never published during his lifetime, it can still give us some insight into why Shelley may have regarded the issue of punishment as a focus of explicitly poetic, as well as political, interest. One of the opening claims of the essay returns us to the reasoning of Lord Kames's *Essays*, with which this chapter began. Shelley claims that there is no "beneficial result" arising from capital punishment because, as a meaningless act of officially sanctioned violence, it cannot establish any "sympathy" between the victim of punishments and the beholder—or between one beholder and another. "The laws in this case lose that sympathy, which it ought to be their chief object to secure, and in a participation of which consists their chief strength in maintaining those sanctions by which the parts of the social union are bound together."[27]

Even a statement this brief from the essay begins to capture the complexity of Shelley's thinking on this subject. He firmly opposes capital punishment and argues for its complete abolition because it detracts from a "sympathy" among public viewers. At the same time, the opposition to the death penalty is itself supported by the maintenance of "sanctions" (157). In other words, Shelley affirms a kind of "sympathy" to be found in the community over which laws govern, but this sympathy is not simply located within the hearts and minds of people themselves. Sympathy is at least in part a construction of the legislator. Laws "secure" sympathy, and the punishment of death depletes the power of the law's sanctions to bind persons together in a "union" (157). This complexity is of course something that connects Shelley's writing quite firmly with the writings of penal reformers I discussed in Chapter 1—more precisely, with the tendency of those writers to make punishment both the product of communal interests and a systematic rule over those interests. But I want to do more than suggest the existence of a relatively simple similarity. What is even more interesting is that Shelley keeps seeing the punishment of death as the usurpation of a decidedly *poetic* design, and this design is in turn inseparable from his attention to the shadings of "distinction" in human crime and guilt (155).

Early in the essay, Shelley boldly asks "what *death* is" (155): the question is directed to ask what the *punishment* of death is or means, but this way of phrasing it draws attention to the author's attempts to hold up death as such as an impossible object of knowledge and thus as an impossible form of punishment. For Shelley, death is "a measure of transgressions of indefinite shades of distinction, so soon as they shall have passed that degree and color of enormity with which it is supposed no inferior infliction is commensurate" (155). The claim that death is "beyond" distinction expands in the text that follows, as he makes it unclear whether it could be declared "good or evil, a punishment or a reward, or whether it be wholly indifferent" (155). The point recalls Plato's claim in his *Apology*, while rejecting Plato's view that a lack of knowledge of death's goodness or evil makes resistance irrational, even when it is inflicted as a punishment, and even when that punishment is unjust.[28] In answer to death's lack of definition or distinction, Shelley constructs an alliance between "inferior infliction" or penalties lighter than death, and a kind of artistic rhetoric of shade and color. Neither author could have read the other's work, but Shelley's terms are close to Taylor's in his discussion of Wordsworth—and, in fact, are consistent with them. If Taylor sees Wordsworth's support of the death penalty as a curious way of dabbing colors onto already established lines (an account that I said Wordsworth resists, or at least troubles), Shelley frames his opposition as if he were rejecting mere outline (what Taylor associates with Providential authority) and creating figures from light, shade, and color.

This aesthetic valence may seem abstract at first, but its connection to Shelley's thinking about retributive penalties is central in the account that follows from it. Further on, for instance, he shifts metaphors to speak not so much of painting, as the earlier example might suggest, but of weaving. To inflict the punishment of death is to deprive the person punished of a distinctive kind of clothing, "to disrobe him at once from all that intertexture of good and evil with which Nature seems to have clothed every form of individual existence" (156). Shelley's words here are reminiscent of the language he uses to describe Beatrice Cenci, whose "crimes and miseries" are the "mask and mantle" clothing her for "the scene of the world."[29] And if the connection is warranted, the essay may suggest to us that the audience for *The Cenci* (1819) must appreciate its poetic textures by upholding the "redress," "aid," and "retribution" of a punishment for the villain that might come from just laws, even though justice has no representation in the play outside the wishful articulations of those who suffer under Cenci's tyranny.[30] Furthermore, the audience, subscribing to such a principle of just law, must denounce Beatrice's resort to murdering her father for his crime, even while they must also denounce the violent punishment of Beatrice herself—a punishment that strips away all "intertexture of good and evil."

What is remarkable in all of these instances, I think, is the way that the essay invokes the power of conscience without naming it; the death penalty extinguishes the "vital principle within us" of good and evil—what we might interpret as the ability to distinguish between right and wrong (156). But the language of conscience or internal deliberation is also, and more importantly for Shelley, a kind of artistic production designed by the poet and legislator. Indeed, this is why much of the essay goes on to address the death penalty as a mismanaged spectacle in need of careful revision. Turning his attention to the death penalty's audiences, Shelley faults their fickleness or variability in sentiment for causing disorder and unrest during the executions of criminals. At first this may seem like familiar fare: he joins forces with many other contemporary reformers who worried over the sentiments of the audiences and the threat they posed to social order. Further on, though, Shelley—like Wordsworth—keeps connecting the punishment of death to a vulgar lack of sensibility or artistic awareness in audiences. It is not merely that those audiences lack control; it is that they produce highly controlled and inappropriate readings. The penalty of death makes traitors into martyrs in the public eye, inspiring "pity, admiration, and sympathy" rather than disapprobation (156). The audience is so utterly sympathetic to the "motives" of the criminal that it has no attention to the "evil, or the purpose itself of those actions, though that purpose may happen to be eminently pernicious" (156). The essay does not simply criticize lower-class readers, though; the "more powerful, and the richer" among the audience are also a problem: they tend to "regard their own wrongs as in some degree avenged and their own rights secured by this punishment, inflicted as the penalty of whatever crime" (157). If the poor and disadvantaged have too much sympathy for criminals, the rich and powerful have no sympathy with them and only a vengeful sentiment (akin to the collective resentment defended in Adam Smith's *Theory of Moral Sentiments*) that they share with each other.

If the audiences for executions are a problem, however, it is because of the flawed text of capital punishment: its uncertain authorship and faulty construction. An execution produces disorder not only because of the audience but also because of the anarchic tendencies of the criminal; criminals submitted to the death penalty become false or suspicious "authors" communing with the anarchic tendencies of their audiences. (Shelley is referring to the tendency of criminals to present elaborate gallows speeches or manage elaborate spectacles, as in Dick Turpin's legendary grand procession to the gallows in 1739.[31]) The criminal, after all, is not really an "author"; he merely looks like one because legislators who preside over the punishment of death seem barely to have authored anything at all. What occupies the place of authorship is thus a false and misleading communication of motives and sympathies between criminals and spectators, since the criminals both demonstrate and encourage a habit of "despising the perils attendant upon consummating the most enormous crimes" because of an "insensibility to fear or pain" (156).

Even if these contingencies could be put under control—that is, even if the death penalty's message were properly conveyed—it would still look to Shelley like an inept piece of workmanship with no internal consistency. The death penalty falsely supposes that death will have a sustained meaning after life, or that the infliction of death imitates a punishment that occurs after death. Even if we were to believe in life after death, Shelley rejects the idea that we could know the rationale of reward and punishment in a future state; he insists upon regarding it as a mere superstition that criminals or audiences might actually benefit from the "art" of punishment after the criminal's death.[32] In identifying all of these problems plaguing executions—unruly audiences, usurping authors, incoherent texts—Shelley does not differ substantially from Hannah More, who also sought to correct what she saw as the corrupting influences of criminal biographies and gallows speeches. But Shelley finally reaches a solution that is both political and poetic rather than restricted to More's domain of Christian theology. Far from opposing punishments generally, he advocates "sanctions" that would provide a stronger sense of "social union." Those sanctions, furthermore, are deliberately and consistently framed as the work of the poet-legislator who helps to organize the "actions" of the reader-spectator. He can thus admit all the variability of sentiment in his audience while affirming the power and responsibility of the ability to punish. Punishment is "an exhibition which, by its known effects on the sensibility of the sufferer, is intended to intimidate the spectators from incurring a similar liability" (156). By embracing a more lenient set of sanctions, Shelley gives shape to an opposition to the death penalty that nevertheless reinforces a "sane polity." The "true art of the legislator" presumably aims to construct "laws founded upon reason," which collectively encourage both "reformation and strict restraint" (156–57).

The Cruelty of the Ideal

Shelley's "Essay on the Punishment of Death," with its emphasis on the replacement of the chaotic effects of the punishment of death with an orderly and legible set of sanctions, may point us toward ways of talking about how and why many of his works revolve around an essentially retributive aesthetic. Indeed, if he makes punishment look like a kind of poetry, we can now turn to the poetry with a heightened awareness of the way it constitutes itself through a highly self-conscious embrace of penal retributivism. Still more specifically, Shelley's work consistently constructs a profound alliance between poetry and retributive penalty of a very specific kind: the imposition of shame, whether in the explicit thematics of punishment in *Prometheus Unbound* (1820), in the satirical scourge of *Peter Bell the Third* (1819), or in the Dantean cosmogony of *The Triumph of Life*. Shaming for Bentham and other reformers was both thoroughly modern and thoroughly archaic; the proliferation of punishments for offenses coincided with the proliferation of emblems furnishing "allusions to poetry, eloquence, drama, and common everyday speech," emblems that would in turn impress social disapprobation upon the criminal (*TL* 3:73). It can hardly surprise us that Hazlitt referred to shame as "the sheet anchor of the law" (*HW* 11:12). For Shelley, the power to shame is built into the poem itself: shame emerges from an elaborate network of literary figures emphasizing the poem's ability to expose and deflect violent attack, returning all hostility with unparalleled aggression. His opposition to violence and injustice, that is, arises alongside his commitment to his poetry's power to produce retributive effects capable of humbling audiences, critics, and fellow writers.

Much of what I say here about the poetics of shame will at first glance seem at odds with the better-documented Shelleyan aesthetics of love.[33] I am not entirely contradicting those accounts; rather, I suggest that shame is love's darker complement in his work.[34] Shame is an aspect of his writing routinely ignored in the attempt to celebrate Shelley's opposition to tyrannical systems of thought and political organization, but it receives inadvertent support from David Bromwich's essay "Love against Revenge in Shelley's *Prometheus*." In this recent articulation of Shelleyan love in *Prometheus Unbound*, Bromwich has little to say about Despotism and Conquest, personified figures that demonstrate the "shame" of Jupiter's "ill tyranny," to which Prometheus refers in the first lines of Shelley's work even as he withdraws his curse and proclaims against hate (1.18–19). He also has little to say about Demogorgon's punishments imposed upon these figures, who are thrown into the earth's abyss and dragged through the deep (4.555–56). But even more intriguing than any of these omissions is the way that Bromwich momentarily halts in order to register the "difficulty" of Shelley's poetry and its chastening result, namely, its power of "shaming" its readers—including Bromwich himself, apparently—into a position of "defensiveness" not unlike that of the quivering critics in *Adonais*.[35] How does Shelley in fact impose this shame, and what is its purpose? Shelleyan shame differs from Coleridgean remorse because it is a version of retribution that does not, strictly speaking, externalize a personal moral feeling. Shelley moves beyond the problem of publicly expressing the internal state of conscience and instead harnesses the power of penality entirely to a public exposure achieved within the poem. That public exposure—of insult or injury perpetrated not only by named subjects but perhaps even by the reader herself—in turn reflects back on an unknowing or unthinking offender: in *The Triumph of Life*, "none seemed to know / Whither he went, or whence he came, or why / He made one of the multitude."[36]

The word "shame" has occupied a central position in recent critical parlance, and I pause here to distinguish those recent accounts from the version of it I am attempting to discuss. Michael Warner's account of shame (adapted from Erving Goffman's notion of stigma) results from one hegemonic group's prejudices—defined as "normal"—directed against a less powerful group for the purposes of social exclusion.[37] Martha Nussbaum's view of shame as a "barrier to compassion," although more abstract than Warner's view, does not depart radically from it.[38] More helpful for my purposes is Jean-Paul Sartre's account of shame as "only the original feeling of having my being *outside*, engaged in another being and as such without any defense, illuminated by the absolute light that emanates from a pure subject."[39] This strangely creative aspect of shame—a kind of *fiat lux* in which shame ushers in the beginning of light and then the beginning of life—bears some resemblance to Bernard Williams's well-known account, which places particular emphasis on the imagination. "The basic experience connected with shame is that of being seen, inappropriately, by the wrong people, in the wrong condition," he begins. But then he goes on to blur the distinction between the right people and the wrong ones: more fundamental to shame is the gaze of others—not simply others who are actually observing one's conduct, but "the imagined gaze of an imagined other will do." It is this "imagined" dimension of shame—not necessarily inspired by a particular person, or even a particular social group, but by a general idea about how we are connected with other people—that secures its "ethical" significance.[40]

The connection between shame and imagination is indeed important in what I want to discuss in Shelley's writing. There, however, it acquires a creative energy that even exceeds the boundaries of Williams's account. For Shelley, shame is not an affect in the possession of individual ethical agents;[41] it is instead coextensive with the production of poetry itself and is imposed or inflicted upon the guilty, who might try to escape its authority. There is a remarkable consistency in Shelley's writing on this issue, and *The Triumph of Life* stands as the culmination of a series of works that, through various strategies, identifies poetry with shaming. Perhaps this power might be tempting to connect with facts from Shelley's biography—both his personal relationships and his outspoken atheism, culminating in his much-discussed Chancery suit, made him no stranger to public opprobrium. But this could hardly account for the ways in which Shelley makes shame into a vitalizing force. His impassioned 1822 verse letter to Edward Williams ("The Serpent Is Out from Paradise"), for instance, shows how even as the *object* of a shame imposed from outside himself—as the object of others' "hatred" and "scorn" for his conduct—Shelley considers shame to be poetically productive and not just an unfortunate predicament.[42]

While recounting the miseries of rejection and ostracism among his friends (Byron called Shelley "the snake," a name that puns on the Italian *bischelli* or "little snake"),[43] the speaker nevertheless rejects "Pity" for his plight, since that would "break a spirit already more than bent." Pity would seem colorless and lifeless—it would "break" the strand (the bent spirit?) of the poem itself. The speaker instead prefers to turn scorn to his advantage. He continues: "The miserable one / Turns the mind's poison into food; / Its medicine is tears, its evil, good" (9–16). Indeed, strange as it may seem, the "comfort" ministered by the speaker's friends in stanza 3 is not the comfort of understanding but the comfort of sustained scorn that propels the speaker's anxiously shifting "griefs" and "hopes" (20).

But isn't the possibility of seeing shame as food and medicine somewhat implausible as a state of affairs shared by all miserable people, and somewhat more plausible as a condition acceptable only to the speaker who inhabits the identity of a poet? The last stanza explicitly refers to the poem itself—the series of "verses" recounting the speaker's "woe"—and it therefore insinuates that the "good" precipitating from shame is good precisely because woe, or the ability to inspire it, has become poetry. The point is a subtle but important one: it is not that the speaker believes that his shame can be turned into good by him personally—there is no suggestion that the poet might use shame in order to improve or reform himself, as if it might be appreciated in terms of its utility to the offender. The point is about the formal rather than the personal status of shame: it becomes medicine when it is absorbed into verse. This is because shame is no longer considered only as a force of opinion outside the speaker, hostile to his interests *as a poet*; it instead solidifies into the poem's structural principle. The poem could not exist without it.

If this temperament comes close to masochism, its most striking attribute is undoubtedly its will to live by a law that the momentary cruelty of the poet's friends, with their inevitable gravitational pull toward pity, could never sustain. Thus the work installs, in that uncompromising gesture, something on the order of what Gilles Deleuze, in his account of masochism, describes as "the cruelty of the Ideal."[44] It is this aspect of the poem—its ability to out-shame those who shame the author—that makes it a particularly compelling starting point for examining other poems in which Shelley arranges the unforgiving public exposure of, and shaming for, faults or injuries caused by others beyond himself.

As in "The Serpent," public exposure in a range of texts is managed to greatest advantage within—and even becomes identified with—the space of poetry; it is only there that injurious actions can be vividly characterized and figuratively turned back upon the offending agents—critics, monarchs, politicians, hostile readers. In *The Mask of Anarchy* (written in 1819 but not published until 1832), for instance, the violence of tyrants shames them. After committing brutal murders of innocent people, tyrants "will return with shame / To the place from which they came / And the blood thus shed will speak / In hot blushes on their cheek" (348–51). And more: the "slaughter to the Nation," three stanzas later, "shall steam up like inspiration, / Eloquent, oracular; / A volcano heard afar" (360–63). We cannot help noticing, of course, that—simply from an empirical standpoint—bloodshed does not necessarily yield blushes, and slaughter does not necessarily result in eloquent volcanoes. Indeed, violence against the powerless instead has a tendency to end in silence, as its victims suffer without their plight being fully known. The fate of victims, Shelley implies, can only be truly "oracular" when manipulated within poetry—poetry that makes the state's violence result in a turning of that violence back against the tyrant, not with an equal measure of violence, but with shaming marks and words. What is required for violence to become oracular, then, is literary figure—the ability to give a voice to objects and persons that were previously unable to speak. The quasi-personifications at work in making entities "oracular" once again return us to the consistent connection between personification and penality: as in Coleridge's use of the figure to invoke a force without a specific agent, it works here to endow the shaming mechanisms of punishment with the attributes of human agency, even while the cruel ideal of poetry refuses to accommodate the variability and inconsistency of humans themselves.

The "chastisement" for the viperous critics in *Adonais* (1821) even more explicitly yet unexpectedly connects shaming and poetry. It is unexpected because of the way that Shelley incorporates an unmistakably punitive element into the elegaic work of providing consolation for loss. Shelley's poem does not restrict itself to Rilke's rule that "Only in the realm of praising should lament / Walk."[45] The poet here is as concerned with punishment as he is with consolation, as concerned with blame as he is with praise. It may even be possible to say that *Adonais* makes praising thoroughly inseparable from blaming, and aesthetics inseparable from retribution.

This may, after all, explain why the poet feels so little need to curtail the hateful energies of Keats's critics. Kim Wheatley's suggestion that the reviewers are simply "left behind" in the poem's pursuit of "aesthetic appreciation" seems slightly wide of the mark; in fact, Shelley welcomes them into the poem with a terrible glee, bidding them "Ever at thy season be thou free / To spill the venom when thy fangs o'erflow" (329–30).[46] This is because the venom, once exposed through the operations of the poem, will turn back upon the vipers. Emotions of "Remorse and Self-contempt," the poet asserts, "shall cling to thee" (331), but remorse is not described here in the same way that it appears in Coleridge. It is instead conscripted into the thoroughly externalized operations of shame, the most powerful and terrifying mechanism here: "Hot Shame shall burn upon their secret brow, / And like a beaten hound tremble thou shalt—as now" (332–33). Shelley is of course describing shame's visible manifestation as a blush, but we must also recognize here that "Hot Shame" is not an internal feeling (as in Coleridge's remorse) but a forcefully imposed act of branding—it shall "burn upon" the hateful critics—not unlike the "blushes" that appear on the tyrant's cheek in *The Mask of Anarchy.* Here, as there, blood—in what we might now call a literalization of the operation of figure—issues forth from the victim and turns back upon the aggressor. In *Adonais*, the brand of shame makes what was previously silent or "secret" leap into a new level of expression because it is conceived quite literally as a flaming record of the critics' spiteful words by virtue of a corresponding imposition on the brow.

The burning and trembling is felt "now," as if imposed by the very fact of reading. And if this openly hints at the shaming brand's connection to great poetry—Keats's, and presumably Shelley's, too—the connection receives further reinforcement from the affiliation between the imagery of burning and the "pure spirit" of which poets partake in stanza 38. Whereas Christopher Ricks points to the rhetoric of blushing and embarrassment in Keats, Shelley not only celebrates the poet but also slyly reverses his logic, making poetry into a cause of blushing rather than a demonstration or symptom of it.[47] The "pure spirit" of those poets "shall flow / Back to the burning fountain whence it came" (338–39). Once again, through this complex logic, poetry takes on the power to shame because it is invested with the power to *trope* or *turn* violent effects back on those who inflicted the suffering, to brand or mark the guilty with flaming signs of retribution. This is why the poem continues to follow through with a similar series of maneuvers in the succeeding stanzas. The lovely "Spirit" of which Keats shares a "portion" turns out to be a rigorous punisher, "torturing" the "dross" of the world that tortured its genius (384), or, two stanzas later, causing each thing of "oblivion" to shrink back "like a thing reproved" (405). What greater reproof could the poem inflict on those reviewers than the shame of having their insults imposed back upon them, while the poem itself—in that very process—rises above, and gorgeously expounds on, their own hopeless oblivion?

Deep Scorn: *The Triumph of Life*

What I have been saying so far about several important poems by Shelley is that they view retribution as something that is poetic, or that requires the aid of poetry. Of course, the issue of satire is very much at stake in what I have been discussing so far, and the poet's technique could be contrasted, I think, with the mode of Augustan satire that we find in Pope, whose *Dunciad* (1728) was obviously a powerful model for *Peter Bell the Third*, and perhaps less obviously for *The Triumph of Life*. The *Dunciad*'s satirical power resides in the possibility of combining low and high. The goddess Dulness presides over her empire of degraded writing and degraded taste; meanwhile, the epic framework—while accentuating the ridicule and shame directed at the poem's satirical objects—honors the poet himself for upholding a literary tradition enforced by great examples. The key here for Pope is that the poet's authority is inseparable from his alliance with that tradition.[48] For Shelley, as I have been suggesting, the engine of shame is self-consciously appropriated by the poet himself and embedded in his work. Shaming is a function of the poem's own self-proclaimed retributive powers of exposure and figurative turning, and is inseparable from what Wheatley rightly identifies as Shelley's later idealization of his own poetry as an "all encompassing beauty."[49]

These are the terms in which we must examine *The Triumph of Life*, a poem that repeatedly summons forth the power of violent and unregulated powers that are chastened or regulated within the space of the poem. Once again we find the imagery of burning associated with something like the "spirit" that appeared in *Adonais*: here, the "living flame," also the source of "knowledge" for which the poet might thirst and follow (194), is held only by those "sacred few," including "they of Athens and Jerusalem" (134), who are not to be found in the "sad pageantry" (176) appearing in the poet's vision. The living light of Socrates and Jesus—which cannot be separated from their virtue and unjust punishment—is not identical to the various sources of light in the poem, but nonetheless stands in a metonymic relation to the light of retribution that burns and blocks vision: the blazing sun (349–50), or the "shape all light" that is simultaneously blinding to those who view it (352). Burning or shining, this imagery of heat and light cannot be divided from the poem's retributive logic through which the Dantean figures of power, greed, and ambition both enact their crimes and react to their perfectly proportionate punishments (the mortal part "expiates" crime—it endures punishment in order to atone for guilt [255]). The poem's figures are intriguingly both drawn to the light and punished by it, "by light attracted and repelled" as they "Oft to new bright destruction come and go" (153–54).

The images of light and heat, reminding us of that "absolute light" that Sartre identifies with shame, are frequently viewed by critics such as Paul de Man and J. Hillis Miller as metaphorical representations of the poet's own "power of figuration." As Karen Weisman has pointed out, their arguments tend to center on the "instability" of these images without examining the extent of their "integrity," and Weisman's claim could be taken still further to examine the way that images of sun, light, heat, and fire appear not merely as deceptive fictions (as they do in deconstructive accounts) but as instruments of pain.[50] Not only fire but also all elements of the earth combine to inflict this punishment, in fact. From the "Ocean's wrath" (163) to the "insulting wind" (166), all collude in the pageantry's "deep scorn" (191), which, as the poet's Virgilian guide Rousseau explains, both leads and scourges those who follow it. "Life" itself is the poem's most consistent punisher of all, and this is because "Life"—as we shall see—is not simply the sum total of living beings and their powers. Shelley makes Life into a larger moral-political force that, joined by all forces of the world, imposes penalties upon those who, merely "living," did not pay the world sufficient heed. Shelley thus reverses the progress from Virgil to Dante, pagan to Christian, returning to the pagan Lucretius, who, in *On Nature*, describes cosmic movement as our law, pilot, or governor.[51] Shelley, moreover, makes the natural features of the cosmos embody the very punitive mechanisms that Kames described as an imposition or fantasy of the remorseful conscience; in *The Triumph of Life*, that cosmos is a conscience.

Shelley's poem also follows the example of Petrarch's *Trionfi*, by modeling its procession after the Roman Triumph, a spectacle of conquerors leading their shamed prisoners of war before a cheering public. But the contrast between Shelley's work and Petrarch's is nonetheless remarkable in that Petrarch focuses his lament on the "wretched" man who "sets his hope on mortal things."[52] Petrarch's moral-political scheme depends upon a Polybian commitment to exposing human futility with reference to the necessary decay and degeneration of human constructions. Not so for Shelley: the condition of mortality, with all of its futile hopes and inevitable disappointments, is simply a given. Here the task is both more concrete and more abstract than Petrarch's—not to lament a basic human condition but to expose and shame those who have brought injury and injustice upon human life. Central to Shelley's purpose in the poem is the way that the figures in the pageantry are objects of shame and scorn; thus in his own vision—and in Rousseau's account of his visions enclosed in this vision—Shelley makes the process of shaming central within the representation of the visionary imagination itself. In the poem's succeeding visions related by Rousseau, that is, Rousseau is confronted by a shape who leaves him "between desire and shame suspended" (394); and the "new Vision" following this is itself a vision, a "wonder" that embodies Dante's words of "hate and awe" (475). In both instances, the fundamental experience of the vision is one not only of mystery but also of being viewed with reproof, contempt, disapproval.

This general association between the poem's vision and the power of retribution is more concretely realized in the specific descriptions of its central figures. Consider Rousseau more closely, for instance. Gregory Dart has recently drawn attention to Rousseau's notoriety among his English readers for confessing his crimes while also excusing them; Shelley's poem inflicts a penalty where none was felt or expected.[53] In Shelley's handling, that is, Rousseau is not simply deluded by false claims to enlightened knowledge, as many recent commentators have suggested.[54] He is a figure doomed by his own criminality, and his pain and failure are imposed by the logic poem in a way that Rousseau himself has refused to do. The poem asserts its punitive forces most visibly in the torturing load of words from which Rousseau suffers: he drags along wearily before the speaker's eyes "like one who with the weight / Of his own words is staggered" (196–97). Later, the words Rousseau has written throughout his life are once more viewed as an analogous cause of suffering: "I / Have suffered what I wrote, or viler pain!" (278–79). The force of these expressions is inseparable from Rousseau's actual refusal of guilt and contempt for punishment in his own work: "I declare before Heaven that I was not guilty" is the typical response to virtually every harm he brings upon others.[55] Rousseau can suffer from what he has written—suffer, indeed, a "pain" that is still "viler" than what may have been the effect of the words themselves—only within the retributive logic of the poem, which produces the figurative turn of the "contagion" of the author's writing back upon him (279, 277).

Another way of putting this would be to say that the punishing inflicted by nature's forces (the ocean's wrath or the wind's insults) is ultimately dominated by the punishing artifice of "Life"—in other words, by the construction of the poem itself. The logic continues in Rousseau's vision, populated by "Phantoms" haunting the "forms" in the procession; these are nothing less than phantoms of "shame" and "hate," mocking the beleaguered crew with symbols and effects of the power that they once wielded in life. The most striking of these are "chattering like restless apes / On vulgar paws and voluble like fire," or else holding forth the symbols of power—"ermined capes / Of kingly mantles" or tiars of pontiffs, or crowns "which girt with empire / A baby's or an idiot's brow" (493–99). The maneuver that is accomplished here not only underlines the fact that power is effected through the artifice of symbols, but also draws attention to the entirely counterfactual poetic use of those symbols for the purposes of mockery. They are turned back upon their agents, just

Chapter 5

as the vision proceeds by imagining the skeletons of the dead—the "old anatomies" that are the dead bodies of those murdered by tyrants—assuming a "delegated power" over the crew in the procession (500, 503).

The "old anatomies" brilliantly refute the legacy of capital punishment not only by raising the dead to punish those that killed them, but also by making the anatomies into poetic delegates that eerily double the delegated power of the state's executioners. Nothing could be more deliberately fantastic than this reversal of, and poetic response to, the logic that Shelley had traced out in his "Essay on the Punishment of Death": death is not the unknown territory bereft of all "distinction,"[56] but recuperated to become part of the poem's representation of "Life"—a stunning, searing product of the imagination. In the same vein, moreover, we must pause to appreciate the general rigor of Shelley's retributive logic, which continually makes poetry provide a series of penalties for those who did not receive them during their natural lives. For "Life" punishes those whose desires were unregulated by "thought's empire over thought" (211), an unrestrained "mutiny within" (213). Yet at the same time, the reader of the poem knows that, empirically speaking, "Life" as history does *not* necessarily serve tyrants with justice, just as Rousseau did not suffer from what he wrote (at least in the way Shelley imagines it).

Maybe it is true that Napoleon—who seems to offer the supreme example of a "power" overcome by "will"—occupies a central position in *The Triumph of Life* as one served justice by history; at least military defeat might seem to offer just deserts for one who has "left the giant world so weak / That every pigmy kicked it as it lay" (226–27). The same cannot be said of the line of other "spoilers spoiled" who follow:

> Voltaire,
>
> Frederic, and Kant, Catherine, and Leopold,
> Chained hoary anarchs, demagogue and sage
> Whose name the fresh world thinks already old—
>
> For in the battle Life and they did wage
> She remained conqueror.

The combination of "anarchs, demagogue and sage" is perhaps most striking because of its odd mixture of accusation and penalty; the notion of an anarch—one who has caused or encouraged disorder rather than actually imposed an obvious harm upon others (Shelley appropriates the word from both Milton and Pope, who use it to describe Chaos)—implies that the precise nature of their crimes and the victims of them is not easily found by looking for dead or injured bodies. The crimes of the demagogue (Voltaire) and sage (Kant) are equally obscure, as is the degree to which the spoilers are spoiled. The anarchs have died, but none has been defeated so dramatically as Napoleon. And what about the writers? They, like the anarchs, have fallen in public estimation, we are told—they are those "whose name the fresh world thinks already old" (238)—and the authors of them are "those who drew / New figures" on the world's "false and fragile glass // As the old faded" (246–48).

But it seems both odd and utterly ingenious for Shelley to announce the obsolescence of rulers and thinkers who are by no means forgotten. The only way this formulation can make sense in the poem is that their historical importance makes them simultaneously unforgettable in the mind of the reader and willed into being forgotten by the poem. (I thus differ from de Man's account of forgetting in the poem as an enactment of an ontological condition.) To put it another way, the lines impose a collective amnesia: the world, as Shelley describes it, has no memory but is "fresh"—indeed, it is so fresh that it renews itself continually, for neither the figures nor the world are deemed to be anything other than false and fragile; that world is a mere "bubble" on which deluded mortals cast their "shadows" (249–51). At the same time, the collective amnesia proposed by the poem is itself presumed to be an indelible statement, a form of decisive retribution not to be found on earth in the passage of historical events. The poem makes forgettings, blanks, or absences into shaming marks; transience works as a punishment for ambition because the poem insists upon a fading that has not yet occurred, and because the poem avoids the very transience it names.

If "Life" is the conqueror, in other words, Shelley does not simply mean—I emphasize my earlier point—that such mortals are doomed by their mortality. Constantin Volney writes in his *Ruins* that "the lot of mortals" is to be punished by inevitable destruction according to "the justice of heaven." The world's evils and consequent suffering are the "experience of past generations" that in turn provide a "spectacle of . . . errors" literally "written on the surface of [the] soil."[57] But Shelley's poem, while undoubtedly influenced by Volney, extends far beyond this, implicitly gesturing toward the incapacity of the mere passage of time to provide justice, and explicitly rendering "Life" as a moral-political system that more consistently brings (through poetry) a retributive force to bear upon its offenders.

Having come this far, we are now prepared to account for the way that the poem does not stop at pointing to a range of criminals to be shamed, or at conscripting Rousseau as one of those shamed figures. Shelley's work also implicates the narrator of the poem, and the reader herself, as targets of the work's shaming effects. All are shamed by the thing that they see or read, and this process has the curious result of making it seem as if the poem can see and judge them. Just as Rousseau is shamed by the shape and vision before him, the poet-narrator is shamed by the spectacle of the somber figures before him. Is it not the case that the poet—whose "cheek" is said to "Alter to see the great form [of Napoleon] pass away" (224–25)—feels himself shamed by this spectacle, or at least feels the power to be shamed by it? We are not told so, but it hardly seems a stretch for us to assume here that the altering of the cheek is indeed a blushing or reddening, not unlike the tyrant's ensanguined cheek in *The Mask of Anarchy* or the critic's branded brow in *Adonais*. The poet's altered cheek attests at once to his identification with the figure of Napoleon, having once connected his own desires and ambitions with him. At the same time, the cheek testifies to his ability to be shamed by the spectacle that also shames Napoleon. Later, and in a slightly different version, the poet/narrator again rehearses this logic of chastened desire: "For despair / I half disdained mine eye's desire to fill / With the spent vision of the times that were / And scarce have ceased to be" (231–34); the "eye" attaches itself to those figures that not only are desired but also are figures of its desire, whereas the "I," identified with the narrative movement from desire to shame, imposes "disdain" upon the eye's impassioned yearnings. In both of these cases, with the cheek's shameful reddening and the eye's disdained desire, the speaker asserts the power of the vision, and hence the power of the poem itself, to exert or impose its chastening effects.

In the latter of these instances, if there is a punitive restriction on the poet/observer's "desire," it is also to be extended to the reader's experience of a "disdain" exerted by following the narrative of the poem. The reader emerges here, in the process of scanning the "chains" of Shelley's stanzas, as the next in the series of shamed beings. What is remarkable about this movement from Rousseau to poet to reader, of course, is that the poet has not perpetrated any harmful action that would merit his shame, and neither has the reader. But perhaps this is precisely the point. Rousseau tells the poet: "Follow thou, and from spectator turn / Actor or victim in this wretchedness, // And what thou wouldst be taught I then may learn / From thee" (305–8). The injunction to be taught by what is seen would hinge upon the ability to "follow" and thus identify with its figures as "actor or victim"; it would also hinge upon the ability to feel the weight of their shame, the observing "I" disdaining the desiring "eye." For only this final result could possibly correct the false "lore" of tyrants, who were not "taught . . . to know themselves" (212). What the poet/narrator would learn, and what could be conveyed to Rousseau, would be exhibited on the poet/narrator's altered cheek. And the reader can "follow" in that quest for self-knowledge by feeling the shame exerted by the retributive apparatus of the poem.

To move from Coleridge to Shelley is to pass through two quite distinct conscience-formations that are inseparable from an issue of genre. *Osorio* makes explicit what is implicit in the shorter lyrical poems, like "The Rime" and "The Eolian Harp": conscience can only make itself visible through a dramatic struggle and compromise. Or, as in "Fears in Solitude," the poet's conscience struggles even to be heard at all in a world filled with those "Who, playing tricks with conscience, dare not look / At their own vices" (158–59). Dramatic poetry, for Coleridge, literalizes the struggle that motivates the conscience-formation in lyric poetry. Shelley's poems demonstrate a lyric form cleansed of dramatic struggle in order to exhibit a retributive power truly terrifying in its grandeur. This is because the work of conscience is not restrained within competing voices or characters; the poet's adversaries cannot offer any resistance, since they lack an awareness of their crimes, just as they lack the remorse to atone for them. Instead, the work of conscience is appropriated by, and coextensive with, the work of the poem. Lyric becomes law. As such, it has an uncontested monopoly on two things: poetic beauty and the authority to impose a strict, vividly rendered punishment.

6

The Two Abolitions

> Remember, Christians, negroes black as Cain
> May be refined, and join th'angelic train.
> Phyllis Wheatley, "On Being Brought from Africa to America"

There was not just one "abolition" debated in the late eighteenth and early nineteenth centuries, but two. The abolition of slavery and the slave trade was relentlessly linked to the abolition of the death penalty, and reformers regularly—even to this day—refer to the second, just as often as first, simply as "abolition." To be sure, there were other injustices to be redressed, other kinds of restrictive legislation to be repealed throughout the nineteenth century: restrictions on free speech, worship, political participation, and so on. But no two projects were as consistently—we might at first glance say "confusingly"—connected as these two movements. I have already hinted at the important affiliation between slaves and criminals in previous chapters; here, I investigate precisely what the nature of this connection was, and argue that the two programs for reform capitalized upon each other's rhetoric and logic, even while their aims (the freeing of slaves and the more effective punishment of convicted criminals) seemed to diverge.

At one level, the connection I am about to discuss here demonstrates the dazzling versatility of penal reform; leaders of the movement, like Romilly, made punishment seem like the *ur*-discourse of the Romantic age, adapting its terms to a range of different issues and debates. With a nearly obsessive regularity, Romilly's *Memoirs* transforms every issue in parliament into a problem of penal law—from colonial administration to parish apprentices and even the Regency (it would subject the regent to a "punishment" unauthorized by any act of Parliament [*MSR* 2:355]). At another—I think deeper—level, it demonstrates the way in which slavery abolition was not simply one among many similar objects of attention but occupied a distinctive role in defining the lineaments of penal reform, even as penal reform revealed a fundamental characteristic of the freed slave's freedom.

We can observe the traces of some kind of privileged affiliation between the two abolitions in the careers of prominent white slavery abolitionists of the late eighteenth and early nineteenth centuries. Thomas Clarkson, Lord Holland, Romilly, and William Wilberforce, to name a few, were in fact advocates of both reforms and seemed to divide their energies between them. But the features defining this connection suggest that it cannot be summed up with the mundane explanation that both were the most important liberal causes of the day.[1] Indeed, the writings of such figures persistently treat the two abolitions not quite as one single issue, but as complementary causes that allow one to be used as a crucial means of explanation for the other. With surprising consistency, political and literary texts of this period change gears, a work about punishment suddenly shifting into a commentary on slavery, or a work on slavery suddenly taking up the cause of penal reform.

How and why did this happen? The discourse of death-penalty abolition could look to the discourse of slavery abolition as an enlivening force for its own claims: the condition of slavery, that is, could provide death-penalty opponents with the archetypal instance of a thoroughly arbitrary denial of humanity. Viewing the slave as an innocent and hapless victim of violence, reformers could bank on the sympathy an audience might have for slaves and make it seem applicable to a less-than-innocent criminal. The discourse of slavery abolition—and I think that this is the most interesting tactic of all—could call upon the discourse of death-penalty abolition for a very different and utterly contradictory reason: because the freed slave could look like a saved criminal. The abolition of slavery came to be a plausible notion because the discourse of penal reform made the very freedom of political subjects depend upon their punishability. The two abolitions, then, required each other's reinforcement: one asked its audience to view criminal subjects as potentially human; the other asked the same audience to view such potential human subjects not simply as free, but as free because of their prior inclusion and inscription within an organized regime of humane punishment.

My argument responds to a number of recent accounts of these two abolitions as they have been separately studied. I continue in this chapter to show how Foucault's work, by emphasizing "general punishment" as a system "replac[ed]" by the ideal of the disciplinary reformatory, occludes the extent to which penal reform continued powerfully to shape political debate and literary production.[2] At a more specific level, I want to respond to the ways in which scholarship on the death penalty, such as Stuart Banner's, addresses the relationship between punishment and slavery. Banner, like most scholars, routinely views the two abolitions as unqualified liberal triumphs, without more closely examining the particular relationship between the end of slavery and the beginning of a reformed penality.[3]

Chapter 6

The argument that I am making about the connection between these two abolitions also aims to contribute to discussions of the abolition of slavery. These have tended to revolve around two arguments that have stressed either the humanitarian or the economically self-interested origins of antislavery. On the one hand, historians like Roger Anstey and David Turley have stressed the importance of religious revival in the work of abolitionist writers.[4] On the other hand, scholars such as Seymour Drescher and Eric Williams have suggested the importance of economic motives for the demise of the slave trade: needs for new markets and more efficient labor were more important than the religious commitments of slave owners and traders.[5] Still other writers on the subject have established a middle road between the two options. David Brion Davis's work establishes the importance of "ideological" commitments that were neither strictly religious nor entirely economic; in his account, it was a combination of religious, economic, and scientific motivations that led to the demise of slavery. Other historians have followed Davis's lead by producing studies that are similarly committed to multiple rather than singular motivations.[6]

Certainly my arguments in this chapter bear some resemblance to Davis's efforts to link slavery abolition with a range of related political causes in the late eighteenth and early nineteenth centuries, while also sharing with his work a more or less skeptical sense of the limits of that humanitarianism. His work accounts, that is, for the importance of sincere and influential philosophical or religious commitments, even as he avoids flattening the issue into an abstract commitment to human rights or attributing a postmodern politics of race and culture to abolitionist reformers.[7] But the similarity ends here. Davis's position tends to regard the connection between multiple "emancipations" and "abolitions" primarily as pointing in one direction: toward laissez-faire capitalism and individualism.[8] He thus finds it most productive to pair the abolition of slavery with the removal of protective legislation governing English workers in 1807 or the Reform Bill of 1832.[9] By connecting slavery abolition to death-penalty abolition, I am not only retrieving an underrepresented historical fact, but also recasting the logic according to which both reforms can be most fruitfully understood. I am less interested here in the larger "ideological" connection between causes than in their tactical combination—one that, despite its specificity, appears throughout a range of important writings of the day. It is only by considering this tactical combination of abolitions that we can appreciate the power of two pervasive and inextricably entwined analogies: the criminal analogized to the innocent slave, and the slave analogized to the properly punished criminal.

Exciting Sympathy

I am certainly not the first to be pointing to the importance of sympathy in the discourse of slavery abolition, but I need to discuss it here in somewhat different terms in order to discern its specific instrumentality in the set of connections I am describing. Many critics have discussed the importance of sympathy as a way of demonstrating the common ground of feeling between self and other, white abolitionist and black slave.[10] But here I am talking about a different and less predictable logic according to which the sympathy already extended to the black slave can be redirected back upon the white criminal. If the blackness of racial difference could hide a pure and innocent soul, why (the logic goes) can't a soul blackened by crime look innocent, too?

Thomas Clarkson's *Cries of Africa* (1822) is exemplary among the author's important writings on abolition: it exposes the cruelties of the slave trade with its haunting diagram (already popularized in previous abolitionist publications) of the slave ship with silhouettes of black bodies packed into its hull and its searing narrative of slaves thrown overboard after losing their eyesight. I will return to the specific interest in the treatment of slaves in a moment; for the time being, however, we must take note of Clarkson's methods for transforming slavery abolition into a forceful commentary on the death penalty. The slave owner is analogized to the executioner, since both are encouraged to extend mercy to others who "feel and think like ourselves"; the criminal, like the slave, is entitled to "a claim upon our deepest sympathy."[11] Little work seems to be required in order to make the shift from one subject to another in Clarkson's argument, and this slipperiness is typical of the intertwining rhetorics of the two abolitions. He continues to expand on the impact of the connection he has made: once the slavers' "hearts become at length hardened" to the cruelty of their actions, they look like the agents of criminal justice at home. "This is the case with all public executioners," he says. "They are shocked when they first enter upon their office, but perform it afterwards with insensibility."[12]

If the abolitionist has already been able to give sympathy to the slave, in other words, the sympathy can be extended to the criminal as well—one who, despite her evil action, is still a person deserving some fellow-feeling. Clearly the question of retributive justice—what the criminal may or may not deserve as punishment for his or her crime—is not the issue here; humanity is. The implication is that capital punishment is possible only because "sympathy" has been withdrawn from the criminal. In turn, Clarkson, in his lightning-fast transition from slavery to the death penalty, treats the criminal not as the perpetrator of injurious action, but as the passive victim of the state's policy of legalized murder.

One of the curious elements of the relationship between the two abolitionist causes is the odd fact that one can be used as the preceding discourse upon which the other can follow and borrow its terms of authority: the point is not that one actually precedes the other but that one is rhetorically framed as the other's support or background. This shift in attention crops up in a whole range of writings. For even though Sir James Mackintosh specifically notes this as a habit of Quakers like Clarkson, suggesting that it was precisely their "spirit of benevolence" that brought together the two reforms, the practice is more pervasive.[13] In his 1814 essay, "Military Torture," in *The Examiner*, Leigh Hunt seeks to excite disgust with the "punishments that mangle and convulse" British soldiers by comparing military discipline to slavery's "indifference to suffering."[14] Bentham's *Rationale of Punishment* criticizes use of the "hook" employed to hang slaves in the West Indies—a particularly gruesome form of punishment that he sets before his reader in order to conjure up the picture of brutalized innocence: the slaves are described as the "weakest" of victims whose rebellion can be excused as a desperate act of "self defense" (*RP* 174). Later in the nineteenth century, advocates of death-penalty abolition could still call upon a reserve of British sympathy for the innocent slave, even after the end of the slave trade in 1807 and the abolition of slavery (in British colonies) in 1833. Albert Midlake's 1850 poem "A Colloquy between the Gallows and the Hangman" rapidly shifts between the situations of slave and convicted criminal. The hangman is like the slave's master, lording over the "sable race of Africa, / Who perish, smarting 'neath the murderous lash."[15] But also presumably the criminal is like the slave, who is murdered rather than justly punished for a crime.

Transportation, Savagery, Criminality

There is a curious tension with this sympathy to be observed in numerous texts on transportation during the period, and, although I have briefly alluded to the punishment of transportation earlier in this book (in Chapter 1), it is time to say more about it. In a slightly earlier episode in the history of attitudes about transportation, George Olyffe in 1731 suggested that criminals simply be sent into transportation and sold as slaves (reviving a solution practiced among the Romans). He liked this idea because criminals could be made to work and also suffer the indignities of marks, brands, and other bodily injuries inflicted on slaves themselves.[16] Promising as it all sounds, opinions on the subject tended to change later in the century (although transportation was not curtailed significantly until the

1840s and did not come to a complete halt until 1870). Although transportation was favored by some politicians, like Burke, for its leniency, the problem was that it could only provide an imperfectly calibrated form of punishment—and would perhaps even produce future crimes.[17] Inseparable from these claims, moreover, was the conviction that transportation would cause an undesirable connection with savages—either native people or slaves—who would encourage new forms of corruption.

Here, then, we encounter at least one way in which the sympathy so easily extended to the slave and rerouted to the criminal encounters a significant contrary impulse. There is little need for writers who comment on the issue to distinguish between slaves and native populations; both, it seems, contaminate.[18] In an *Edinburgh Review* article on Bentham, Henry Brougham remarks on the "mismanagement of punishments" in Botany Bay, a mismanagement that has not only wasted money but also has produced a community that is "radically vicious and miserable," growing increasingly "depraved and wretched."[19] Sydney Smith is more particular about the issue: he locates the problem with New South Wales specifically in native populations, who create a "dangerous . . . encouragement to offenses."[20] Some version of this account appears in virtually all late eighteenth-century critiques of transportation. Montagu speaks of the dangers of American "savages" whose cruelty and depravity lead men in their midst to "horrid excesses";[21] a poem of the same period portrays the degradation of convicts who live with slaves and become tainted by their barbaric manners and culture.[22] The possibility of having one's Britishness corrupted abroad only aggravates the general climate within Britain itself, Lord Grenville warns, where crime proliferates and makes the nation's subjects more "truculent" and "savage" every day.[23]

Brougham's real point about savagery, though, concerns the mismanagement of punishments; similarly, Grenville's real point is that savage citizens are named as such because of "the hardness and savageness of the laws."[24] Here, then, is a further twist to prevailing anxieties about transporting criminals. In the much-publicized trial of the Reverend John Smith, Sir James Mackintosh sides with the defendant, accused of involvement with a slave rebellion in Demerera. As he does so, it becomes increasingly clear that the violations of justice that led to Smith's trial are, in Mackintosh's argument, the result of a subversion of British law by foreign procedures of justice, thus depriving Smith of "all the safeguards which are the birthright of British subjects."[25] A whole range of writing enforces a similar reasoning: slaves and foreign savages are not simply corrupt, they are in violation of English law. We can hardly wonder, then, at J. Sydney Taylor's indictment of the death penalty for displaying "the moral principles of savages."[26] Even Bentham, while at first legitimating the slave revolt against their captors, makes an abrupt shift of attention in his text to a more efficient use of penalties, as if he were taming the rebellious impulses he had just sought to legitimate. He contrasts those impulses with the "enlightened" and "softened" manners of Western Europeans, proof of their capacity to adopt more just and equitable criminal legislation (*RP* 191). Surely Clarkson is one of the subtlest of writers when it comes to the supposed savagery of African slaves, for he views the savage laws of non-Europeans as a product of European domination. "The jurisprudence of Africa," he writes, "has been made to accommodate itself to the demands of the slave trade; so that now every offence, even of the most trivial kind, is punished with slavery." But if African jurisprudence is England's offspring, Clarkson ultimately disowns this progeny: he sees the foreign system as an enemy, a system in which "crimes are invented, and accusations multiplied, for the purpose of procuring condemnations; nay, that ever the unwary are tempted and seduced into crime."[27]

In prints and political tracts from the period, representations of black slaves have a curious way of reflecting the complex position they occupy in the conjunction of slavery and death-penalty abolitionist discourses. On the one hand, slaves are the objects of compassion; on the other hand, they are themselves portrayed as the perpetrators of lawlessness—injury and death. In William Blake's illustrations for John Stedman's *Narrative of a Five Years' Expedition against the Revolted Negroes of Surinam* (1796), the series of images depicting punishments of slaves repeatedly shows its subjects as victims of a range of tortures and methods of execution, yet slaves are also the guilty agents of the brutality they suffer. In one engraving, "The Execution of Breaking on the Rack" (Fig. 1), one black slave beats another; in "The Flagellation of a Female Samboe Slave" (Fig. 2), a female slave hanging from a tree with a rope about her wrists writhes in the foreground, while two slaves in the background carry whips. The images are not specific to Stedman's account—the text of which repeatedly accuses slaves of criminal "excesses"—but they appear everywhere in abolitionist prints.[28] Throughout Hugh Honour's survey of eighteenth- and nineteenth-century European graphic representations of slaves, black slaves are willing spectators or active participants in the violence against their own people, wielding whips or other instruments of pain and torture.[29]

Documentation of the practices of punishment suggests that either natives or slaves were in fact forced to flog at the master's bidding. In admiralty law cases, for instance, the printed accounts of the trials expose a scandalous transfer of authority from colonial governors and their regiments to either slaves or colonial subjects; the British military men are guilty of relying upon, and submitting themselves to, the criminal indulgences of those who are supposedly under their control.[30] But if admiralty

Figure 1. William Blake, "The Execution of Breaking on the Rack."
By permission of the Milner Library, Special Collections, Illinois State University.

Chapter 6

Figure 2. William Blake, "The Flagellation of a Female Samboe Slave."
By permission of the Milner Library, Special Collections, Illinois State University.

law makes it quite clear that yielding the authority to punish is a potentially criminal act for the agents of colonial dominion, abolitionist images—far too regular and systematic merely to represent historical "fact"—would suggest that a slave beating a slave incriminates the black slaves themselves. This can best be described as a potent product of the legal imagination. Slaves simultaneously play the part of victim and agent of punishment; meanwhile, white owners are either absent or angelically hover somewhere at a safe distance from the scene of the crime, as if to disavow their own involvement in it. Central to the abolitionist cause on behalf of the slave's freedom, in other words, is a fantasy that depends upon the slave's presumed guilt.

Slave Crimes

Saidiya Hartman's *Scenes of Subjection* has explored the relationships between guilt, power, and enslavement in the context of nineteenth-century American literature; my argument about the presumption of guilt makes a closely related but quite different point. Hartman—who inaccurately sums up the Western liberal tradition as a defense of "unencumbered individuality"—makes it seem as if guilt is what deprives the slave of complete freedom.[31] But my point here is that guilt is coextensive with the very form of freedom with which it appears to be in contradiction: it in fact provides the necessary condition for that slave's freedom. More needs to be said here about the way that the discourse of slavery abolition insistently looks beyond its terms to the (fictionally) anterior discourse of death-penalty abolition, the latter lending a distinctive and disturbing shape to the former.

Slavery abolition paradoxically calls upon the language of penal reform in order to show that the very slave that seems innocent is also—or instead—tainted with guilt. It cannot escape our notice that, even at first glance, slavery is connected to the penalty of death simply because slavery literally meant death to so many of those subjected to it: as reformers continually reported, half or more of the slaves on each ship were likely to perish.[32] At the same time, though, what I am arguing is that the massive mortality rate in the transportation and forced labor of slaves occupied a crucial logical role in the discursive connection between slavery and penality. For the point of abolition is not simply to free slaves from death and fatal torture, but to offer a replacement for slavery consisting of more rigorous and systematic punitive measures. Reformers thus look to the criminal freed from the gallows as an analogue to the freed slave: both can be allowed to live, but both are necessarily criminalized and subjected to a more lenient but carefully measured form of punishment. If slavery depends upon the social death of its victims, as Orlando Patterson has claimed, punishment becomes the sign of the (potentially) freed save's social life.[33]

If we look more closely at how this works, it becomes clear that, in a whole range of political writing among abolitionists, the slave is considered guilty even though the nature of the crime may be entirely obscure. Nowhere is this more amply demonstrated than in the tendency of slavery abolitionists to concentrate primarily on the issue of propriety in punishment; the entire discourse of antislavery depends upon the horrors and excesses of the slave's punishment, which are not to be removed but simply alleviated and systematized. There is a vivid contrast here, in other words, between the early abolitionist strain of thought and the theory of natural right outlined in John Locke's *Second Treatise of Government* (1689–90), in which slavery is defined not according to the slave's conditions but according to the absence of her consent to them.[34] James Ramsay's *An Essay on the Treatment and Conversion of African Slaves* (1784) painstakingly documents a range of offenses with disproportionately cruel penalties; the "ordinary punishments" inflicted by masters on their slaves for "crimes" like eating harvested sugar cane (that is, for eating the product of their labor) ranged from cart whipping to castration.[35] In a similar fashion, Clarkson's *Essay on the Slavery and Commerce of the Human Species* (1786), which explicitly acknowledges Ramsay as a source of inspiration, surveys a dense catalogue of cruel and immoderate punishments inflicted on slaves: "Ears have been slit, eyes have been beaten out, and bones have been broken" for even the most negligible offenses.[36]

The work that some recent historians have pursued on slave law in the colonies provides us with an important starting point for explaining this particular aspect of abolitionist thinking. Penal codes governing slaves were a subject of public attention, yet they were seldom enforced. Joan Dayan shows how the *Code Noir* in Saint Domingue both stipulated specific penalties for slaves and ultimately ceded virtually limitless power to the master: "Since slaves are construed as a special kind of property, no amount of amputation, torture, or disfiguring can matter."[37] Diana Paton argues still further that, even with the multiplication of slave laws and the institution of slave courts in Jamaica regulating procedures of justice and modes of punishment, such regulations often did little to protect slaves.[38] Excess and brutality, Dayan and Paton show, *was* the law. These accounts help to sharpen our image of abolitionist discourse. Central in the logic set forth in the work of Ramsay and Clarkson from which I quoted above is precisely the sense that punishments imposed upon slaves are excessive—not because slaves are innocent, but because punishments are excessive in relation to a particular prior offense. As if to reform the injustices of slave law and its implementation, abolitionist writers imply that what is needed is not the removal of sanctions, but the correction of them—a correction that still depends upon the slave's necessary culpability.

These accounts of improper punishment, moreover, continued to fuel the energy of other reformers. One of the grandest gestures of William Wilberforce's speech "The Slave Trade; and The Elevation of the Colored Race" (1789) is the author's contemptuous ridicule of the claims that slaves "rejoice[d] in their captivity"—feasting, dancing, and perfuming themselves with "frankincense and lime juice." Instead, he explained, the slaves were "loaded with chains and oppressed with disease" while subjected to regular flogging.[39] Charles James Fox, in a parliamentary speech of 1791, quotes from an eyewitness report of

> a young female tied to a beam by her wrists, entirely naked, in the act of involuntary writhing and swinging, while the author of her torture was standing below her with a lighted torch in his hand, which he applied to whatever parts of her body swung near. What crime this miserable woman had perpetrated he knew not; but the human mind could not conceive a crime warranting such a punishment.[40]

The list could go on of works in which the torture or execution of the slave is the main object of the reformer's critique. But Fox's account provides one of the most vivid and disturbing instances of the logic I am describing: the basic presumption of the slave's guilt is summed up in the witness's claim that "what crime this miserable woman had perpetrated he knew not." The famous case to which Fox refers is the incident, represented in an etching by Isaac Cruikshank, involving a Captain Kimber, who flogged a slave to death after she refused to "dance" on deck for him.[41] Most important in Fox's account, though, is that he does not identify the "crime." Doing so might essentially show that the slave did not commit one—the only guilty party was the captain, who had attempted rape and committed murder. What Fox shows is that he is less interested in the facts of the case than in the larger protocols of slavery abolition: the guilty slave is in need of a punishment that the reformer commits himself to modifying.

It is not my point to deny that abolitionists could still in fact compare slaves to innocent children: in one fairly typical instance, William Smith claims, "I would as soon affiance myself in the bonds of friendship with a man who had strangled my infant child, as lend my . . . support to an administration disposed to violate the sacred duty of adhering to and enforcing the Abolition of the Slave Trade."[42] It is my point, however, that statements of this kind about innocence are necessarily and paradoxically combined with, and inseparable from, assertions of guilt. The question is not whether slaves are guilty, but whether their guilt is punished by "unmerited severity," in Clarkson's words, which could then be revised under a more equitable and lenient system of penalties.[43]

Now it might at first seem as if historians like Davis have a way of explaining the paradox I am describing by showing how slavery abolitionists regarded slaves as objects of Christian compassion, yet inferior to white Christians. Perhaps, after examining this evidence, it would be tempting to suggest that the purpose of criminalizing the slave was to demonize her. But something more is at work here, a further layer of complexity in the connection between punishment and slavery. Writers make it clear that both masters and their slaves need to be punished for their crimes. What is at stake in these arguments, I suggest, is a pervasive system of punishment that would comprehend slaves and masters in its scope. If we return to the prints I mentioned earlier, we can see with a second glance how they pictorially represent a more complex accountability for the death of the slave, even while, as I showed above, the slave is more obviously construed as the agent of brutal floggings and death. Blake's engravings are unusually potent for the way they repeatedly depict black slaves not only as agents and victims, but also—or instead—as instruments of pain and death detached from any agent. Some agent or agents, that is, are either absent or (as in the ship sailing away in "A Negro Hung Alive by the Ribs to a Gallows," Fig. 3) drifting away from the scene. Blake will not give his readers a clear answer to the obvious question that arises here: who is the unrepresented agent of this death? His point is not to provide that answer but to ask the reader to interrogate the possible suspects that widen out into larger and larger circles of responsibility: the slavers sailing away in their ships, the plantation owners, the reader herself.

In a wide range of writings, furthermore, we find an emphasis not only on accountability, but also on the need to punish those accountable. Ramsay's *Essay* thus complains of the "the capricious cruelty of an ignorant, unprincipled master, or a morose, unfeeling overseer,"[44] and suggests that both slaves and their masters should become objects of a new form of "civil government" in which all will be "subject only to the laws."[45] A poetic version of the argument, Hugh Mulligan's "The Slave, An American Eclogue" (1788), presents a speaker—a male slave named Adala— who calls not merely for the freedom of slaves, but for "justice" to be brought upon the "lawless" slave owners. This "justice" will only be distributed by a "stronger race" that will inflict just punishments upon the guilty.[46]

In still more specific terms, Brougham declares in an 1810 parliamentary speech that "the slave trade should at once be made felony," and possibly a capital crime. He expands upon that idea by arguing that, if capital punishment is still being upheld as a punishment applicable for

Figure 3. William Blake, "A Negro Hung Alive by the Ribs to a Gallows."
By permission of the Milner Library, Special Collections, Illinois State University.

Chapter 6

some crimes, it surely must be applicable to slave owners. The report on the speech proceeds as follows:

> When he considered how easily laws were passed, declaring those acts even capital offences, which had heretofore been either permitted, or slightly punished; when scarce a session ended without some such extension of the criminal code; when even capital offences were among the most numerous progenies of our legislative labours; when he saw that difficulty experienced by an honourable and learned friend of his [Sir Samuel Romilly] in doing away the capital part of the offence of stealing five shillings; when it was remembered that lord Ellenborough, by one act (and he honoured him for it) had created somewhere about a dozen capital felonies; when, in short so many comparatively trivial offences were so severely visited, could one, who knew what Slave Trading meant, hesitate in admitting that it ought at length to be punished as a crime?[47]

This aspect of the relation between the discourses of slavery and death-penalty abolition—the issue of the slave owner's punishability—was just as common as discussion of the punishability of the slave herself. Anthony Benezet clearly frames his abolitionist rhetoric in *Some Historical Account of Guinea* (1771) as an impulse to apply penal sanctions everywhere they are due. Anyone who transports, owns, or otherwise uses slaves "is actually guilty of murder," he writes. But the slave is guilty, too. Cohabitation without marriage, and marriage followed by lawless dissolution, are practices both prohibited by "the laws of the land" and produced by the slave system itself. Those depriving slaves of freedom are above the law, whereas slaves are below it; Benezet brings both to account, making an argument for freedom coincide with an argument for proper punishment.[48]

This pervasive strain in slavery abolition criminalizes slaves and their masters, inserting both in an omnipresent and inescapable scale of penal sanctions. The result is a delicate balancing act. For how can reformers suggest a way for the slave master to be punished adequately for the murders he has committed, if they also must oppose (or at least have ambivalent feelings about) the use of the death penalty? Should slaves be dealt lenience for their crimes, while slave traders and plantation owners are put to death for their crimes of still greater enormity? Brougham suggests that perhaps some of those engaged in slavery do indeed deserve death— but couldn't the same lenience applied to the slave be applied to the mass murderer of slaves? Indeed, few reformers thought to apply the death penalty to slave traders or owners, and in fact, little consensus is to be found among these writers on how to punish those implicated in the inhumanity of slavery and the slave trade. (Current debate about reparations shows that the case is still far from closed.) But the lack of clarity about punishment only demonstrates how rationales of punishment create loci of tension rather than clearly defined solutions. The guilty master is deserving of the ultimate punishment, yet benefits from the utilitarian skepticism about the purpose that such punishment would actually serve; the slave is released from the sentence of death but judiciously punished. We can only conclude that the discourse of penal reform is important to slavery not because it recommends specific remedies for the crimes of masters or slaves, but because in a more general way it devotes itself to an all-encompassing spectrum of penalties through which all subjects—those actually free, and those potentially free—might be identified and individualized through their criminal actions.

Freedom's Fatal Joy

Although I have discussed some examples of the way that literary works came to the defense of the two abolitions, we have now approached a point at which it would be possible to say something more general about a range of works beyond these political tracts—works of poetry and fiction that weave together the two discourses of abolition in mutually animating ways. While the political texts designated for the support of one issue could repeatedly offer support for the other—death-penalty abolition for slavery abolition, and vice versa—works of fiction and poetry devoted to addressing these issues are particularly fascinating because of the way that slaves are imaginatively rendered as criminals tried and punished by masters, or by legislators who subject the masters themselves to punishment.

Sarah Scott's *The History of Sir George Ellison* (1766) will provide one example, the poetry of Cowper another. Early in the Scott's novel, her hero takes it upon himself to adopt more humane methods of managing the Jamaican plantations he acquires through marriage. Young George Ellison's treatment of his slaves does not take the form of freeing them, however poignantly he regrets having to enslave others.[49] Instead, his tactic is to intervene within the customary practices of the island and repeatedly curtail the "most severe punishment" that his slaves receive at the hands of masters and stewards (10). Ellison contends that "cruelty was not necessary," but the antidote is not simply lenience. It is an increasingly systematic disposition toward punishment: "I would have the punishment bear some proportion to the offence," he argues, "and till it does so, it cannot be effectual" (11–12).

As the narrative proceeds, Ellison repeatedly demonstrates his lenience and his commitment to increasing the "liberty" of his slaves by lightening their punishments (14). But I take issue with Moira Ferguson's claim that his policy is primarily defined by treating slaves with "charity."[50] At the same time that Ellison "abolish[es] all corporal punishments," his humanity wins the hearts of his slaves precisely because of his refusal to waver from the scale of punishments that is the product of lenience (15). The sign of the master's humanity is inextricable from his adherence to an art of legislation: the ability to grant his slaves limited freedom is inseparable from his ability to grant them punishment:

> He did not expect them to be exempt from faults; and for such slight offences as in England he would have thought deserved only reproof, he inflicted no other punishment; not using the power received from the custom of the country, but in relation to more material offenses. (20)

We could very easily say that not only does Ellison not expect his slaves to be exempt from faults, he forbids that exemption. For without fault, how could the slaves receive Ellison's lenient rigor?

There is an upsetting series of events that at first seems to trouble Ellison's system, though. Ellison announces that the punishment for a third offense is to sell the slave to "the first purchaser, however low the price offered; and this sentence is irreversible; no prayers, no intreaties shall move me" (15). This works well enough at first. But when one "poor wretch" is punished on his third offense with "strict adherence" to his regulations by being sold, Ellison eventually relents and buys him back from the master who has almost killed him with poor treatment. He relents once more with another slave, and by this time it has become clear enough that a future pattern of lenience might actually undo Ellison's wisely constructed scale of punishments. This is not allowed to happen, of course; we are finally told, somewhat mysteriously, that the slaves "carefully avoided" committing other offenses, not wanting to risk a third possibility of being sold to another master. But this hardly seems satisfying: why wouldn't the slaves depend upon further instances of the master's forbearance?

The answer is simply that the master, while he seems merely to exercise mercy by saving his slave from the other master, actually does so in order to combine greater lenience with greater severity; he is, like Shelley's poet-legislator, a successful author of law. First, note that Ellison's punishment for his slaves is not death but sale to another master—a punishment that is designed to be less extreme than the sentence of death, but still the most extreme form of punishment that the slave owner can inflict. At the same time, removing the slave from Ellison's plantation exiles the slave from the master's observation and distracts his own slaves from their work; it is therefore also regarded as inefficient and potentially subversive of the law (18). Sale seems to be at once the most severe punishment and the least severe—or at least, it appears questionable in its severity. Buying the slave back demonstrates the slave owner's mercy, but also reinforces his powerful system of sentencing.

There is a second dimension to these cases of slaves who are objects of both punishment and mercy. It is a curious fact about both instances that, in keeping with the master's combination of relaxation and rigor, the slaves seem to have escaped a severe punishment (of being sold) at the same time that the simultaneous threat and avoidance of sale means either imagining or desiring punishment by death. The first slave, when informed that he is to become Ellison's "property" once again, experiences a "joy" that was "near proving fatal" (18); the second slave "prefe[rs] death to slavery under another master" and refuses to take the medical remedies offered him to cure his fever (19). Being released from the possibility of an arbitrary death at the hands of another slave master, in other words, results in a freedom that is experienced as a strange brush with the death that was avoided. Brought back into the master's fold, the slave experiences a virtual death, the actuality of which the master's program of punishment both raises as a terrifying specter and then generously proscribes.

Sarah Scott's novel has been described by Markman Ellis as a work devoted to an "ameliorist" position on the subject of slavery, rather than an "abolitionist" one.[51] I argue, however, that the positions are not so easily distinguishable, and that Scott's novel, with its moderate opposition to slavery, is utterly consistent with the abolitionist discourses that made the freedom of slaves inseparable from their punishability. Scott makes it clear in the preface to the novel that her work is meant not merely as entertainment but as an ideal type for her readers to follow. Its open appeal to a white readership that might read and follow the example of Sir George Ellison therefore aims to revise existing structures of power. Its campaign for individual reform, moreover, extends into a campaign for social reform that will (the author hopes) gather more adherents: "Such exertion will not fail of being rewarded by the necessary assistance" (4).

If we turn to the poetry of Cowper, we find a still more aggressive strategy to interweave the logic of the two abolitions as an explicitly national campaign. It is for this reason that we find his poetry repeatedly making Britain itself (rather than an individual like Sir George) into the compassionate guarantor of the slave's freedom *and* the distributor of a more systematic mode of punishment encompassing both slave and master. Imitable individual action in Scott becomes imitable national policy in Cowper.

Britain, in Cowper's poetry, can be modeled as a kind of savior that will right the wrongs of slavery; at the same time, righting these wrongs requires nothing other than a new, consistent, and severe form of restraint. The connection between slavery and punishment vividly emerges in "Table Talk" (1782), a poem in which the two speakers discuss both the need for liberty and the proper boundaries for it.[52] The slave emerges

Chapter 6

here with particular urgency, since she is deprived of both physical and mental freedom; even the consolation of religion, which "stands most reveal'd before the freeman's eyes" (269), is unavailable. To be sure, Cowper's poetry—most notably "The Negro's Complaint" (1788)—fervently articulates a wish for the slave to be freed from instruments of torture and murder: "knotted scourges, / Matches, blood-extorting screws" (29–30). Yet nothing could be further from the aims of a poem like "Table Talk" than encouraging mere "anarchy and terror" (303) or the oppression of tyrants, both of which seem like possible results of the slave's fight for unrestricted freedom. If freedom from all legal authority were the aim, then slaves would be fighting "for what were better cast away" (282). They would be fighting for a greater cruelty than slavery itself.

In fact, it would be more accurate to say that wherever we turn in Cowper's abolitionist poetry, the problem with slavery is not simply that slaves are unfree, but that it is the cause of anarchy and violence. A potentially self-destructive cycle of imperial ambition and destruction can finally be staved off by Britain's more enlightened "pow'r" that "secures what industry has won," as Cowper writes in 1782 in "Heroism" (87). But what is the nature of that power? The object, even in "The Negro's Complaint," is not to overturn British government and the "duty" it exacts from its "agents" (29, 32). Quite the opposite: duty is to be extended everywhere, so that freedom coincides with a reinforcement of the slave's obligation. "Peace for Afric," Cowper writes in his "Sonnet to William Wilberforce, Esq." (1792), is to be achieved by being "fenc'd with British laws" (12). Rather than withdrawing British power from Africa, he urges readers of *The Task* (1785) to "Spread it, then / And let it circulate through ev'ry vein / Of all your empire; that where Britain's pow'r / Is felt, mankind may feel her mercy too" (2.44–47).

What becomes perfectly clear, moreover, is that the new commitment to lawfulness must not encompass simply the slave but also the slave owner—and indeed all "mankind." "The Negro's Complaint" calls out for an accounting of previously hidden injuries—"Think how many backs have smarted / For the sweets your cane affords" (23–24). Cowper's pun points out not only that the English reader's pleasure in sugar "cane" comes at the cost of the slave's painful labor, but also that such pleasure is inextricable from—afforded by—the master's "cane" lashing on the slave's back. The correction of laws that would regulate the master's brutality, however, cannot come from the master himself, as in Sarah Scott's novel. The poem's intriguing strategy is to appeal to Providence as an inspiration for, and ally in, Britain's legal cure.

Southey, among others, appropriates a similar line of thought in his *Poems Concerning the Slave Trade* (1794–1810): he appeals not to any individual person, and not even to Britain itself, but to the "God of Justice," who will adjudicate the slave's complaint in court, "Before the Eternal."[53] There is a difference, though. Southey can only hopelessly imagine a liberty that appears after the slave's death ("Bless with liberty and death the Slave!"), and we find a similar sentiment in Thomas Day's suggestion in his famous poem "The Dying Negro" (1773), when he speaks of "slumbering justice," a "Power" that has deserted the wronged people of Africa and only comes to their aid in hazy "Prophetic visions" at the end of the poem.[54]

Cowper moves in a slightly more radical direction: he enlists Providence as a higher court, a perfected mechanism for trial, conviction, and punishment that the state itself might take as an example. The "answer" of the heavens to British slavery is nothing less than a rational, measured, and decisive series of punishments that take place in nature itself, which is endowed with human or superhuman agency: "wild tornados . . . / Strewing yonder sea with wrecks; / Wasting towns, plantation, meadows, / Are the voice with which he speaks" (33–36). The voice, in other words, is retribution itself. The will to fashion Britain as a Providential protector in Cowper's poetry leads us, moreover, to the judicious "Heroes of Truth" in Wordsworth's *Salisbury Plain*. In Wordsworth's poem, though, the reformed punisher coming to the rescue of the enslaved and oppressed is not Britain itself, and not Providence, but a force of reform that is constructed by the legislating impulses of the poem's closing stanza.

Sin, Individuality, and Equiano's *Interesting Narrative*

There is yet another dimension to the two abolitions that I want to pursue in the final pages of this chapter. Although I have been concentrating on the work of white death-penalty and slavery abolitionists, I now turn to the work of Olaudah Equiano to show how a black slave could incorporate the conjoined terms of these discourses, arguing for the guilt of both slave traffickers and—most surprising of all—himself. Equiano's *Interesting Narrative* has received substantial critical attention in the last ten years, but with all of the focus on the author's literary education and intellectual milieu, criticism of Equiano, like histories of the slave trade, has not accounted for the connection between slavery and the death penalty. Even Adam Potkay's account of the law of revenge, or *lex talionis*, in the *Narrative*, which approaches the terms of criminal law, does so in a way that completely disconnects Equiano's argument from the actual context of legal debate in which the work was written.[55]

Equiano's narrative participates in the logic of the texts I have been mentioning, but it intervenes in their claims in a complex way. A great deal of this complexity, I think, derives from the manner in which the narrative dramatizes tensions between different accounts of Providence and the extent to which Providence in those accounts authorizes different kinds of human action. Does Providence authorize slavery? If so, is anyone justified in opposing it? One approach that Equiano offers to these questions rigorously applies the logic of Providential guidance. In that account, Equiano can explain—one might say rationalize—his "present situation" of misery constantly as a "judgment of Heaven" requiring him to "acknowledge[e] my transgression to God."[56] The fact that Equiano observes punishments applied to slaves by white masters, even while those masters themselves escape any repercussions for their murders and abuses, simply demonstrates that whatever standards of justice we might have, they may not be the same as God's, whose standards are ineffable to us. This is why Equiano, accepting that the state of affairs conforms to God's will, repeatedly arrives at the conclusion that he cannot expect "any right among men here" (94). He must simply submit to whatever "fate" has in store for him—"what no mortal on earth could prevent" (98)—rather than actively seek out any "means or hope to obtain my freedom" (119).

Certainly these responses might remind us of Hannah More's tracts or Southey's poems; although it is quite possible that these two authors were familiar with Equiano's text, the point to be made here is one not of influence but of a shared logic through which these writers show a commitment both to God's justice and to its utter unavailability to humans. Meanwhile, the very commitment to God's justice looks barely distinguishable—if distinguishable at all—from a simple support of conventional law and its provisions for protecting the system of slavery. But there is less stability in Equiano's narrative than there is in Southey's, and even in More's; indeed, the same sufferings Equiano explains as Providentially authorized can be examined from yet another perspective. Equiano sees himself—as he sees other African slaves destined for the colonies—primarily as a prisoner subjected to inhumane treatment that is capable of being criticized and altered (97). Thus it is profoundly appropriate for Equiano to be adapting the speech from *Paradise Lost* (1674) in which Beelzebub complains of his treatment at the hands of God: "No peace is given / To us enslav'd, but custody severe" (112). The scandal of framing the author's voice as the prince of the devils comports with the author's challenge to a system that may (from one point of view) be sanctioned by God.

The difference between the first perspective and this one is a difference between seeing humans as instruments of God's ineffable punishments and viewing them as responsible and creative moral-political agents of punishment. In his account of the West Indies, Equiano joins the white abolitionists of his day (he relied here on many of their accounts) by concentrating on the *poor treatment* of slaves rather than the mere fact that they are slaves and therefore not rights-bearing subjects. Chapter 6 produces one account after another of floggings and amputations of ears, legs, and other body parts, many of which ultimately end in death: they are "reduced so low, that they are turned out as unfit for service, and left to perish in the woods, or expire on a dunghill" (103). In other cases, the repetitious applications of "torture"—brands, iron muzzles, thumb screws, and so on—drive a slave to "despair" and thus to "seek a refuge in death from those evils which tender their lives intolerable" (107). In both cases, in fact, Equiano's point about slave masters is that virtually all penalties end up as the death penalty; his point, in other words, coincides with and reinforces the claim of death-penalty reformers who continually criticized the excessive application of capital punishment and its lack of effect on its audience of political subjects.

This treatment is in fact sanctioned by law, as Equiano goes on to claim in his quotation from the 329th act of the Assembly of Barbados, which provides that a master who willfully kills a slave of his own "*shall pay into the public treasury fifteen pound sterling*" (109; Equiano's italics). This act, frequently cited in abolitionist literature, in effect proclaims, as Equiano openly states, "the small account in which the life of a negro is held in the West Indies" (109). But the act is also disturbing because of the way that it frankly allows the master the power to enforce the penalty of death at his pleasure: a slave "under punishment by his master" may be killed without any fine at all. The law, in other words, does not merely deal leniently with a master for treating his slaves cruelly; it makes the master into the agent of the law over his slaves, and thus into their legal murderer.

As I suggested earlier, it would be entirely plausible to say that the legal murder of slaves, both in Equiano's text and in the texts of white reformers, is not simply a *possible* outcome of the ownership of other human beings; it is virtually coextensive with that ownership, and therefore literalizes Patterson's account of the slave's "social death" at the hands of white masters. At the same time, however, Equiano's account does not center primarily on securing life for the slave exclusively through the acquisition of liberty or property in one's own person. Indeed, neither of Equiano's two eloquent responses to slavery involves a simple and direct claim for self-ownership; both, however, depend upon a logic of penality. The narrative thus turns punishment into problem and solution, both an injurious effect of ownership and a response to injury itself.

The first response is Equiano's not always successful but nonetheless powerfully stated emphasis on "redress," on compensation for damages or return of property taken by fraudulent merchants and masters. All too often, Equiano is subjected to punishments—such as the dramatic and horrifying hanging from the wrists and ankles that he suffers on board a ship bound for the Musquito coast—"merely because I was a freeman, and could not by the law get any redress from a white person in those parts of the world" (212). In other instances, such "redress" is to some extent possible, and it is significant that Equiano draws the narrative to a close with two particularly successful pleas for compensation (230).[57] In the first, he obtains payment withheld from him for his position in the transportation of the "Black Poor" to Sierra Leone. "Because he knows not of what crimes he is accused," he pleads for a "vindication of . . . his conduct" and a restoration of the money prejudicially withheld (230). In the second, he pleads in a letter to the Queen for "redress" for the "oppression and cruelty" suffered by his "injured countrymen," coupled with a commitment to "vindicate the honour of our common nature." The redress and vindication of his fellow Africans provides the perfect complement for his personal redress and vindication of his own character (231). Although it is widely accepted that Equiano is in fact mistaken to believe that the 1792 Consolidated Slave Act of Jamaica represented an improvement of conditions for slaves, the particular terms of the act are largely irrelevant for our understanding of the way he wants to make us think of the role of redress in the narrative. For the narrative reaches its conclusion not simply by accepting the punishments of this world, but by seeking compensation from those who have caused injury.

To seek redress (in this context) is to imagine a new set of legal obligations for those who seemed exempt from them; this imaginative act accompanies yet another. Inseparable from the continued emphasis on redress from his captors, employers, and government is Equiano's persistent and more wide-ranging imagining of an appropriate punishment for criminal acts or criminal negligence. Even when he does not actively pursue the cause of justice, in other words, Equiano finds a way in his account to conjure up a vehicle for retribution. The suicides of slaves in one instance are converted in his account from a collective act of despair (as it is in Day's "The Dying Negro") into a more principled attempt to "retaliate on their tyrants" (105). In other cases, the narrative constructs corrective measures that appear only as a kind of wish for their institution: in one instance, he wishes that the unruly Indian governor who strikes one of the ship's party had been "tied fast to a tree, and flogged" (208). Later in the same section (once again on Equiano's voyage to the Musquito coast), he even speculates that he would be entirely "justified" in killing the ship's captain, who has subjected Equiano to repeated physical abuse (217).

Equiano's narrative thus finds multiple ways of asserting or imagining legal redress that intervenes in the account of Providence, and the kind of inaction that such an account might recommend. Legal redress, moreover, supplements the abstract right of the slave, a right that exists only on paper and is repeatedly denied even in the final expeditions reported in the narrative. But there is still a wrinkle here: isn't the retaliation of the slave merely a vengeful repetition of the slave owner's application of power? What could elevate the slave to a higher level of moral authority than the master himself if the slave were to kill the ship's captain? In a way, the questions might seem to have an obvious answer—the captain would be getting what he deserves—but that answer is not acceptable within the domain of this narrative. When Equiano speculates on killing the ship captain, an important revision to the account of retributive justice appears: while believing at first that retaliation of this kind would be "justifiable," he reports that he "prayed to God" and was thus prevented from a supposedly justifiable homicide by respecting the "times" and "bounds" of life on earth, which are set only by God, and by trusting "in the name of the Lord" (217).[58]

The intrusion of God's authority as a corrective to Equiano's imagined recourse to retribution is truly important. Although I first introduced the issue of divine Providence as if it merely supported a cruelly retributive force in the narrative—and hence a support of slavery itself—the account of Providence actually appears to be a bit more complicated. Equiano's conversion to Christianity and the view of Providence it supports has been much debated by scholars: for Srinivas Aravamudan, it is evidence of a nationalist ideology alien to the author's native culture; for Helen Thomas, it is evidence of the author's cultural "hybridity."[59] I tend to agree with Dwight A. McBride's general sense that Christianity has a more functional role in the *Narrative* than either of these static alternatives allows, although I differ slightly from McBride in that what is at stake is not Equiano's performing the role of a "saint" (a form of identity alien to Equiano's particular brand of Protestantism).[60] Sainthood may indeed describe Hannah More's characters, with their tendency to make religion into an erasure of guilt—and any characteristic form of action. But the case is different for Equiano, in whose work Methodism emerges not as an identity but as a penal logic.

For him, conversion under the auspices of Methodism provides a model for a rigorous awareness of criminality combined with a faith in God as a source of forgiveness. Even for those justified and sanctified by faith, sin "is only suspended, not destroyed," John Wesley writes. But justification provides the possibility for renewed pardons: "It is the forgiveness of all our sins and, what is necessarily implied by this, our acceptance with God."[61] On the one hand, then, Equiano continually sees himself as "a condemned criminal under the law" (190). Or, as the "Miscellaneous Verses" at the end of chapter 10 put it, the slave stands "Like some poor pris'ner at the bar, / Conscious of guilt, of sin, and fear, / Arraign'd, and self condemn'd, I stood, / 'Lost in the world and in my blood' " (196). Equiano's account of his attempts at legal redress, moreover, serves as a metaphor for the broader commitment in the narrative—a secularized version of Methodist doctrine—to exposing lawlessness within law. One of the great creative acts of the text, after all, is to arraign and condemn those whose violence and injury hide behind devotion and propriety.

On the other hand, the God to whom Equiano prays orders him to stay the hand of retaliatory violence; taking a life would mean setting its "bounds," which only He may do. The result of prayer, in other words, is an attention to human utility. This is not to say that Equiano simply forgives injury, any more than he expects such forgiveness on earth for himself. Returning to the moment I mentioned earlier—when the captain of a schooner hoists him up by his wrists and ankles as punishment for disobeying his orders—Equiano's objection is not to punishment itself but to the lack of any "judge or jury" that would curb the "impropriety of this conduct." And while he prays to God to "forgive this blasphemer," this heartfelt plea cannot prevent him from also wishing to see the captain brought to justice—by obtaining a counteracting "redress" from his fellow shipmates or any "white person in those parts of the world" (212). This is utterly consistent with Wesley's pronouncements in his *Thoughts on Slavery* (1774); God is a "wise, powerful, merciful Being," but he is also a "just God" who will "reward every man according to his works" and impose "retribution" on those who "showed no mercy."[62] Welsey's two aims are inseparable: to free slaves from bondage, and to impose punishment on all those "guilty of frauds, robberies, and murders."[63]

Equiano's *Interesting Narrative* provides a compelling concluding text for a discussion of Romantic writers on the death penalty because its wavering between retribution and a "stay" to retribution returns us to the central problematic of punishment that I have been discussing throughout this book. But it also emphasizes a sustained yet subdued theme throughout my discussions, namely, the role of religion in discussions of punishment.[64] Equiano's inspiration from his Christian conversion provides a religious companion to Romilly's overtly secularizing arguments. They offer somewhat different rationales for opposition and reform, producing compatible logics while appealing to different readerships. There is a two-part political lesson to be learned from this compatibility. First, we must realize that religion is not necessary to oppose the death penalty: all that is needed is some commitment to the inherent value of an individual human life. Second, secular defenses of the death penalty may look to religions as further reinforcements of their claims: they do not need them, but—as John Rawls has suggested—many religions of the world easily accommodate themselves as allies of a secular pursuit of justice.[65]

The function of religion in Equiano's writing also must return us to the more specific moral-political aesthetics at work in Romantic treatments of the death penalty and penal reform. Saying how a higher power wants us to conduct political life is a great risk for the range of writers I have been discussing: Wordsworth comes close to imagining God authorizing the death penalty, then steps away; Coleridge rejects it in *Osorio*. Religion presents such a risk in these cases because claiming the direct influence of or submission to Providential agency compromises punishment as a construction of human beings. It also robs literary fictions of their power to defend that construction as a self-consciously aesthetic assertion of a valid political order. Equiano's adventurous way of making Providence look like a proponent of lenient but measured punishment, even for a heinous crime, runs the risk of fanaticism, to be sure. And his confidence in Providence might even seem occasionally to challenge the very interest that a reader might take in the human struggle waged throughout this self-styled "interesting" narrative. But such a complaint against Equiano must be considered alongside his text's profoundly austere sense of the human, a sense conveyed through its steady demand upon its readers to acknowledge what persons owe to each other. For Equiano ultimately addresses, repeatedly and urgently, agents of justice that live on this earth, and nowhere else. Why, after all, would the author criticize white people for neglecting the black slave's demand for redress, if he did not believe—as much as he believes in his God—in the capacity of his readers, someday, to provide it?

CODA

The Culture of the Death Penalty

        I dreamt I saw a caravan of the dead
   move on wheels touching rails without sound.
         To each eye as they pass: You betray us.
             Frank Bidart, "To the Republic"

Romanticism's importance in the history of punishment, I have been arguing, is to be understood as an early and decisive opposition to the broad and unsystematic use of the death penalty. But this opposition could only emerge through a reconfiguration of punishment in wider terms. Punishing, in the work of writers from Bentham to Byron, was less coherently grasped as a theory than as a problematic: an uneasy combination of rationales that emphasized both the specific "utilitarian" value of punishment and the specific measure of punishment as "desert." The instability is visible in all of the most prominent writing on penal reform, and is imaginatively reinforced in literary works of the period.

Nineteenth-century literature following the penal reforms embraced by the Romantics is characterized by a subtle yet important shift. If Romantic writers are concerned with how—or if—punishment works, later writers begin to move in a different direction, accompanied by an interest in strategies of detection and elaborated mechanisms of policing. The concern is no longer what punishment is, but on whom it should be inflicted. This shift is inseparable from another one, a move from the view of punishment as a problematic, to punishment as a more firmly defined affront to innocence or just desert for the guilty. In Sir Edward George Bulwer Lytton's *Eugene Aram* (1831), as in Charles Dickens's *Oliver Twist* (1838), the novel becomes the self-conscious advocate for abused innocence. Eugene Aram, who interested Hazlitt for his "staggered imagination" as he contemplated his own murder (as I suggested in Chapter 1), takes on a quite different role in the redemptive scheme of Bulwer Lytton's novel. As the author explains in his series of prefaces to the work, the novel displays the convicted criminal's innocence, despite his trial and penalty of execution. For "in the murder itself," the author declares, Aram "had no share, borne out by the opinion of many eminent lawyers by whom I have heard the subject discussed."

The case of Eugene Aram—convicted and executed for murder in 1759, fourteen years after the event—was the occasion for significant controversy and subsequent literary invention. In his poem "The Dream of Eugene Aram" (1829), Thomas Hood takes a radically different view of the murderer whom Bulwer Lytton devotes himself to exonerating. Much of the distinction between treatments of Aram centers on the significance of his learning; as various editions of *The Newgate Calendar* were fond of pointing out, Aram was a self-taught man of "high erudition" worthy of the "shoulders of our Atlas, Dr. Johnson"; he even embarked on a "comparative Lexicon" of Celtic and Eastern languages.[1] Certainly this fact adds an important emphasis to Hazlitt's account, which suggests that even a man guilty of murder would stagger in estrangement from a word that he might have intricately defined. For Bulwer Lytton, Aram's learning offers more straightforward proof of his higher morality and sensitive heart. But Hood slyly depicts Aram reading Solomon Gessner's version of the Cain and Abel story (*The Death of Abel* [1758]), as if to emphasize Aram's crime as a replication of Cain's. Hood is not interested in stressing the criminal's innocence; he also is not concerned to use the Biblical text to suggest that Aram (like Cain) deserved lenience. He is more interested in representing Aram's penalty for his guilt: the criminal suffers a "horrid, horrid dream" of an "avenging Sprite" that tortures him for his crime and even extends his suffering in waking life. The vengeful sprite, demanding that only "blood for blood" will "aton[e]" for the crime, turns out be the harbinger of the death penalty itself.[2]

Hood's poem, I think, joins forces with detective novels and "sensation" fiction, which align the work of the narrator more or less consistently with a structure of retribution that gives due punishment for the guilty. It might even be argued that the frustrations arising in the process of detection and punishment in a novel like Anthony Trollope's *The Eustace Diamonds* (1873) still depend upon the narrator's and reader's confidence in Lizzie Eustace's guilt, as if their certainty compensated for the lack of legal recognition. The emphasis on wronged innocence and deserved guilt in later nineteenth-century fiction contrasts powerfully with Romantic paradigms of punishment, in which innocent subjects seek out punishment (as in Austen's *Mansfield Park*) or guilty subjects receive lenience (as in Byron's *Cain*): the purpose of depicting such troubling figures is not to devalue punishment or simply to register skepticism about it, but to reveal punishment's unsettled internal logic.

Because my aim was to write a book about political, legal, and literary history, I have not extensively engaged current thinking about the death penalty or about punishment more generally. But, following some of my hints from Chapter 1, we could still indulge in some speculation about the impact a study of Romanticism might have on our understanding of today's ongoing debates. In the United States, the politics and culture surrounding the death penalty represent yet another shift in thought. On the one hand, contemporary political writing and cultural production have adopted a heightened interest in the aims and purposes of punishment—particularly capital punishment. On the other hand, that interest is most frequently typified by a polarization and ossification of punishment's rationales, so that opposing points of view are ultimately blinded to their necessary interconnection.

An example of that trend could be seen in the more or less weak positions of many who oppose the death penalty. Characteristic of abolitionist arguments is their attempt to deny the power of retributivist arguments for the death penalty without engaging with them. Some endorse a form of sentimentalism—as if the unique claims of human experience alone might constitute an argument against death or any form of punishment.[3] Others try too quickly to dismiss the death penalty as if it were simply irrational, an arcane and empty ritual; Stephen B. Bright thus suggests that, like "whipping," "branding," and other "primitive forms of punishment," it will disappear.[4] Still others, mostly postmodern critics of capital punishment like Austin Sarat and Peter Fitzpatrick, claim that the death penalty is not merely a relic of state authority but actually is subversive of it, since its finality denies the incalculable specificity of human subjects.[5] All of these critiques are joined by the claim that utility could one-sidedly trump the claims of retributivism; at the same time, such critiques decline to explain how any law whatsoever could avoid the taint of dehumanized ritual, or how any law could ever be made to account for the infinite variety of human subjects.[6]

The extremism of abolitionists has often been evenly matched by the extremism of retentionists. The primary difficulty encountered by retentionists is that they suppose the death penalty to have a meaning that is stable beyond its effects. It has been common enough to question the actual relief that can be achieved through the closure of the death penalty, the "vindication," as Alex Kozinski calls it, for the families and loved ones of victims of violent crime.[7] And it is just as common to suggest that the violence of the death penalty simply repeats the cycle of violence rather than providing any real satisfaction for the parties involved.[8] Abolitionists and retentionists can continually carry out a battle over whether people are or are not satisfied by the punishments they, or others, receive. But the underlying problem with the retentionist's defense is that what counts as "vindication" is a matter of contingent cultural and historical consensus—a consensus that may vary culturally, that may change in the future, or that may not even exist in the present.

Yet one more variation on the death-penalty argument requires some mention, since it has attracted a significant amount of attention. This is the view of the death-penalty "agnostic." This position, popularized by Scott Turow, focuses primarily on the problem of wrongful conviction, so that recommendations for reform tend to center on the reduction of the death penalty for cases with uncorroborated testimony or other factors (like class difference, racial difference, and inadequacy of legal representation) that might cast doubt on the justice of a capital sentencing. The agnostic's case is not significantly different from the death-penalty supporter's; the agnostic limits the death penalty only because of the problem with the imprecise knowledge leading to capital conviction, and not because of capital conviction itself.[9] Turow's position is not an ontological one—he does not mean to say that we can never be sure of any murderer's guilt; thus, if all murders were videotaped, fingerprinted, or documented in some way that overcame his uncertainty, the rationale for his argument would collapse.

The characteristic suppressions and occlusions in many opinions about the death penalty in the United States, I argue, are not confined to political debate but in fact inform an important trend in cultural representations of capital punishment. Film treatments in the 1990s and early 2000s are particularly revealing in this respect. The current philosophical and political inability to account for the positioning of arguments within the problematic of modern penalty finds cinematic expression in a mode of aphasia—a disconnect between criticism of the death penalty's inhumanity and an ultimate, contradictory approval of that inhumanity.[10] As if both sides of the debate were present without acknowledging their positions, film tends to show that there is something wrong with the death penalty, but no one can figure out exactly what it is, and no one wants to try. Some films may be more critical of the death penalty than others, but I argue that whatever critical energies may be present are defeated by a cynical detachment, a confusing competition of affections and interests, or a spiritual consolation that makes peace with the injustices elsewhere opposed. *The Life of David Gale* (2003), a film about narcissistic, fanatical death-penalty reformers playing tricks on the criminal-justice system, is an example of the first.[11] *The Chamber* (1996) is an example of the second: the protagonist's attempt to free a grandfather from the death penalty produces such a welter of conflicting emotions that sending the old man to his death can only seem like a relief.[12]

The Green Mile (1999), adapted from a Stephen King novel, is an example of the third type—combining criticism with consolation—and I think it demonstrates the problem with current debate on the death penalty in the United States most vividly.[13] At the center of the film is Paul Edgecomb (Tom Hanks), the friendly executioner and officer on death row; he treats those who are waiting for their executions with the utmost dignity and respect, and he severely punishes those who do not do the same. There are suggestions that Paul is uncomfortable with his job: a nagging urinary-tract infection prevents intimacy with his wife, and his physical condition thus appears as a metaphor for the death penalty's moral corruption. His internal conflicts are more pronounced once John Coffey (Michael Clark Duncan) is added to the group of inmates. John, a massive black man, at first looks like a threat, but Paul ultimately finds out that he is gentle and childlike, and—as we suspected all along—falsely accused of his crimes. Still more, Paul discovers that John has a particular knack for working miracles: helping both meek and powerful, he revives a dead mouse and banishes Paul's ailments (apparently enhancing his sexual performance).

All of this inspires Paul to wonder whether killing someone with John's special gifts might be against God's command. It is certainly weird enough that a black man—and one falsely accused—requires superhuman powers in order to be treated with humanity, as if blackness depletes humanity so much that miracles are required to reinforce it. But it turns out that John's status as a Christ-figure is not simply instrumental in earning him the treatment due to human beings more generally. Indeed, John's exemplary humanity is taken so far that it is almost entirely overturned once we get to the end of the film, when he becomes a full-blown agent of sacrifice: a negation of common humanity rather than an embodiment of it.

At some level, the film seems to understand that there is something fraudulent about this spiritualizing gesture. The recurring segment of Fred Astaire singing "I'm in Heaven" while whirling around the floor with Ginger Rogers in *Top Hat* might be taken as a comment on the vast reduction and trivialization of the very spirituality that the film also, at other moments, wants to take seriously. Indeed, the film treats its fraudulent spirituality with substantial veneration. On the eve of his execution, John refuses Paul's offer to facilitate his escape from prison and from death. Although Sarat claims in his illuminating reading that John sacrifices himself for human salvation (like Christ), this perhaps relies too heavily on the film's own superficial symbolism.[14] In fact, John dies for nothing other than for the integrity of a criminal-justice system, which grinds on undisturbed. The film, while at first seeming to question the justice of the death penalty for anyone, comes close to the thought that it may be not only acceptable but also in fact consistent with God's commands.

The logic of critique and self-effacement—an exposure of fraud followed by a sacramentalizing of fraud—dominates the arc of *The Green Mile*. Toward the end of the film, we realize that the aging prison executioner, along with the mouse, are now living well past their natural life spans, having received a dose of John's miraculous energy. Paul speaks of the transfer of this energy as a kind of "curse," and the choice of words is interesting. First, the agonizing prolongation of life correlates with the prolonged life of the death penalty itself: the unspoken truth in the film is that even while the film's action takes place primarily in the past, the institutional fact—the "curse"—of the death penalty has not died. The death penalty's bias against racial minorities has not died either, despite the brief respite of capital punishment in the United States from 1972 to 1976 on the grounds of its unconstitutionality. And neither has any element of capital punishment's brutality—amply represented everywhere in this film's representations of gruesome but "successful" executions, its portrayal of agents of the law satisfying their bloodlust.

The critical potential of the analogy between the prolonged life of the executioner and the prolonged life of executions remains only implicit. Indeed, the second and more overt level of significance attached to the prolongation of life concerns the mystical transfer of life itself. While described as a "curse," it is a literalization of memory in which Paul does not just remember John; he—and the mouse—*are* John. Sharon Holland argues that the space of death is, for black Americans, an "imaginative replacement" for slavery, and this film steadily subscribes to that logic, making the legacy of slavery visible first by killing Coffey and then by raising his spirit. The mystical transfer perfectly reverses the logic that can be found in the memoirs of executioners like Donald Cabana, who experience a personal loss of life during each killing. After he put Edward Earl Johnson to death, Cabana claims in *Death at Midnight*, "a little piece of me died."[15] In *The Green Mile*, moreover, John Coffey contradicts every known fact about the "living death" of prisoners on death row;[16] he feels inspiration rather than defeat as he contemplates his execution, and he transfers that energy into others as a strange kind of transubstantiation for a small community of believers: one man and one rodent.

The rodent is crucial in the film's insistence on seeing Coffey as subhuman and superhuman at the same time. Further, the parallel between Coffey and Christ only reinforces the fact that what is memorialized is precisely John's pointless sacrifice. What is memorialized, in other words, is simply the selfless devotion to the very system of destruction that continues to burden Paul with guilt. Thus, while in one sense the prolongation of life curses Paul with the memory of his hand in John's death, in another sense those feelings of guilt have no significance. They do nothing to alter the film's general verdict on the death penalty: it is not a crime but a social fact, hallowed, perhaps, by the will of God.

A related aphasia haunts other cinematic treatments of the death penalty in a variety of different ways: in *Dead Man Walking* (1995), the prolonged contact between Sister Helen Prejean (Susan Sarandon) and the murderer Matthew Poncelet (Sean Penn) reinforces the criminal's human qualities that are denied by the death sentence.[17] But religion in this film, as in *The Green Mile*, so easily turns upon itself that Sister Helen eventually provides only spiritual consolation and reconciliation, with little or no hope of political reform or even protest. Something different happens in the brilliantly tangled cynicism of *Identity* (2003): there, it is the murderer who unpredictably shifts before the viewer's eyes.[18] At the end of the film, the audience is tricked into thinking that the killer has reformed himself. We then find out that his reform was in fact a symptom of the same mental disorder that originally inspired his crime; the film ends with a rapid sequence in which he unpredictably shifts into the personality of a murdering monster bent on a new rampage of killing.

It might be possible to anatomize these different films according to their political stances on the death penalty; if so, perhaps a film like *Dead Man Walking* could be taken as a more sincere criticism of the death penalty than *Identity*, which simply sees the criminal as an alien form of consciousness. In the same way, *The Green Mile* might seem more committed to criticism than *The Life of David Gale*. What interests me more, however, is the way in which these films inventively, but pathologically, both mount and dismantle critiques of the death penalty. This collective sense of blockage cinematically enacts a broader habit in our political culture: the habit of framing philosophical commitments on one side of the death-penalty divide or the other, while refusing to acknowledge the implication of those claims within a larger problematic established since late eighteenth century and continued in the United States by the likes of Benjamin Franklin, Benjamin Rush, and Thomas Upham. To take account of punishment on these terms is to realize that the problem with current debate is not that the sides don't speak the same language; it is that they don't realize they are speaking exactly the same one.

To take account of punishment on these terms may also help us to examine the problematic of punishment rather than simply inhabit it by immobilizing and sanctifying its terms. Examining it could reveal that what is wrong with the death penalty may be what is wrong with common beliefs and practices of punishing in far more general terms. Ruth Wilson Gilmore does something like this when she shows how prison sentences fail because of both their uneven benefits and their uneven application. Her analysis of the race-based mechanisms of social control at the heart of the American prison industrial complex suggests a decisive lack of confidence in the perspective adopted by Equiano, who could maintain a healthy optimism about the possibility of serving justice for the victims of racism by working with, rather than against, a legal system of rewards and punishments.[19] Rather than depend upon the kind of lenient penalty advocated in Equiano's text, Angela Y. Davis rejects the idea of punishment entirely: she opposes prisons not in order to replace them with "prisonlike substitutes" but to challenge "the conceptual link between crime and punishment." She thus calls for a range of solutions to crime—an expansion of rights, an increase in protections, a redistribution of wealth—that place a greater burden on the power of distributive justice to improve social welfare.[20] Davis's argument, and others compatible with it that emphasize the importance of socializing criminals rather than punishing them, asks society to reexamine its thoughts about what people are and why they do the things they do. All of that is well beyond the scope of this book. But we can simply acknowledge that, by recognizing the continued yet obscured influence of Romantic paradigms, we may be led not merely to honor those paradigms, but to analyze, criticize, and possibly reject them.

Notes

INTRODUCTION

1. Lord Byron, *Cain: A Mystery*, in Byron 1970, 3.1.512, 517–19.
2. Blackstone 1979, 4:8.
3. I quote from the King James version of Genesis 4.
4. Byron, Polidori writes, "corrected the English of my essay in The Pamphleteer." See William Marshall Rosetti, ed., *The Diary of Dr. John William Polidori* (London: Elkin Matthews, 1911), 180.
5. John William Polidori, "On the Punishment of Death" (1816), 288, 300.
6. Society for the Diffusion of Information on the Subject of Capital Punishment, *Substance of the Speeches of S. Lushington, LLD and J. Sydney Taylor, AM* (Edinburgh: W. Oliphant, n.d.); Lord Nugent, *On the Punishment of Death by Law* (London: James Ridgway, 1840), 6.
7. For a more complete reading of the play focusing on the issue of blasphemy and personal injury, see Canuel 2002, 256–63.
8. My view thus offers a perspective that differs from Regina Schwartz's reading of Cain as a persistent instance of "otherness" opposing the "violent identity formation" in the nation-state. A more historical view shows that Cain's reception is more complex, situated, at least in this instance, within a Western attempt to forge a liberal structure of the state against its own violent heritage. See Schwartz, *The Curse of Cain: The Violent Legacy of Monotheism* (Chicago: University of Chicago Press, 1997), 9.
9. It is hardly a coincidence, moreover, that Byron's God echoes the author's "Frame Work Bill Speech" of 1812, in which he asks for "conciliation and firmness" in punishment, in opposition to the cruelty and inefficiency of the death penalty. Byron 1991, 25.
10. William Blake, *The Death of Abel*, in Blake 1977, pl. 2.
11. Foucault 1977, 73–131.
12. Ibid., 131, 139.
13. Dumm 1987, 111.
14. Siskin 1988; Alan Liu, *Wordsworth: The Sense of History* (Stanford: Stanford University Press, 1989); Lynch 1998; Thomas Pfau, *Wordsworth's Profession: Form, Class, and the Logic of Early Romantic Cultural Production* (Stanford: Stanford University Press, 1997).
15. Rose 1984, 171–207.
16. Foucault's clearest characterization of the juridical as a concealment of the political can be found in Foucault 2003, 37.
17. Foucault 1977, 131.
18. Roger Hood, *The Death Penalty: A Worldwide Perspective*, 3d ed. (Oxford: Oxford University Press, 2002), 243.

Notes to Chapter 1

19. Agamben 1998; Judith Butler, *Precarious Life: The Powers of Mourning and Violence* (London: Verso, 2004); Michael Hardt and Antonio Negri, *Empire* (Cambridge, Mass.: Harvard University Press, 2000).

20. Nietzsche 1969, 80.

21. Nietzsche's connection between punishment and the "bad conscience" is relevant to my remarks here (1969, 86).

22. I should add here that my claims contrast with Frances Ferguson's important emphasis on utilitarian effectiveness in both institutions and discourses. I am interested in how punishment included this utilitarian view as only one of its vantage points. See Ferguson 2004, 1–33.

23. My argument thus differs from accounts of literature and penality that stress the opposition between imaginative sympathy and the impartial functioning of criminal law. See, for instance, Martha Nussbaum's *Poetic Justice: The Literary Imagination in Public Life* (Boston: Beacon Press, 1995), 53–78.

CHAPTER 1
"THE HORRORS OF MY DREAMS"

1. Wakefield 1831, 78.
2. Anon. 1830, 35.
3. Douglas Hay suggests, however, that this concern was less grave than it seemed, since landed property owners had their own means of protection. See Hay, Linebaugh, Rule, and Thompson 1975, 59.
4. Jeffrey 1804, 21.
5. Fielding 1988, 83.
6. Radcliffe 1968, 168.
7. William Cowper, *The Task*, in Cowper 1931, 1.735–38, 4.462.
8. Radzinowicz 1948, 1:453.
9. James Boswell, *Life of Johnson* (1952), 832.
10. Burke 1968b, 130.
11. Burke 1894, 6:246–47.
12. See, for instance, McAllister 2003, 153–63.
13. The careful reader of Madan will find that his adversaries slightly misrepresented him; though he defended the execution of laws as they were, he was not entirely opposed to altering them through the legislature. See *TEJ* 132–33.
14. Dagge *1772*, 270.
15. Dawes 1782, 234.
16. Sir James Mackintosh, "Speech on Moving for a Committee to Inquiry into the State of the Criminal Law," in Mackintosh 1846, 3:385, 380.
17. Polidori 1816, 303.
18. *Memoir of the Late Sir Samuel Romilly, M.P.* (London: John Fairburn, 1818), 20, 5.
19. Count de Mirabeau 1785, 8.
20. This is the general argument of Douglas Hay's "Property, Authority, and the Criminal Law," in Hay, Linebaugh, Rule, Thompson, and Winslow 1975, 17–64.

21. Mandeville 1964, 16–20.
22. William Blake, *Jerusalem*, in Blake 1977, pl. 27, line 30.
23. Scott 1932, 7:409–19.
24. Foucault 1977, 32–69; Gatrell 1994; Thomas W. Laqueur, "Crowds, Carnival, and the State in English Executions, 1604–1868," in Beier, Cannadine, and Rosenheim 1989, 305–55.
25. Conquergood 2002, 339–67.
26. Ten 1987. I discuss the philosophical positions more extensively in the coda to this book.
27. My view also differs from those that stress incompatibility; see B. Honig, "Rawls on Politics and Punishment," *Political Research Quarterly* 46 (1993): 99–125.
28. See Alex Kotlowitz, "In the Face of Death," *The New York Times Magazine*, July 6, 2003.
29. See the postings by Human Rights Watch, *http://www.hrw.org/campaigns/chile98*.
30. English writers at least as far back as More wished to replace the death penalty with a more "convenient and humane" form of punishment. Sir Thomas More, *Utopia* (1965), 53.
31. See Karl Shoemaker's account of the transformation of pain's meaning from a transcendent religious significance to a secular consequential significance, in "The Problem of Pain in Punishment," in Sarat 2001, 15–41.
32. Oliver Goldsmith, *The Vicar of Wakefield* (1982), 162.
33. Byron, *Marino Faliero*, in Byron 1991, 1.2.79.
34. Mary Stockdale, *A Plume for Sir Samuel Romilly; or, The Offering of the Fatherless* (1818), 9.
35. I essentially agree with Mary Poovey's claim that the statistic "depends upon and produces that which lies beyond representation," in "Figures of Arithmetic, Figures of Speech: The Discourse of Statistics in the 1830s," *Critical Inquiry* 19 (1993): 275.
36. See, for example, Stanley Fish's claim (1989, 519) that "you can never get away from force, from the pressure exerted by a partial, non-neutral, nonauthoritative, ungrounded point of view."
37. Charles Lamb, "On the Inconveniences Resulting from Being Hanged," in Lamb 1935, 385–92.
38. Beccaria 1986, 11; see Frances Ferguson's account of the obscurity of both crime and punishment in Ferguson 1987, 248–63.
39. Blackstone 1979, 4:16–17.
40. John Deane Potter's *The Art of Hanging* (1969) provides a detailed account of different procedures in hanging and other executions.
41. On the changing fortunes of the guillotine, see Janes 1991, 21–51.
42. The division here might be understood as a division between moral reasons and legal rules, as outlined by Larry Alexander and Emily Sherwin (2001, 204). This division is usually ignored in accounts of penal reform; Michael Ignatieff inaccurately portrays the movement as a rejection of "retributive theory" in favor

of utilitarian "calculation" of benefits in *A Just Measure of Pain: The Penitentiary in the Industrial Revolution* (New York: Columbia University Press, 1978), 74.

43. Blackstone 1979, 4:396.
44. Montagu 1814.
45. Girard 1977, 21.
46. Montesquieu 1989, 28–29.
47. Hobbes, *Leviathan* (1968), 343.
48. On punishment as an avoidance of "general fear," see Robert Nozick, *Anarchy, State, and Utopia* (New York: Basic Books, 1971), 65–71.
49. Robert Southey, *Botany Bay Eclogues*, in Southey 1840, 2:71–89.
50. Godwin 1977, 325–26.
51. Montgomery 1854, 32.
52. See also Buxton 1818, for a similar emphasis on the need to have punishment coincide exactly with the sentence (9).
53. Scarry 1985, 4; Derrida 1992, 3–67.
54. Engelmann 2003, 51.
55. Eden 1771, 287.
56. Engelmann 2003, 74.
57. Foucault 1977, 101, 130.
58. Ibid., 128.
59. Wilson 1830, 870.
60. Akenside *1845*, book 1, lines 259, 261.
61. Hazlitt, "On the Punishment of Death," in Hazlitt 1998, 9:15.
62. Ibid., 9:12.
63. Ibid., 9:8–9.
64. Ibid.
65. Pinch 1998, 413–28.
66. Hazlitt 1998, 9:13.
67. Ibid., 9:14.
68. Ibid.

CHAPTER 2
UNCERTAIN PROVIDENCE AND CERTAIN PUNISHMENT: HANNAH MORE

1. François Marmontel, "The Shepherdess of the Alps," in Hunt 1802, 4:148.
2. Edgeworth and Edgeworth 1823, 147. This passage suggests an account of the Edgeworths' work that differs from Alan Richardson's view of the emphasis on "domestic regulation" in *Literature, Education, and Romanticism: Reading as Social Practice, 1780–1832* (Cambridge: Cambridge University Press, 1994), 185.
3. See, for instance, Catherine Grace Godwin's *Cousin Kate; or, The Punishment of Pride: A Tale* (London: John W. Parker, 1836).
4. [Hannah More], *Strictures on the Modern System of Female Education* (1799), 1:147.
5. Barbauld 1977, 36, vii.

6. Trimmer 1786, 68–69.
7. Gatrell 1994, 125, 380.
8. More 1799, 1:201.
9. Poovey 1984, 9–10; Elizabeth Jay, *The Religion of the Heart: Anglican Evangelicalism and the Nineteenth-Century Novel* (Oxford: Clarendon Press, 1979), 131–48; Elizabeth Kowaleski-Wallace, *Hannah More, Maria Edgeworth, and Patriarchal Complicity* (New York: Oxford University Press, 1991), 64.
10. Mellor 2000, 24. See also Elliott 2002, 54–80; Mitzi Myers, "Hannah More's Tracts for the Times: Social Fiction and Female Ideology," in *Fetter'd or Free? British Women Novelists, 1670–1815*, ed. Mary Anne Schonfield and Cecilia Macheski (Athens: Ohio University Press, 1986), 264–84.
11. Christine L. Krueger, *The Reader's Repentance: Women Preachers, Women Writers, and Nineteenth-Century Social Discourse* (Chicago: University of Chicago Press, 1992), 94–124.
12. Jones 1990, 47.
13. Ibid., 105.
14. Janet Todd, *A Wollstonecraft Anthology* (Bloomington: Indiana University Press, 1977), 30, 34, 37.
15. Haywood 1745, 1:53.
16. Ibid., 1:57.
17. Jones 1990, 11.
18. More 1830, 4:161. All further references to the *Tracts* are from this edition and are noted by volume and page number in parentheses, unless stated otherwise.
19. Gallagher 1985, 36–61.
20. [More] 1800, 270.
21. Ibid., 284.
22. Although Gary Kelly takes note of such figures, he focuses less on tensions and more on their ability to resolve the "chanciness of life" with personal responsibility. See Kelly, "Revolution, Reaction, and the Expropriation of Popular Culture: Hannah More's Cheap Repository," *Man and Nature* 6 (1987): 153.
23. Weber 1930, 155–83.
24. More 1799, 1:xviii. All further references to this work are from this edition and are noted by volume and page number in parentheses.
25. [More], *Coelebs in Search of a Wife: Comprehending Observations on Domestic Habits and Manners, Religion and Morals* (1808), 1:18. All further references to the novel are from this edition and are noted by volume and page number in parentheses.
26. Gilmartin 2003, 493–50.
27. Elliot 2002, 55.
28. Fish 1972, 229. Also relevant here is Pierre Bourdieu's distinction between habitus and juridical code in *Outline of a Theory of Practice*, trans. Richard Nice (Cambridge: Cambridge University Press, 1977), 17.
29. McKeon 1987, 297.
30. For a discussion of rounded character in the Romantic period, see Lynch 1998, 123–63.

CHAPTER 3
"SHUDDERING O'ER THE GRAVE": WORDSWORTH, POETRY, AND THE PUNISHMENT OF DEATH

1. Bataille 1973, 27.
2. Welsford 1966, 25.
3. Janowitz 1990, 233. See also Janowitz, *England's Ruins: Poetic Purpose and the National Landscape* (Cambridge: Basil Blackwell, 1990), 92–144.
4. Stephen Gill, "'Adventures on Salisbury Plain' and Wordsworth's Poetry of Protest, 1795–97," *Studies in Romanticism* 11 (1972): 62.
5. Manning 1990, 291.
6. All quotations from the sonnets are from Wordsworth, *Sonnet Series and Itinerary Poems* (2004), and are noted by sonnet number.
7. Stephen Gill, introduction to *Wordsworth* 1975, 7. All further references to the Salisbury Plain poems are noted by line number in parentheses.
8. My account here leans on the version of allegory in Alex Preminger and T.V.F. Brogan, eds., *The New Princeton Encyclopedia of Poetry and Poetics* (Princeton: Princeton University Press, 1993), s.v. "allegory."
9. Wordsworth carries the figure into *Guilt and Sorrow*, only substituting "ravenous plague" for "fiery fever."
10. Andrea Henderson, "A Tale Told to Be Forgotten: Enlightenment, Revolution, and the Poet in 'Salisbury Plain,'" *Studies in Romanticism* 30 (1991): 82.
11. Steven Knapp points out Wordsworth's approval for this specific form of personification—observed in Spenser—in *Personification and the Sublime: Milton to Coleridge* (Cambridge, Mass.: Harvard University Press, 1985), 105–6.
12. Martin Jay, *Downcast Eyes: The Denigration of Vision in Twentieth-Century French Thought* (Berkeley: University of California Press, 1993).
13. Dworkin 1986, 171.
14. Swann 1988, 811–34; Kurt Fosso, "The Politics of Genre in Wordsworth's Salisbury Plain," *New Literary History* 30 (1990): 172.
15. Beccaria 1986, 47.
16. Wordsworth, *The Prelude* 9.110. All quotations from *The Prelude* are from Wordsworth 1991, and are noted by book and line number in parentheses.
17. Scarry *1985*, 69.
18. I differ here from James Chandler's view that the primary enemy in *Salisbury Plain* is "Superstition": "It is by defeating superstitious error that the hero of truth defeats oppression. Superstition *is* the deepest base of the oppressor's dungeon." See Chandler 1984, 137.
19. Edmund Spenser, *The Faerie Queen* (1978), 5.1.12, 5.4.1. I am grateful to Mary Beth Rose for suggesting the relevance of Spenser's Book 5 to Wordsworth's poem.
20. Shklar 1998, 11. A somewhat different, but still relevant account of fear (as a marker of injustice) can be found in Dumm 1990, 29–57.
21. See, for instance, John Rieder's "Civic Virtue and Social Class at the Scene of Execution: Wordsworth's Salisbury Plain Poems," *Studies in Romanticism* 30 (1991): 325–43.
22. Radzinowicz 1948, 1:206–7, 215.

23. Godwin 1985, 635. Further references are from this edition and are noted parenthetically in the text by page number.
24. Marilyn Butler, *Romantics, Rebels, and Reactionaries: English Literature and Its Background, 1760–1830* (Oxford: Oxford University Press, 1981), 79.
25. Cooper 1974, 3, 55.
26. Stephen Gill, *William Wordsworth: A Life* (Oxford: Oxford University Press, 1989), 91.
27. Akenside *1845*, 1:564–66.
28. Wordsworth to Henry Taylor, 8 November 1841, in Wordsworth 1993, 258n.
29. [Taylor] 1841, 51.
30. Wordsworth to Henry Taylor, 19 November 1841, in Wordsworth 1993, 262.
31. Wordsworth to Henry Taylor, 17 January 1842, in Wordsworth 1993, 284.
32. Setzer 1996, 428.
33. Francis Bacon, *Essays, Advancement of Learning, New Atlantis, and Other Pieces*, ed. Richard Foster Jones (New York: Odyssey Press, 1937), 13–14.
34. Wordsworth 1867, 4.
35. Setzer 1996, 439.
36. Galperin 1989, 238, 242.
37. [Taylor] 1841, 43–45.
38. Burke 1968a, 47.
39. Seraphia D. Leyda mentions the death-penalty reformers, but does not go further than to suggest that Wordsworth was opposed to their views; see Leyda 1983, 48–53.
40. *Hansard Parliamentary Debates*, 3d ser., vol. 52 (1840), cols. 916, 922.
41. Pinch 1996, 51–71.

CHAPTER 4
JANE AUSTEN, THE ROMANTIC NOVEL, AND THE IMPORTANCE OF BEING WRONG

1. Jane Austen, *Mansfield Park* (1996a), 306. Further references are from this edition and are noted parenthetically in the text by page number.
2. *Oxford English Dictionary*, 2d ed., s.v. "pain."
3. I adopt the phrase from Herbert Morris, "Persons and Punishment," in Baird and Rosenbaum 1995, 69; Butler 1997, 63.
4. Foucault 1977, 242.
5. Butler 1975, 219–49.
6. Tanner 1986, 17. Clara Tuite's account of the novel's support of "the hierarchical relations of the landed estate" agrees in many respects with Tanner's (2002, 106).
7. Said 1993, 87.
8. Trumpener 1997, 182.
9. *Oxford English Dictionary*, 2d ed., s.v. "disposition."
10. Because of this kind of paradoxical thinking that I attribute to Austen, the subject of this chapter differs from—even while it shares some concerns with—David Southward's account of "embarrassment" in Austen's fiction; for him, embarrassment yields a kind of attention to propriety, or "impression management."

See David Southward, "Jane Austen and the Riches of Embarrassment," in *Studies in English Literature* 36 (Autumn 1996): 775–82.

11. Austin 1962, 104.

12. Jane Austen to Cassandra Austen, 24 January 1809, in Le Faye 1995, 170.

13. Samuel Richardson, *Pamela or, Virtue Rewarded* (1971), 164. Further references are from this edition and are noted parenthetically in the text by page number.

14. Armstrong 1987, 113.

15. Elizabeth Inchbald, *A Simple Story* (1967), 315. The quotation is from Rushbrook's tutor, Mr. Sandford.

16. Austen 1996a, 309.

17. Agamben 1993, 68.9.

18. Austen 1996a, 395n.

19. I adopt the terms in this formulation from Bernard Williams: see Williams 199 5, 35–45; and "Internal and External Reasons," in *Williams* 1981, 101–13.

20. Bersani 1976, 76–77.

21. Jonathan Wordsworth, introduction to August von Kotzebue, *Lovers' Vows*, adapted by Elizabeth Inchbald (1798; reprint, 1990). Further references to the play are from this edition and are noted parenthetically by page number.

22. Tanner 1986, 157.

23. David Marshall, "True Acting and the Language of Real Feeling: *Mansfield Park*," *Yale Journal of Criticism* 3 (1989): 87–106.

24. See, for instance, Elizabeth's ability to be "mortified" by reading Darcy's letter, which is also "haughty," "all pride and insolence." Austen 1996b, 198–99.

25. Montagu 1830, 201.

26. On the relation between the eighteenth-century novel and criminal biography, see Davis 1996, 123–37.

27. Austen, *Sense and Sensibility* (1995), 317.

28. On the relationship between the actual and social death of slaves, see Patterson 1982.

29. The connection is reinforced by Fanny's questioning of Sir Thomas about the slave trade (165).

30. *Oxford English Dictionary*, 2d ed., s.v. "mortify."

31. Although William Galperin analyzes this incident, he concentrates primarily on the absence of direct reference to it rather than on the figurative or formal level of response with which I am primarily concerned here. See Galperin 2003, 17–44.

32. Sir Frank Douglas MacKinnon, *Grand Larceny: Being the Trial of Jane Leigh Perrot, Aunt of Jane Austen* (London: Oxford University Press, 1937), 32–50.

33. My reading of the novel is the reverse of Miller's (2003, 39, 50). He claims that it is Mary Crawford who most clearly resembles Austen's style, and this is because he insists that "censure" signals the loss of style.

34. Bender 1987, 223.

35. Ferguson 2000, 165.

36. Austen 1996b, 18.

37. Von Kotzebue 1990, 23–24.

38. Trilling 1950, 210.

39. Johnson 1988, 112.

40. Roland Barthes, *A Lover's Discourse: Fragments*, trans. Richard Howard (New York: Hill and Wang, 1978), 118.

41. Austen, *Sense and Sensibility* (1995), 310; *Pride and Prejudice* (1996b), 264, 276, 93.

42. Austen, *Emma* (1966), 401.

43. Jane Austen to Francis Austen, 26 July 1809, in Le Faye 1995, 178.

44. See Kathryn Sutherland, introduction to Austen, *Mansfield Park* (1996a), xxvi–xxvii. Sutherland sees the discussion of reading as a conflict between the more conservative morality and tastes of Fanny, William, and Edmund, and the "metropolitan" morality and tastes of the Crawfords (xxvi).

45. Radcliffe 1968, 365.

46. Hogg 1990, 139, 137.

47. Mary Shelley, *Frankenstein*, in Fairclough 1968, 354. Further references to the novel are from this edition and are noted parenthetically by page number.

48. Scott 1932, 1:371. All further references to *The Waverly Novels* are from this edition and are noted parenthetically by volume and page number.

49. Peter Garside discusses the influence of "philosophical" history on Scott in "Scott and the 'Philosophical' Historians," *Journal of the History of Ideas* 36 (1975): 497–512. Scott's emphasis on progress is often neglected in accounts of his view of history. Ina Ferris, for instance, sees history defined by such terms as fact, truth, and nature, in *The Achievement of Literary Authority: Gender, History, and the Waverly Novels* (Ithaca, N.Y.: Cornell University Press, 1991), 79–104.

50. Jacques Derrida, "The Century and the Pardon," *Le monde des débats* (http://fixion.systes.net//pardonEng.htm).

51. Bruce Biederwell (1992, 20) sees Talbot and Scott as less complicated advocates of the death penalty.

52. Graham McMaster, *Scott and Society* (Cambridge: Cambridge University Press, 1981), 81.

53. Giorgio Agamben, *State of Exception*, trans. Kevin Attell (Chicago: University of Chicago Press, 2005). I refer to Agamben's view of the "state of exception" as a "suspension of the juridical order," in opposition to Scott's view of exceptions as an instance of juridical order itself (4).

54. Scott *1891*, 633, 641.

55. See, in Scott's *Journal* (1891), the account of the farmer's wife (355), or the tale of Malcom Gillespie (482).

56. Scott *1891*, 355.

57. Ibid., 541.

58. John Lawrence, *A History of Capital Punishment* (New York: Citadel Press, 1963), 30.

CHAPTER 5
COLERIDGE, SHELLEY, AND THE POETICS OF CONSCIENCE

1. Kames, of course, would only have known public executions; these were not ended until 1868.

2. Henry Home, Lord Kames, *Essays on the Principles of Morality and Natural Religion, in Two Parts* (1751), 1–31. All further references to this work are to this edition and are noted by page number in parentheses.

3. Potter 1969, 78–79.

4. Smith 2000, 120.

5. Nietzsche 1969, 57–96; Smith 2000, 130.

6. Hobbes 1968, 132; Pufendorf 2003, 29. Pufendorf's account is similar to Helvetius's in *De L'Esprit* (1970, 134). For a related account of conscience, focusing primarily on Hobbes, see Orlie 1997, 98. My account, moreover, gives a more complex view of conscience than that put forward in Judith Butler's more conservative view of conscience as a private form of subjection prior to any legal enforcement, as argued throughout *The Psychic Life of Power* (1997, 63–82, 106–31).

7. This negotiation, I believe, connects the work I do in this chapter, by way of a specific instance, to James Chandler's interest in casuistry in Chandler 1998.

8. Joseph Fawcett, "Elegy III: The Miseries of a Guilty Mind," in *Fawcett 1798*, 17–18.

9. Ibid., 21.

10. George Crabbe, *The Borough*, in Crabbe 1991, Letter 21, line 100.

11. This chapter therefore follows through on the promising suggestion that Seamus Deane makes about Shelley's "obsession with conscience and remorse" (Deane 1988, 112), although my interpretation turns out to be the opposite of his.

12. All quotations from Coleridge's poetic and dramatic writings are taken from *Coleridge's Poetical Works* (1912). They are noted parenthetically by act and line number, or by line when appropriate.

13. Jewett 1997, 99–130.

14. Thus, although I claim that the play counters violent punishments, I tend to see it as less radical than Marjean Purinton does in "The English Pamphlet War of the 1790s and Coleridge's Osorio," in *British Romantic Drama: Historical and Critical Essays*, ed. Terence Allan Hoagwood and Daniel P. Watkins (Madison, N.J.: Fairleigh Dickinson University Press, 1998), 159–81.

15. Although my view of remorse as a "passion" is less psychological than Adela Pinch's account of mimetically repeated affect, our views coincide insofar as I understand emotion to be prompted by visible and exchangeable text. See Pinch 1996, 1–50.

16. *Oxford English Dictionary*, 2d ed., s.v. "pang."

17. In this sense, Coleridge follows Kant's example in his account of moral law in *The Critique of Practical Reason* (1956). See particularly Kant's account of the man who controls his passion when he is led to imagine a "gallows" in front of the house where he would satisfy it, and "where he would be hanged immediately after gratifying his lust" (30).

18. Kenneth Burke, *The Philosophy of Literary Form: Studies in Symbolic Action* (New York: Vintage, 1957), 3–117. Burke's reference point is actually *Remorse*, but his quotations and commentary apply also to the earlier version of the work.

19. Coleridge, *Lectures 1795 On Politics and Religion*, ed. Lewis Patton and Peter Mann (Princeton: Princeton University Press, 1971), 33–42. I am thus in-

sisting on Coleridge's representation of a movement (even while it is made more complex in this paragraph) from one regime of punishment to another; this gives a different view of the play than does Reeve Parker, who has documented the play's many ironic doublings and repetitions. See Parker, "Osorio's Dark Employments: Tricking Out Coleridgean Tragedy," *Studies in Romanticism* (1994): 119–60.

20. Holmes 1998, 377.

21. I am introducing some complication into Julie Carlson's claim (1994, 94–133) that Coleridge leaves action up to women and reflection up to men.

22. Coleridge to Robert Southey, 8 February 1813, in Coleridge 1895, 2:607.

23. This, at least, is Hamlet's aim. It seems to me that Stephen Orgel's skeptical account of the scene, in which he claims that Claudius "refuses" this confession, is somewhat of an overstatement. See Orgel, "The Play of Conscience," in *Performativity and Peformance*, ed. Andres Parker and Eve Kosofsky Sedgwick (New York: Routledge, 1995), 146.

24. Coleridge 1912, 2:555n.

25. Ibid., 2:564n.

26. Carlson 1994, 103.

27. Percy Bysshe Shelley, "Essay on the Punishment of Death," in Shelley 1988, 156. All further references to the prose works, unless noted otherwise, are from this edition and are cited parenthetically by page number.

28. In fact, the wisdom Socrates demonstrates by accepting death is itself taken to contradict the charges of folly and corruption brought against him. Plato 1961, 15.

29. Shelley 1977, 242. All further references to Shelley's poetry are from this edition and are cited by line number in parentheses.

30. Percy Bysshe Shelley, *The Cenci*, in Shelley 1977, 3.1.166, 204.

31. Potter 1969, 53.

32. See also Shelley, "Essay on a Future State," in Shelley 1988, 176.

33. Some prominent examples of scholarship on this aspect of Shelley's work include Cronin 1986; Frances Ferguson, "Shelley's Mont Blanc: What the Mountain Said," in *Romanticism and Language*, ed. Arden Reed (London: Methuen, 1984), 202–14; Ulmer 1990.

34. This is supported by Shelley's short essay "On Love" (not published until 1828, after the poet's death), which connects love to emotions of both "hope" and "fear." Shelley 1988, 169–71.

35. Bromwich 2002, 239. Bromwich's argument echoes Seamus Deane's view of Shelley's resistance to revenge and guilt (1988, 95–129).

36. Shelley, *The Triumph of Life*, in Shelley 1977, lines 47–49. All further references to the poems are from this edition and are noted parenthetically by line number.

37. Warner 1999, 24–33.

38. Martha Nussbaum, *Upheavals of Thought: The Intelligence of Emotions* (Cambridge: Cambridge University Press, 2001), 344.

39. Sartre 1956, 288.

40. Williams 1993, 82, 84.

41. My account thus also differs from Eve Kosofsky Sedgwick's "performative" account of shame in *Touching Feeling: Affect, Pedagogy, Performativity* (Durham, N.C.: Duke University Press, 2003), 35–65.

42. Richard Holmes describes the situation that gave rise to the poem as follows: "The almost complete failure of feeling between Shelley and Mary; and the increasing strain of the friendship with Byron." The fact that Shelley had no reason to blame himself for his deteriorating ties with Byron would support my basic claim that the poem is not about coming to terms with an actual situation; the shame is less important in terms of its origin than in terms of its poetic effects. Holmes, *Shelley: The Pursuit* (London: Quartet Books, 1976), 699.

43. Shelley 1977, 447n.

44. Gilles Deleuze, "Coldness and Cruelty," in Deleuze 1991, 55. See also Deleuze's and Felix Guattari's comments on the masochist's appropriation and application of an artificially constructed "assemblage" of codes and regulations, in *A Thousand Plateaus*, trans. Brian Massumi (Minneapolis: University of Minnesota Press, 1987), 149–66. Although Shelley uses his poems to shame others, Deleuze's account of the idealism in masochism suggests how inappropriate it would be to call this shift "sadistic."

45. Rainer Maria Rilke, *Sonnets to Orpheus* 1.8, in Rilke 1984, 237.

46. Wheatley 1999, 8, 152.

47. Ricks 1984.

48. I provide a different view here from Steven E. Jones's account of the Augustan roots of Shelley's works (1994, 1–14).

49. Wheatley 1999, 152.

50. Weisman 1994, 160–61.

51. See especially books 5 and 6. Lucretius 1965.

52. Petrarch 1962, 56–57.

53. Dart 1999, 52. Dart's account gives a more convincing context in which to read Shelley than Edward Duffy's more exclusive attention to Rousseau's vanity and mental infirmity (1979).

54. See, for instance, Wang 1996, 37–143.

55. Rousseau 1954, 29.

56. Shelley 1988, 155.

57 Volney 1979, 1:14, 41, 40.

CHAPTER 6
THE TWO ABOLITIONS

1. A loose connection on the grounds of humanitarian interest has been noticed before; see, for instance, Robert Jay Lifton and Greg Mitchell, *Who Owns Death? Capital Punishment, the American Conscience, and the End of Executions* (New York: HarperCollins, 2000), 33.

2. Foucault 1977, 131.

3. Banner 2002, 112–43.

4. Anstey 1975; Turley 1991.

5. Drescher 1987; Williams 1944.

6. Davis 1999. For a similarly nuanced view of multiple motivations, see Robin Blackburn, *The Overthrow of Colonial Slavery, 1776–1848* (London: Verso, 1988).

7. Davis 1999. The counterintuitive gesture of reading postmodernism into antislavery has been popular mostly in literary studies. See, for instance, Debbie Lee's reading of antislavery through the framework of phenomenology and deconstruction, from Husserl and Levinas to Spivak and Taylor (2002, 37).

8. Davis 1999, 414–15.

9. Ibid., 357, 452.

10. Lee 2002, 42. See also Adam Lively, *Masks: Blackness, Race, and the Imagination* (Oxford: Oxford University Press, 2000); Wood 2002.

11. Clarkson 1822, 9–10.

12. Ibid., 31.

13. Sir James Mackintosh, "Speech on Moving for a Committee to Inquire into the State of the Criminal Law," in Mackintosh 1846, 3:387.

14. Leigh Hunt, "Military Torture," in *Shelley-Leigh Hunt: How Friendship Made History*, ed. R. Brimley Johnson (London: Ingpen and Grant, 1928), 131.

15. Midlake 1851, 23.

16. Olyffe 1731, 13.

17. Debates about transportation are discussed in Devereaux 1999, 405–33.

18. For a more thorough account of the relationship between slavery and colonial disease, see Bewell 1999, 66–130.

19. [Henry Brougham] 1813, 17.

20. [Sydney Smith] 1803, 32.

21. Montagu 1830, 51.

22. [Anonymous], *The Poor Unhappy Transported Felon's Sorrowful Account* (n.d.), 5.

23. Grenville 1840, 36.

24. *Ibid.*, 36. By the middle of the nineteenth century, reformers describe criminals as savages that will be made more savage by transportation, which may explain why, as Elaine Hadley notes, "an argument in favor of emigration suddenly turns into an argument against emigration." Hadley, "Natives in a Strange Land: The Philanthropic Discourse of Juvenile Emigration in Mid-Nineteenth-Century England," *Victorian Studies* (1990): 432.

25. Mackintosh, "Speech on Mr. Brougham's Motion for an Address to the Crown," in Mackintosh 1846, 3:411.

26. *Substance of the Speeches of S. Lushington, LLD and J. Sydney Taylor, AM* (Edinburgh: W. Oliphant, n.d.), 27.

27. Clarkson 1822, 4–5.

28. John Stedman, *Narrative of a Five Years' Expedition against the Revolted Negroes of Surinam* (Amherst: University of Massachusetts Press, 1972), 18.

29. Honour 1976.

30. See, for instance, *The Authentic Trial of Joseph Wall* (London: J. Roach, n.d.), which asserts that "black men," rather than men of Wall's regiment, flogged a man to death.

31. Hartman 1997, 122.

32. Wilberforce 1970, 26.

33. Patterson 1982, 17–34.
34. Locke 1960, 283–85.
35. Ramsay 1784, 85–86.
36. Clarkson 1786, 149.
37. Joan Dayan, "Code of Law and Bodies of Color," *New Literary History* 26 (1995): 287.
38. Diana Paton, "Punishment, Crime, and the Bodies of Slaves in Eighteenth-Century Jamaica," *Journal of Social History* 34 (2001): 926–27.
39. Wilberforce 1970, 8–10.
40. Ibid., 44.
41. Marcus Wood, *Blind Memory: Visual Representations of Slavery in England and America* (London: Routledge, 2000), 160–61.
42. *Hansard Parliamentary Debates*, 1st ser. 17 (1810), col. 678.
43. Clarkson 1786, 163.
44. Ramsay 1784, 63.
45. Ibid., 105, 282.
46. Hugh Mulligan, "The Slave, An American Ecologue," in Mulligan 1788, lines 121, 147, 122.
47. *Hansard Parliamentary Debates*, 1st ser. 17 (1810), cols. 672–73.
48. Benezet 1968, 110, 112.
49. Scott 1996, 10. All further references to this work are to this edition and are noted by page number in parentheses. It is entirely likely that Scott's work influenced Edgeworth, whose "Grateful Negro" explores similar themes.
50. Ferguson 1992, 94.
51. Ellis 1996, 87–128.
52. William Cowper, *The Poems of William Cowper* (1931). All references to the poems are from this edition and are quoted by line number in parentheses.
53. Southey 1840, 2:56, 58.
54. Ibid., 2:56; Thomas Day, "The Dying Negro," in *The Works of the British Poets*, ed. Thomas Park, 36 vols. (London: John Sharpe, 1828), 18:12.
55. Adam Potkay, "Olaudah Equiano and the Art of Spiritual Autobiography," *Eighteenth-Century Studies* 27 (1994): 689.
56. Olaudah Equiano, *The Interesting Narrative* (1995), 95. All further references to this work are from this edition and are noted parenthetically by page number.
57. By stressing the extent to which Equiano's economic actions are circumscribed by legalism, I depart here from Houston Baker's account of Equiano's bourgeois individualism, and Joel Fichtelberg's critique and recuperation of that account. See Baker, *Blues, Ideology, and Afro-American Literature: A Vernacular Theory* (Chicago: University of Chicago Press, 1984), 35; Joseph Fichtelberg, "Words between Worlds: The Economy of Equiano's Narrative," *American Literary History* 5 (1993): 474–76.
58. Equiano invokes a similar argument to defuse violent conflict earlier in the narrative (1995, 208).
59. Aravamudan 1999, 233–88; Thomas 2000, 6.
60. McBride 2001, 120.

61. John Wesley, "The Scripture Way of Salvation," in *English Spirituality in the Age of Wesley*, ed. David Lyle Jeffrey (Grand Rapids, Mich.: William B. Eerdmans, 1987), 211, 210.

62. Wesley, "Thoughts upon Slavery," in *Views of American Slavery, Taken a Century Ago* (Philadelphia: Society for the Diffusion of Religious and Useful Knowledge, 1858), 93–94.

63. Ibid., 97.

64. For additional discussion of religion and alterations in penal law, see Randall McGowen, "'He Beareth Not the Sword in Vain': Religion and the Criminal Law in Eighteenth-Century England," *Eighteenth-Century Studies* 21 (1987–88): 192–211.

65. See, for instance, John Rawls, "The Law of Peoples," in *John Rawls: Collected Papers* (Cambridge, Mass.: Harvard University Press, 1999), 529–64.

CODA
THE CULTURE OF THE DEATH PENALTY

1. George Theodore Wilkinson, *The Newgate Calendar* (London: Sphere Books, 1991), 291, 294.

2. Thomas Hood, *Poetical Works* (New York: A. L. Burt, n.d.), lines 199, 193, 194.

3. Lifton and Mitchell 2000.

4. Stephen B. Bright, "Why the United States Will Join the Rest of the World in Abandoning Capital Punishment," in Bedau and Cassell 2004, 152. See also Dwight Conquergood's view of the death penalty as ritual in "Lethal Theatre" (2002).

5. For some typical arguments in this vein, see the essays in Austin Sarat, ed., *The Killing State: Capital Punishment in Law, Politics, and Culture* (New York: Oxford University Press, 1999), particularly Peter Fitzpatrick, "'Always More to Do': Capital Punishment and the (De)Composition of Law," 117–36.

6. Hugo Bedau's views are slightly different from these arguments; he privileges human utility simply as a general principle of lenience: a punishment is justified only if it imposes a "minimal invasion" upon the human subject. But Bedau's view cannot counter the argument that some crimes might require no less an "invasion" than death. See Hugo Adam Bedau, *Death Is Different: Studies in the Morality, Law, and Politics of Capital Punishment* (Boston: Northeastern University Press, 1987), 92–128.

7. Alex Kozinski, "Tinkering with Death," in Bedau and Cassell 2004, 14.

8. For a particularly incisive critique of the "myth" of satisfaction provided by the death penalty, a myth contradicted by actual experiences of murder victims' families, see Judith W. Kay, *Murdering Myths: The Story Behind the Death Penalty* (Lanham, Md.: Rowman and Littlefield, 2005), 1–15.

9. See Scott Turow, *Ultimate Punishment: A Lawyer's Reflections on Dealing with the Death Penalty* (New York: Farrar, Straus and Giroux, 2003). This is why Turow's argument is founded on a contradiction: voting against retention of the death penalty in Illinois, he nevertheless claims, "I admit I am still attracted to a

death penalty that would be available for the crimes of unimaginable dimensions like [John Wayne] Gacy's" (114–15).

10. I take issue with Lifton and Mitchell's characterization of such films as straightforward stories about lawyers criticizing the death penalty (2000, 112).

11. *The Life of David Gale*, 35 mm, 130 min., Universal Pictures, Universal City, 2003.

12. *The Chamber*, 35 mm, 113 min., Universal Pictures, Universal City, 1996.

13. *Stephen King's The Green Mile*, 35 mm, 188 min., Warner Brothers, Burbank, 1999.

14. Austin Sarat, *When the State Kills: Capital Punishment and the American Condition* (Princeton: Princeton University Press, 2001), 232.

15. Donald A. Cabana, *Death at Midnight: The Confession of an Executioner* (Boston: Northeastern University Press, 1996), 187.

16. Robert Johnson, *Death Work: A Study of the Modern Execution Process*, 2d ed. (Belmont, Calif.: Wadsworth, 1998), 63.

17. *Dead Man Walking*, 35 mm, 122 min., Working Title Films, London, 1995. See also Sister Helen Prejean's book on which the film is based, *Dead Man Walking* (New York: Vintage, 1994). The book displays similar tensions between a radical opposition to the death penalty and a commitment to working within the existing boundaries of "remedial legal help" (32).

18. *Identity*, 35 mm, 90 min., Columbia Pictures, New York, 2003.

19. Ruth Wilson Gilmore, "Globalisation and U.S. Prison Growth: From Military Keynesianism to Post-Keynesian Militarism," *Race and Class* 40 (1998–99): 171–88.

20. Angela Y. Davis, *Are Prisons Obsolete?* (New York: Seven Stories Press, 2003), 107, 112.

Selected Bibliography

Agamben, Giorgio. 1993. *Coming Community.* Trans. Michael Hardt. Minneapolis: University of Minnesota Press.
———. 1998. *Homo Sacer: Sovereign Power and Bare Life.* Trans. Daniel Heller-Roazen. Stanford: Stanford University Press.
Akenside, Mark. 1845. *Pleasures of the Imagination.* London: Bell and Daldy. (Original ed. 1744.)
Alexander, Larry, and Emily Sherwin. 2001. *The Rule of Rules: Morality, Rules, and the Dilemmas of Law.* Durham, N.C.: Duke University Press.
[Anonymous.] 1830. *Anti-Draco, or Reasons for Abolishing the Punishment of Death in Cases of Forgery.* 2d ed. London: James Ridgeway.
Anstey, Roger. 1975. *The Atlantic Slave Trade and British Abolition, 1760–1810.* London: Macmillan.
Aravamudan, Srinivas. 1999. *Tropicopolitans: Colonialism and Agency, 1688–1804.* Durham, N.C.: Duke University Press.
Armstrong, Nancy. 1987. *Desire and Domestic Fiction: A Political History of the Novel.* New York: Oxford University Press.
Austen, Jane. 1966. *Emma.* Ed. Ronald Blythe. Harmondsworth: Penguin.
———. 1995. *Sense and Sensibility.* Ed. Ros Ballaster. Harmondsworth: Penguin.
———. 1996a. *Mansfield Park.* Ed. Kathryn Sutherland. Harmondsworth: Penguin.
———. 1996b. *Pride and Prejudice.* Ed. Vivien Jones. Harmondsworth: Penguin.
Austin, J. L. 1962. *Sense and Sensibilia.* Oxford: Oxford University Press.
Baird, Robert, and Stuart E. Rosenbaum, eds. 1995. *Punishment and the Death Penalty: The Current Debate.* Amherst, N.Y.: Prometheus Books.
Banner, Stuart. 2002. *The Death Penalty: An American History.* Cambridge, Mass.: Harvard University Press.
Barbauld, Anna Laetitia. 1977. *Hymns in Prose for Children.* New York: Garland. (Original ed. 1781.)
Bataille, Georges. 1973. *Literature and Evil.* Trans. Alastair Hamilton. London: Marion Boyars.
Beccaria, Cesare. 1986. *On Crimes and Punishments.* Trans. David Young. Indianapolis: Hackett.
Bedau, Hugo Adam, and Paul G. Cassell, eds. 2004. *Debating the Death Penalty: Should America Have Capital Punishment? The Experts on Both Sides Make Their Best Case.* New York: Oxford University Press.
Beier, Al, David Cannadinne, and James M. Rosenheim, eds. 1989. *The First Modern Society.* Cambridge: Cambridge University Press.
Bender, John. 1987. *Imagining the Penitentiary: Fiction and the Architecture of Mind in Eighteenth-Century England.* Chicago: University of Chicago Press.

Benezet, Anthony. 1968. *Some Historical Account of Guinea . . . With an Inquiry into the Rise and Progress of the Slave Trade*. London: Frank Cass. (Original ed. 1771.)

Bentham, Jeremy. 1802. *Traités de legislation*. Ed. Etienne Dumont. 3 vols. Paris: Bossange, Masson, et Besson. (Abbreviated *TL*.)

———. 1830. *The Rationale of Punishment*. London: Robert Heward. (Abbreviated *RP*.)

———. 1948. *An Introduction to the Principles of Morals and Legislation*. New York: Hafner. (Abbreviated *PML*.)

Bersani, Leo. 1976. *A Future for Astyanax: Character and Desire in Literature*. Boston: Little, Brown.

Bewell, Alan. 1999. *Romanticism and Colonial Disease*. Baltimore: The Johns Hopkins University Press.

Biederwell, Bruce. 1992. *Power and Punishment in Scott's Novels*. Athens: University of Georgia Press.

Blackstone, William. 1979. *Commentaries on the Laws of England*. 4 vols. Chicago: University of Chicago Press. (Original ed. 1765–69.)

Blake, William. 1977. *The Complete Poems*. Ed. Alicia Ostriker. Harmondsworth: Penguin.

Boswell, James. 1952. *Life of Johnson*. Ed. R. W. Chapman. Oxford: Oxford University Press.

Bromwich, David. 2002. "Love against Revenge in Shelley's *Prometheus*." *Philosophy and Literature* 26:239–59.

[Brougham, Henry]. 1813. Review of Jeremy Bentham, *Theorie des Peines et des Recompenses*. *Edinburgh Review* 43:1–31.

Burke, Edmund. 1894. *Works of the Right Honourable Edmund Burke*. 12 vols. Boston: Little, Brown. (Abbreviated *EBW*.)

———. 1968a. *A Philosophical Enquiry into the Origin of Our Ideas of the Sublime and Beautiful*. Ed. James T. Boulton. Notre Dame, Ind.: University of Notre Dame Press.

———. 1968b. *Reflections on the Revolution in France*. Ed. Conor Cruise O'Brien. Harmondsworth: Penguin.

Butler, Judith. 1997. *The Psychic Life of Power: Theories in Subjection*. Stanford: Stanford University Press.

Butler, Marilyn. 1975. *Jane Austen and the War of Ideas*. Oxford: Clarendon.

Buxton, Thomas Fawell. 1818. *An Inquiry, Whether Crime and Misery Are Produced or Prevented, By Our Present System of Prison Discipline*. London: John and Arthur.

Byron, George Gordon, Lord. 1970. *Poetical Works*. Ed. John Jump. Oxford: Oxford University Press.

———. 1991. *Complete Miscellaneous Prose*. Ed. Andrew Nicholson. Oxford: Oxford University Press.

Canuel, Mark. 2002. *Religion, Toleration, and British Writing, 1790–1830*. Cambridge: Cambridge University Press.

Carlson, Julie. 1994. *In the Theater of Romanticism: Coleridge, Nationalism, Women*. Cambridge: Cambridge University Press.

Chandler, James. 1998. *England in 1819: The Politics of Literary Culture and the Case of Romantic Historicism*. Chicago: University of Chicago Press.

Selected Bibliography

———. 1984. *Wordsworth's Second Nature.* Chicago: University of Chicago Press.
Clarkson, Thomas. 1786. *Essay on the Slavery and Commerce of the Human Species, Particularly the African.* London: J. Phillips.
———. 1822. *The Cries of Africa, To the Inhabitants of Europe.* London: Harvey and Darton.
Coleridge, Samuel Taylor. 1895. *Letters of Samuel Taylor Coleridge.* Ed. Ernest Hartley Coleridge. 2 vols. Boston: Houghton Mifflin.
———. 1912. *Poetical Works.* 2 vols. Ed. Ernest Hartley Coleridge. Oxford: Oxford University Press.
Conquergood, Dwight. 2002. "Lethal Theatre: Performance, Punishment, and the Death Penalty." *Theatre Journal* 54:339–67.
Cooper, David D. 1974. *The Lesson of the Scaffold: The Public Execution Controversy in Victorian England.* Athens: Ohio University Press.
Cowper, William. 1931. *Poems of William Cowper.* New York: J. M. Dent.
Crabbe, George. 1991. *Selected Poems.* Ed. Gavin Edwards. Harmondsworth: Penguin.
Cronin, Richard. 1986. *Shelley's Poetic Thoughts.* New York: St. Martin's.
Dagge, Henry. 1772. *Considerations on the Criminal Law.* London: T. Cadell.
Dart, Gregory. 1999. *Rousseau, Robespierre, and English Romanticism.* Cambridge: Cambridge University Press.
Davis, David Brion. 1999. *The Problem of Slavery in the Age of Revolution, 1770–1823.* New York: Oxford University Press. (Original ed. 1975.)
Davis, Lennard J. 1996. *Factual Fictions: The Origins of the English Novel.* Philadelphia: University of Pennsylvania Press. (Original ed. 1983.)
Dawes, M. 1782. *An Essay on Crimes and Punishments.* London: C. Dilly.
Deane, Seamus. 1988. *The French Revolution and Enlightenment in England, 1789–1832.* Cambridge, Mass.: Harvard University Press.
Deleuze, Gilles. 1991. *Masochism.* Trans. Jean McNeil. New York: Zone.
Derrida, Jacques. 1992. "The 'Mystical Foundation of Authority.'" In *Deconstruction and the Possibility of Justice,* ed. Drucilla Cornell, Michael Rosenfeld, and David Gray Carlson, 3–67. New York: Routledge.
Devereaux, Simon. 1999. "The Making of the Penitentiary Act, 1775–1779." *The Historical Journal* 42:405–33.
Drescher, Seymour. 1987. *Capitalism and Antislavery: British Mobilization in Comparative Perspective.* New York: Oxford.
Duffy, Edward. 1979. *Rousseau in England: The Context for Shelley's Critique of the Enlightenment.* Berkeley: University of California Press.
Dumm, Thomas. 1987. *Democracy and Punishment: Disciplinary Origins of the United States.* Madison: University of Wisconsin Press.
———. 1990. "Fear of Law." In *Studies in Law, Politics, and Society,* ed. Susan S. Silby and Austin Sarat, vol. 10. Greenwich, Conn.: JAI Press.
Dworkin, Ronald. 1986. *Law's Empire.* Cambridge, Mass.: Harvard University Press.
Eden, William. 1771. *Principles of Penal Law.* London: B. White and T. Cadell.
Edgeworth, Maria, and Richard Lovell Edgeworth. 1823. *Practical Education.* Boston: Samuel H. Parker.

Selected Bibliography

Elliott, Dorice. 2002. *The Angel Out of the House: Philanthropy and Gender in Nineteenth-Century England*. Charlottesville: University Press of Virginia.
Ellis, Markman. 1996. *The Politics of Sensibility: Race, Gender, and Commerce in the Sentimental Novel*. Cambridge: Cambridge University Press.
Engelmann, Stephen G. 2003. *Imagining Interest in Political Thought: Origins of Economic Rationality*. Durham, N.C.: Duke University Press.
Equiano, Olaudah. 1995. *The Interesting Narrative*. Ed. Vincent Carretta. Harmondsworth: Penguin.
Fairclough, Peter, ed. 1968. *Three Gothic Novels*. Introduced by Mario Praz. Harmondsworth: Penguin.
Fawcett, Joseph. 1798. *Poems, to Which are added Civilised War*. London: J. Johnson.
Ferguson, Frances. 1987. "Coleridge and the Deluded Reader." In Richard Machin and Christopher Norris, eds., *Post-Structuralist Readings of English Poetry*, 248–63. Cambridge: Cambridge University Press.
———. 2000. "Jane Austen, *Emma*, and the Impact of Form." *MLQ* 61:157–80.
———. 2004. *Pornography, The Theory: What Utilitarianism Did to Action*. Chicago: University of Chicago Press.
Ferguson, Moira. 1992. *Subject to Others: British Women Writers and Colonial Slavery, 1670–1834*. London: Routledge.
Fielding, Henry. 1988. *An Enquiry into the Causes of the Late Increase of Robbers and Other Writings*. Ed. Malvin R. Zirker. Middletown, Conn.: Wesleyan University Press.
Fish, Stanley. 1989. *Doing What Comes Naturally: Change, Rhetoric, and the Practice of Theory in Literary and Legal Studies*. Durham, N.C.: Duke University Press.
———. 1972. *Self-Consuming Artifacts*. Berkeley: University of California Press.
Foucault, Michel. 1977. *Discipline and Punish: The Birth of the Prison*. Trans. Alan Sheridan. New York: Vintage.
———. 2003. *"Society Must Be Defended": Lectures at the Collège de France, 1975–1976*. Trans. David Macey, ed. Mauro Bertani and Alessandro Fontana. New York: Picador.
Gallagher, Catherine. 1985. *The Industrial Reformation of English Fiction: Social Discourse and Narrative Form, 1832–67*. Chicago: University of Chicago Press.
Galperin, William. 1989. *Revision and Authority in Wordsworth: The Interpretation of a Career*. Philadelphia: University of Pennsylvania Press.
———. 2003. *The Historical Austen*. Philadelphia: University of Pennsylvania Press.
Gatrell, V.A.C. 1994. *The Hanging Tree: Execution and the English People, 1770–1868*. Oxford: Oxford University Press.
Gilmartin, Kevin. 2003. "'Study to Be Quiet': Hannah More and the Invention of Conservative Culture in Britain." *ELH* 70:493–540.
Girard, René. 1977. *Violence and the Sacred*. Trans. Patrick Gregory. Baltimore: The Johns Hopkins University Press.
Godwin, William. 1977. *Caleb Williams*. New York: W. W. Norton.
———. 1985. *Enquiry Concerning Political Justice*. Ed. Isaac Kramnick. Harmondsworth: Penguin.

Selected Bibliography

Goldsmith, Oliver. 1982. *The Vicar of Wakefield*. Ed. Stephen Coote. Harmondsworth: Penguin.
Greenblatt, Stephen, Walter Cohen, Jean E. Howard, and Katherine Eisaman Maus, eds. 1997. *The Norton Shakespeare*. New York: Norton.
Grenville, George, Lord. 1840. *On the Punishment of Death by Law*. London: James Ridgeway.
Hartman, Saidiya. 1997. *Scenes of Subjection: Terror, Slavery, and Self-Making in Nineteenth-Century America*. Oxford: Oxford University Press.
Hay, Douglas, Peter Linebaugh, John G. Rule, E. P. Thompson, and Cal Winslow, eds. 1975. *Albion's Fatal Tree: Crime and Society in Eighteenth-Century England*. New York: Pantheon Books.
Haywood, Eliza. 1745. *The Female Spectator*. 4 vols. London: T. Gardner.
Hazlitt, William. 1902–4. *Collected Works of William Hazlitt*. Ed. A. R. Waller and David Glover. 21 vols. London: J. M. Dent. (Abbreviated *HW*.)
———. 1998. *The Selected Writings of William Hazlitt*. Ed. Duncan Wu. 9 vols. London: Pickering and Chatto.
Helvetius. 1970. *De L'Esprit*. New York: Burt Franklin.
Hobbes, Thomas. 1968. *Leviathan*. Ed. C. B. Macpherson. Harmondsworth: Penguin. (Original ed. 1651.)
Hogg, James. 1990. *The Private Memoirs and Confessions of a Justified Sinner*. Ed. John Carey. Oxford: Oxford University Press. (Original ed. 1824.)
Holmes, Richard. 1998. *Coleridge: Darker Reflections, 1804–1834*. New York: Pantheon.
Home, Henry, Lord Kames. 1751. *Essays on the Principles of Morality and Natural Religion, in Two Parts*. Edinburgh: R. Fleming.
Honour, Hugh. 1976. *The Image of the Black in Western Art*. Vol. 4. New York: W. Morrow.
Hunt, Leigh. 1802. *Classic Tales, Serious and Lively*. 5 vols. London: n.p.
Inchbald, Elizabeth. 1967. *A Simple Story*. Ed. J.M.S. Tompkins. Oxford: Oxford University Press.
Janes, Regina. 1991. "Beheadings." *Representations* 35:21–51.
Janowitz, Anne. 1990. "'A Night on Salibury Plain': A Dreadful, Ruined Nature." In *Revolution and English Romanticism: Politics and Rhetoric*, ed. Keith Hanley and Raman Selden, 225–240. Hemel Hempstead: Harvester Wheatsheaf.
Jeffrey, Francis. 1804. Review of Bentham, *Traités de Legislation Civil et Penale*. *Edinburgh Review* 7:1–26.
Jewett, William. 1997. *Fatal Autonomy: Romantic Drama and the Rhetoric of Agency*. Ithaca, N.Y.: Cornell University Press.
Johnson, Claudia S. 1988. *Jane Austen: Women, Politics, and the Novel*. Chicago: University of Chicago Press.
Jones, Steven E. 1994. *Shelley's Satire: Violence, Exhortation, and Authority*. DeKalb: Northern Illinois University Press.
Jones, Vivien. 1990. *Women in the Eighteenth Century: Constructions of Femininity*. London: Routledge.
Kant, Immanuel. 1956. *Critique of Practical Reason*. New York: Macmillan.
Lamb, Charles. 1935. *The Complete Works of Charles Lamb*. New York: Random House.

Selected Bibliography

Lee, Debbie. 2002. *Slavery and the Romantic Imagination*. Philadelphia: University of Pennsylvania Press.

Le Faye, Deidre, ed. 1995. *Jane Austen's Letters*. 3d ed. Oxford: Oxford University Press.

Leyda, Seraphia D. 1983. "Wordsworth's *Sonnets upon the Punishment of Death*." *Wordsworth Circle* 14:48–53.

Lifton, Robert Jay, and Greg Mitchell. 2000. *Who Owns Death? Capital Punishment, the American Conscience, and the End of Executions*. New York: Harpercollins, 2000.

Locke, John. 1960. *Two Treatises of Government*. Ed. Peter Laslett. Cambridge: Cambridge University Press.

Lucretius. 1965. *On Nature*. Trans. Russel M. Geer. Indianapolis: Bobbs-Merrill.

Lynch, Deidre. 1998. *The Economy of Character: Novels, Market Culture, and the Business of Inner Meaning*. Chicago: University of Chicago Press.

Mackintosh, Sir James. 1846. *The Miscellaneous Works of the Right Honourable Sir James Mackintosh*. 3 vols. London: Longman.

Madan, Martin. 1785. *Thoughts on Executive Justice*. London: J. Dodsley. (Abbreviated *TEJ*.)

Mandeville, Bernard. 1964. *An Enquiry in the Causes of the Frequent Executions at Tyburn*. Introduction by Malvin R. Zirker, Jr. Los Angeles: Augustan Reprints Society. (Original ed. 1725.)

Manning, Peter. 1990. *Reading Romantics*. New York: Oxford University Press.

McAllister, Pam. 2003. *Death Defying: Dismantling the Execution Machinery in Twenty-First Century U.S.A*. New York: Continuum.

McBride, Dwight. 2001. *Impossible Witnesses: Truth, Abolitionism, and Slave Testimony*. New York: New York University Press.

McKeon, Michael. 1987. *Origins of the English Novel, 1600–1740*. Baltimore: The Johns Hopkins University Press.

Mellor, Anne K. 2000. *Mothers of the Nation: Women's Political Writing in England, 1780–1830*. Bloomington: Indiana University Press.

Midlake, Albert. 1851. *A Colloquy between the Gallows and the Hangman: A Poem on the Evils of Capital Punishment*. London: C. Gilpin.

Miller, D. A. 2003. *Jane Austen, or the Secret of Style*. Princeton: Princeton University Press.

Mirabeau, Count de. 1785. *Considerations on the Order of Cincinnatus*. London: J. Johnson.

Montagu, Basil. 1811. *A Brief Statement of the Proceedings . . . Upon the Several Bills Introduced with a View to the Amendment of the Criminal Law*. London: Longman. (Abbreviated *BSP*.)

———, ed. 1814. *The Debate in the House of Commons, April 25, 1814, Upon Corruption of Blood*. London: Longman.

———. 1830. *Thoughts on the Punishment of Death for Forgery*. London: William Pickering.

Montesquieu, Charles de Secondat, Baron de. 1989. *The Spirit of the Laws*. Trans. Anne M. Cohler, Baisa C. Miller, and Harold Stone. Cambridge: Cambridge University Press.

Montgomery, James. 1854. *Poetical Works*. Boston: Phillips, Sampson, and Co.

Selected Bibliography

[More, Hannah.] 1799. *Strictures on the Modern System of Female Education.* 7th ed. 2 vols. London: T. Cadell.

———. ed. 1800. *Cheap Repository Shorter Tracts.* London: F. and C. Rivington.

———. 1808. *Coelebs in Search of a Wife: Comprehending Observations on Domestic Habits and Manners, Religion and Morals.* 2 vols. London: T. Cadell and W. Davies.

———. 1830. *The Works of Hannah More.* 11 vols. London: T. Cadell.

More, Sir Thomas. 1965. *Utopia.* Trans. Paul Turner. Harmdonsworth: Penguin.

Mulligan, Hugh. 1788. *Poems Chiefly on Slavery and Oppression.* London: W. Loundes.

Nietzsche, Friedrich. 1969. *On the Genealogy of Morals.* Trans. Walter Kaufmann and R. J. Hollingdale. New York: Vintage Books.

Olyffe, George. 1731. *An Essay . . . For an Act . . . to Prevent Capital Crimes.* 2d ed. London: J. Downing.

Orlie, Melissa. 1997. *Living Ethically, Acting Politically.* Ithaca, N.Y.: Cornell University Press.

Paley, William. *Principles of Moral Philosophy.* New York: Garland, 1978. (Original ed. 1785; abbreviated *PMP.*)

Patterson, Orlando. 1982. *Slavery and Social Death: A Comparative Study.* Cambridge, Mass.: Harvard University Press.

Petrarch. 1962. *The Triumphs of Petrarch.* Trans. Ernest Hatch Wilkins. Chicago: University of Chicago Press.

Pinch, Adela. 1996. *Strange Fits of Passion: Epistemologies of Emotion, Hume to Austen.* Stanford: Stanford University Press.

———. 1998. "Learning What Hurts: Romanticism, Pedagogy, Violence." In *Lessons of Romanticism: A Critical Companion*, ed. Thomas Pfau and Robert Gleckner, 413–28. Durham, N.C.: Duke University Press.

Plato. 1961. *The Collected Dialogues of Plato.* Ed. Edith Hamilton and Huntington Cairns. Princeton: Princeton University Press.

Polidori, John. 1816. "On the Punishment of Death." *The Pamphleteer* 8:281–304.

Poovey, Mary. 1984. *The Proper Lady and the Woman Writer. Ideology as Style in the Works of Mary Wollstonecraft, Mary Shelley, and Jane Austen.* Chicago: University of Chicago Press.

Potter, John Deane. 1969. *The Art of Hanging.* New York: A. S. Barnes.

Pufendorf, Samuel. 2003. *The Whole Duty of Man, According to the Law of Nature.* Ed. Ian Hunter and David Saunders. Indianapolis: Liberty Fund. (Original ed. 1691.)

Radcliffe, Ann. 1968. *The Italian.* Ed. Frederick Garber. Oxford: Oxford University Press.

Radzinowicz, Sir Leon. 1948. *A History of English Criminal Law and Its Administration from 1750.* 5 vols. London: Stevens and Sons.

Ramsay, James. 1784. *An Essay on the Treatment and Conversion of African Slaves in the British Sugar Colonies.* London: James Phillips.

Richardson, Samuel. 1971. *Pamela or, Virtue Rewarded.* Ed. T. C. Duncan Eaves and Ben D. Kimpel. Boston: Houghton Mifflin.

Ricks, Christopher. 1984. *Keats and Embarrassment.* Oxford: Clarendon.

Rilke, Rainer Maria. 1984. *The Selected Poetry of Rainer Maria Rilke.* Ed. and trans. Stephen Mitchell. Introduction by Robert Hass. New York: Vintage.

Romilly, Sir Samuel. 1786. *Observations on a Late Publication, Entitled, Thoughts on Executive Justice*. London: T. Cadell. (Abbreviated *OLP*.)
———. 1811. *Observations on the Criminal Law of England, as it Relates to Capital Punishments, and on the Mode in Which it is Administered*. 2d ed. London: T. Cadell. (Abbreviated *OCL*.)
———. 1820. *The Speeches of Sir Samuel Romilly in the House of Commons*. 2 vols. London: James Ridgway. (Abbreviated *SSR*.)
———. 1840. *Memoirs of the Life of Sir Samuel Romilly*. 3 vols. London: John Murray. (Abbreviated *MSR*.)
Rose, Gillian. 1984. *Dialectic of Nihilism: Poststructuralism and Law*. London: Basil Blackwell.
Rousseau, Jean-Jacques. 1954. *Confessions*. Ed. J. M. Cohen. Hardmondsworth: Penguin.
Said, Edward. 1993. *Culture and Imperialism*. New York: Knopf.
Sarat, Austin, ed. 2001. *Pain, Death, and the Law*. Ann Arbor: University of Michigan Press.
Sartre, Jean-Paul. 1956. *Being and Nothingness*. Trans. Hazel E. Barnes. New York: Philosophical Library.
Scarry, Elaine. 1985. *The Body in Pain: The Making and Unmaking of the World*. New York: Oxford University Press.
Scott, Sarah. 1996. *The History of Sir George Ellison*. Ed. Betty Rizzo. Lexington: University Press of Kentucky.
Scott, Sir Walter. 1891. *The Journal of Sir Walter Scott*. Edinburgh: David Douglas.
———. 1932. *The New Crown Edition of the Waverly Novels*. 25 vols. London: A & C Black.
Setzer, Sharon. 1996. "Precedent and Perversity in Wordsworth's Sonnets upon the Punishment of Death." *Nineteenth-Century Literature* 50:427–47.
Shelley, Percy Bysshe. 1977. *Shelley's Poetry and Prose*. Ed. Donald H. Reiman and Sharon B. Powers. New York: Norton.
———. 1988. *Shelley's Prose, or The Trumpet of a Prophecy*. Ed. David Lee Clark. London: Fourth Estate.
Shklar, Judith N. 1998. "The Liberalism of Fear." In *Political Thought and Political Thinkers*, ed. Stanley Hoffman, 3–20. Chicago: University of Chicago Press.
Siskin, Clifford. 1988. *The Historicity of Romantic Discourse*. New York: Oxford University Press.
Smith, Adam. 2000. *The Theory of Moral Sentiments*. Amherst, N.Y.: Prometheus Books. (Original ed. 1759.)
[Smith, Sydney]. 1803. Review of Lieutenant-Colonel Collins, *Account of the English Colony of New South Wales*. *Edinburgh Review* 3:30–42.
Southey, Robert. 1840. *Poetical Works of Robert Southey*. 10 vols. London: Longman.
Spenser, Edmund. 1978. *The Faerie Queen*. Ed. Thomas P. Roche, Jr. Harmondsworth: Penguin.
Stephen, James Fitzjames. 1883. *A History of the Criminal Law of England*. 3 vols. London: Macmillan. (Abbreviated *HCL*.)
Stockdale, Mary. 1818. *A Plume for Sir Samuel Romilly; or, The Offering of the Fatherless*. London: Mary Stockdale.

Swann, Karen. 1988. "Public Transport: Adventuring on Wordsworth's Salisbury Plain." *ELH*: 811–34.
Tanner, Tony. 1986. *Jane Austen*. Houndmills: Macmillan.
[Taylor, Sir Henry.] 1841. Review of The Sonnets of William Wordsworth. *Quarterly Review* 9:1–51.
Ten, C. L. 1987. *Crime, Guilt, and Punishment: A Philosophical Introduction*. Oxford: Clarendon Press.
Thomas, Helen. 2000. *Romanticism and Slave Narratives: Transatlantic Testimonies*. Cambridge: Cambridge University Press.
Trilling, Lionel. 1950. *The Opposing Self: Nine Essays in Criticism*. New York: Viking.
Trimmer, Sarah. 1786. *Fabulous Histories Designed for the Instruction of Children*. London: T. Longman.
Trumpener, Katie. 1997. *Bardic Nationalism: The Romantic Novel and the British Empire*. Princeton: Princeton University Press.
Tuite, Clara. 2002. *Romantic Austen: Sexual Politics and the Literary Canon*. Cambridge: Cambridge University Press.
Turley, David. 1991. *The Culture of English Anti-Slavery*. London: Routledge.
Ulmer, William. 1990. *Shelleyan Eros: The Rhetoric of Romantic Love*. Princeton: Princeton University Press.
Volney, Constantin François. 1979. *Ruins*. 2 vols. New York: Garland. (Original ed. 1802.)
Von Kotzebue, August. 1990. *Lovers' Vows*. Adapted by Elizabeth Inchbald. Ed. Jonathan Wordsworth. Oxford: Woodstock Books. (Original ed. 1798.)
Wakefield, Edward Gibbon. 1831. *Facts Relating to the Punishment of Death in the Metropolis*. London: J. Ridgway.
Wang, Orrin N.C. 1996. *Fantastic Modernity: Dialectical Readings in Romanticism and Theory*. Baltimore: The Johns Hopkins University Press.
Warner, Michael. 1999. *The Trouble with Normal: Sex, Politics, and the Ethics of Queer Life*. Cambridge, Mass · Harvard University Press.
Weber, Max. 1930. *The Protestant Ethic and the Spirit of Capitalism*. Trans. Talcott Parsons. New York: Harper Collins.
Weisman, Karen A. 1994. *Imageless Truths: Shelley's Poetic Fictions*. Philadelphia: University of Pennsylvania Press.
Welsford, Enid. 1966. *Salisbury Plain: A Study in the Development of Wordsworth's Mind and Art*. New York: Barnes and Noble.
Wheatley, Kim. 1999. *Shelley and His Readers: Beyond Paranoid Politics*. Columbia: University of Missouri Press.
Wilberforce, William. 1970. *The Enormity of the Slave Trade; and The Duty of Seeking Moral and Spiritual Elevation of the Colored Race: Speeches of Wilberforce, and Other Documents and Records*. Freeport, N.Y.: Books for Libraries Press.
Williams, Bernard. 1981. *Moral Luck*. Cambridge: Cambridge University Press.
———. 1993. *Shame and Necessity*. Berkeley: University of California Press.
———. 1995. *Making Sense of Humanity*. Cambridge: Cambridge University Press.

Selected Bibliography

Williams, Eric. 1944. *Capitalism and Slavery.* Chapel Hill: University of North Carolina Press.

Wilson, John. 1830. "On the Punishment of Death." *Blackwood's Edinburgh Magazine* 27:865–78.

Wood, Marcus. 2002. *Slavery, Empathy, and Pornography.* Oxford: Oxford University Press.

Wordsworth, Christopher. 1867. *On the Punishment of Death for Wilful Murder: A Sermon, Preached in Westminster Abbey.* London: Rivington.

Wordsworth, William. 1975. *The Salisbury Plain Poems of William Wordsworth.* Ed. Stephen Gill. Ithaca, N.Y.: Cornell University Press.

———. 1991. *The Prelude.* 2 vols. Ed. Mark Reed. Ithaca, N.Y.: Cornell University Press.

———. 1993. *Letters of William and Dorothy Wordsworth: The Later Years, Part 4, 1840–1853.* Ed. Ernest De Selincourt, rev. Alan Hill. Oxford: Clarendon.

———. 2004. *Sonnet Series and Itinerary Poems.* Ed. Geoffrey Jackson. Ithaca, N.Y.: Cornell University Press.

Index

abolition: of death penalty; 12, 13, 24, 142–67, 170; of slavery, 9–10, 142–67
Agamben, Giorgio, 5, 92, 185n53
Akenside, Mark, 29, 72
Alexander, Larry, 179n42
Alighieri, Dante, 136
allegory, 53, 90
Anstey, Roger, 144
Austen, Jane, 6, 8, 81–106; works: *Emma*, 104, *Mansfield Park*, 21, 33, 81–106; *Pride and Prejudice*, 89, 98, 99, 104; *Sense and Sensibility*, 99, 104
Austin, J. L., 81

Bacon, Sir Francis, 74
Baker, Houston, 190n57
Barbauld, Anna Laetitia, 36
Barthes, Roland, 103
Beccaria, Cesare, 17, 23, 63
Bedau, Hugo, 191n6
Bender, John, 100
benefit of clergy, 105
Benezet, Anthony, 156
Bentham, Jeremy, 3, 13, 17, 21, 28, 32, 34, 63, 77, 146–47
Bible, 1, 2, 75
Blackstone, William, 1–2, 23
Blake, William, 3, 19, 148–50, 154–55
Bonaparte, Napoleon, 138–40
Bromwich, David, 130
Brougham, Henry, 24, 147, 154, 156–57
Bunyan, John, 53
Burke, Edmund, 15, 19, 26–27, 31, 76, 78, 147
Burke, Kenneth, 120
Butler, Judith, 1, 5, 186n6
Butler, Marilyn, 71, 85
Byron, George Gordon, Lord, 1–3, 21, 23, 121

capital punishment. *See* death penalty
Carlson, Julie, 124, 187n20
Chander, James, 182n18, 186n7
Chapone, Hester, 39

Clarkson, Thomas, 9, 145–46, 148, 152
Coleridge, Samuel Taylor, 9, 23, 119–26; works: "The Dungeon," 120; "The Eolian Harp," 125, 141; "Fears in Solitude," 141; *Osorio*, 119–26, *Remorse*, 123–24; "The Rime of the Ancient Mariner," 120
Colquhoun, Patrick, 26
Conquergood, Dwight, 191n4
conscience, 14, 117–26
Cowper, William, 10, 14, 159–61
Crabbe, George, 118
Cruikshank, Isaac, 153

Dagge, Henry, 17
Dart, Gregory, 137
Davis, Angela Y., 174–75
Davis, David Brion, 144, 154
Dawes, Manesseh, 17
Day, Thomas, 161, 164
Dayan, Joan, 152
death penalty, 2, 12–15, 27, 29–33, 55–80, 99, 107–14, 115–18, 126–29, 142–67. *See also* abolition
Deleuze, Gilles, 132, 188n44
DeMan, Paul, 136, 139
Derrida, Jacques, 27, 112
Dickens, Charles, 168
didactic literature, 34
Drescher, Seymour, 144
Druids, 58–59
Dworkin, Ronald, 62

Eden, Sir William, 28
Edgeworth, Maria, 17, 35
Edgeworth, Richard Lovell, 17, 35
Eldon, Lord, 15
Elliott, Dorice, 37, 52
Ellis, Markman, 159
Engelmann, Stephen, 28
enlightenment, 60–61
Equiano, Olaudah, 161–67
Ewart, William, 24, 73, 77

203

Index

execution, 14, 19–20, 25, 31, 115–16, 128. *See also* death penalty

Fawcett, Joseph, 118
fear, 25, 67, 69
Ferguson, Frances, 100, 178n22
Ferguson, Moira, 157
Ferris, Ina, 185n49
Fielding, Henry, 12, 13
film, and death penalty, 10, 171–74
Fish, Stanley, 53, 179n36
form, literary, and penal law, 18–29
Fosso, Kurt, 63
Foucault, Michel, 3–4, 19, 29, 84, 143
Fox, Charles James, 153
French Revolution, 23, 64–66, 68–69, 75

Galperin, William, 75, 184n31
Garside, Peter, 185n49
Gattrell, V.A.C., 19, 36
Genet, Jean, 34
Gessner, Solomon, 169
gibbet, 68–69
Gill, Stephen, 56, 71
Gilmartin, Kevin, 52
Gilmore, Ruth Wilson, 174
Girard, Ren, 25
God. *See* Providence
Godwin, William, 26, 70–71
Goffman, Erving, 131
Goldsmith, Oliver, 21
Gothic, 58, 76, 107–10
Gregory, John, 38
Grenville, William Wyndham, Lord, 147
guillotine, 23, 65

habit, 31, 53
Hadley, Elaine, 189n24
hanging. *See* death penalty, execution
Hardt, Michael, 5
Hartman, Saidiya, 151
Hay, Douglas, 178n3
Haywood, Eliza, 39, 41
Hazlitt, WIlliam, 6, 22–23, 29–33, 130, 168
Henderson, Andrea, 60
Hobbes, Thomas, 25, 117
Hogg, James, 108–9
Holland, Henry, Lord, 143
Holland, Sharon, 173
Holmes, Richard, 188n42
Honour, Hugh, 148
Hood, Thomas, 169
Hunt, Leigh, 146

imagination, 6–13, 28–33, 56, 76–77, 80, 117–19, 131, 157, 164–65
Inchbald, Elizabeth, 90–91, 96

Janowitz, Anne, 56
Jay, Elizabeth, 37
Jay, Martin, 62
Jeffrey, Francis, 13
Jewett, William, 119
Johnson, Claudia, 102
Johnson, Samuel, 15
Jones, Vivien, 39
juvenile delinquency, 25

Kafka, Franz, 23
Kames, Henry Home, Lord, 115–17, 118–19, 126
Kant, Immanuel, 138, 186n17
Kay, Judith, 191n8
Keats, John, 133–34
Kelly, Gary, 181n22
Kowaleski-Wallace, Elizabeth, 37
Kozinski, Alex, 170
Krueger, Christine, 37

Lamb, Charles, 23
landscape architecture, 93
Laqueur, Thomas, 19
law, 14; as judge-made, 14, 26; as literary text, 26
Lee, Debbie, 189n7
Leyda, Seraphia, 183n39
Locke, John, 152
love, 130
Lucretius, 136
Lytton, Sir Edward George Bulwer, 168

Mackintosh, Sir James, 17, 146
Madan, Martin, 14–16, 18–19, 22
Mandeville, Bernard, 19
Marmontel, Jean François, 35
Marshall, David, 96
Methodism, 165–66
Midlake, Albert, 146
Miller, D. A., 100, 184n33
Miller, J. Hillis, 136
Milton, John, 48, 52–53, 138, 162
Mirabeau, Count de, 18
Montagu, Basil, 13, 26, 71, 147
Montesquieu, Charles de Secondat, Baron de, 23, 25
Montgomery, James, 26

Index

More, Hannah, 7, 17, 34–54, 74, 90, 129, 162; works: *Cheap Repository Tracts*, 36, 38, 39–43, 45–47; *Coelebs in Search of a Wife*, 36–38, 47–54; *Strictures on the Modern System of Female Education*, 43–45
More, Sir Thomas, 179n30
Mulligan, Hugh, 154
Myers, Mitzi, 37

Negri, Antonio, 5
Nietzsche, Friedrich, 5–6, 116
novel, 54
Nozick, Robert, 180n48
Nussbaum, Martha, 131, 178n23

Olyffe, George, 146
Orgel, Stephen, 187
Orlie, Melissa, 186n6

Paley, William, 15–16, 21–22
pardon, 111–12
Parker, Reeve, 187n19
Paton, Diana, 152
personification, 62–63, 65–66, 122, 133
Petrarch, 75, 136
Pinch, Adela, 31, 79, 186n15
Plato, 127, 187n28
Polidori, John William, 2, 17, 109
Poovey, Mary, 27
Pope, Alexander, 135, 138
postmodernism, 62
Potkay, Adam, 161
Potter, John Deane, 179n40
prison, 4, 26
progress, 110–14
Protestantism, 45, 119
Providence, 21, 34–54, 74, 75, 127, 161–62, 165–66
Pufendorf, Samuel, 117
punishment: codification of, 13; conflicting rationales of, 2–3, 6, 20–21, 22–24; lenience in, 13, 15, 120
Purinton, Marjean, 186n14

Radcliffe, Ann, 14, 107
Ramsay, James, 152
Rawls, John, 166
reading, and penality, 26–33, 103–7, 140
reform, penal, 5, 16, 24–25
retention, of death penalty, 170–71
retributivism, 2–3, 20, 22–24, 168
Richardson, Alan, 180n2

Richardson, Samuel, 90–91
Ricks, Christopher, 134
Rilke, Rainer Maria, 133
Romilly, Sir Samuel, 3, 9, 11–12, 16–25, 27, 142–43
Rose, Gillian, 4
Rousseau, Jean-Jacques, 136–38

sacrifice, 25, 55
Said, Edward, 85
Sarat, Austin, 170
Sartre, Jean-Paul, 34, 131, 136
Scarry, Elaine, 27, 65
Schwartz, Regina, 177n8
Scott, Sarah, 10, 156–59
Scott, Sir Walter, 8–9, 19, 81, 110–14
secularization, 55
Setzer, Sharon, 75
Shakespeare, William, 49, 105, 115, 117, 122
shame, 129–41
Shelley, Mary, 8, 81, 108–10
Shelley, Percy Bysshe, 6–7, 9, 23, 126–41; works: *Adonais*, 130, 133–34; *The Cenci*, 127–28; "Essay on the Punishment of Death," 126–29, 138; "On Love," 187n34; "The Mask of Anarchy," 133; *Peter Bell the Third*, 120, 135; *Prometheus Unbound*, 120–21, 130–31; "The Serpent Is Out from Paradise," 132–33; *The Triumph of Life*, 130, 131, 135–41
Sherwin, Emily, 179n42
Shklar, Judith, 55, 67
slavery, 9–10, 142–67
Smith, Adam, 116, 128
Smith, Charlotte, 79
Smith, Sydney, 147
Smith, William, 153
Southey, Robert, 26, 160–61, 162
Southward, David, 183n10
sovereignty, 5
Spenser, Edmund, 66
statistics, 22
Stephen, Sir James Fitzjames, 29
sublime, 76, 78
suicide, 164
Swann, Karen, 63
sympathy, 115–16, 126–28, 145–46

Tanner, Tony, 85, 96
Taylor, J. Sydney, 147
Taylor, Sir Henry, 72–73, 75, 127
theater, and theatricality, 76, 94–97

205

transportation, as punishment, 2, 26, 46, 146–48
Trilling, Lionel, 102
Trimmer, Sarah, 36
Trollope, Anthony, 169
Trumpener, Katie, 85–86
Turley, David, 144
Turow, Scott, 191n9
Tyburn, 19, 46

utilitarianism, 2–3, 20–21, 22–24, 78–79, 83–84, 168

Virgil, 136
Volney, Constantin, 139
Voltaire, 138

Wakefield, Edward Gibbon, 12
Warner, Michael, 131
Welsford, Enid, 56
Wesley, John, 165–66
Wheatley, Kim, 133–34
Wheatley, Phyllis, 142
Wilberforce, William, 9, 143, 153
Wilde, Oscar, 23
Williams, Bernard, 131, 184n19
Williams, Eric, 144
Wilson, John, 29
Wollstonecraft, Mary, 39
Wordsworth, Christopher, 74–75
Wordsworth, Jonathan, 96
Wordsworth, William, 7–8, 55–80, 127; works: *Adventures on Salisbury Plain*, 67–70; *Guilt and Sorrow*, 67–70; *Lyrical Ballads*, 59; *The Prelude*, 64–66, 68, 117–18; *Salisbury Plain*, 56, 57–71, 117; *Sonnets upon the Punishment of Death*, 72–80
Wu, Duncan, 20